GEOSOPHIA

THE ARGO *of* MAGIC

JAKE STRATTON-KENT

GEOSOPHIA
THE ARGO *of* MAGIC

ENCYCLOPÆDIA GOETICA VOLUME II

from the Greeks to the Grimoires

BOOKS V, VI, VII & VIII

BIBLIOTHÈQUE ROUGE

MMX

Published by Scarlet Imprint
under the *Bibliothèque Rouge* banner
/rouge
Copyright © Jake Stratton-Kent, 2010
Design by *fofó*
Printed & bound by CPI Antony Rowe.
ISBN 978-0-9567203-1-3

CONTENTS

VOLUME II

BOOK FIVE

The Barbarian Interpretation   I

The Hero   4

The Great Mother of the Gods   5

Hieros Gamos and Deification   8

Goetic Gallery: Barbaricæ   13

Cosingas   13

Abaris   14

Zalmoxis   14

Aristeas   17

Argonautica III: Jason and Medea   20

Goetic Gallery: Sympathia   35

Empedocles   37

Goetic Gallery: Maters de Mysteria   46

Melissa   46

Medea as Scarlet Woman   51

Papyrus Parallels   53

Implications for Modern Practice   62

BOOK SIX

Volcanic Conjurations   68

Argonautica IV: Homeward Bound   86

Nebiros and Hermes Chthonios   131

BOOK SEVEN

The Magical Papyri   156
Typhon-Set   170
Theurgia   179
Goetic Gallery: Metamorphica   191
  Pythagoras   191
Interlude: Reformers & Backsliders   197
Familiar & Unfamiliar Spirits   201

BOOK EIGHT

The Magic of the Picatrix   227
Sabean Practices   233
Sabean Rites of the Planets   236
Al-Istamatis   244
Works of the Moon in the Twelve Signs   250
Talismans & Works of the Lunar Mansions   262
Astrological Talismans   269
Correspondences I   272
Correspondences II   278
The Figures of the Stones   284

Appendix
  Astrological Notes   298
  Typhonian Star Lore   305

Bibliography   313
Index   319

Sagatana has the power to render you invisible, to transport you anywhere, to open locks, to make visible to you all that occurs in houses, to teach you all the paths and subtle skills of the Shepherds.

Le Grand Grimoire

THE BARBARIAN INTERPRETATION

T HE EXPRESSION INTERPRETATIO GRECÆ refers to the Classical Greek
habit of interpreting the religions, deities and languages of other nations in terms of their own. For example, various Greek scholars said
of the Thracians that they worshipped three deities, Artemis, Dionysus
and Ares, who are of course all Greek deities. This is all the more problematic since a good many Greek gods came from elsewhere in the first
place. The myths of the origin of Cybele and the supposedly castrated god
Attis are largely Greek; even though the deities concerned are not.

In recent studies of the Thracians the necessity of putting aside old assumptions and finding the Thracian interpretation has been powerfully
underlined. Applying this barbarian interpretation to the Greeks, in reversal of the Greek habit, may appear a little strange. This is not really the
case, for two very cogent reasons. The first is that the Thracians, and other 'barbarians', were an extremely important influence on Greek religion,
particularly the aspects of it directly relevant to this study. The second is
that many urbanised and literate Greeks in the Classical and Hellenistic
eras were moving away from the state cults. In consequence, the older
strata of Greek religion, and supposedly backward areas of their own culture, underwent a tremendous renaissance. Both had more in common
with 'barbarian' rather than Classical Greek ideas and practices. While
Dionysus was not a foreign god, and Orphism is more likely to have begun in Southern Italy, both cults consciously adopted Thracian motifs
and rites. An interpretation based on Thracian, Scythian or Pelasgian
motifs therefore has numerous advantages, not least being a useful balance to the employment of classical literary sources.

The key role of Thrace in this study is exemplified by several elements indicated already: the selection of hierophants for the Eleusian Mysteries from the Eumolpidæ, a Thracian family; the similar primacy of the Thracidæ family at Delphi; the Thracian influences on the cults of Dionysus and Orpheus; the Mysteries of Samothrace and Lemnos on the Thracian coast. Of nearly equal importance is the role of Phrygia, its cult of the Mother, and the Thracian element in its civilisation.

The Classical Greeks tended to portray the Thracians as bloodthirsty barbarians. While they were certainly great warriors, this estimation cannot be taken at face value. Homer's account of the Trojan War accurately portrays the Thracians as at least equal in cultural advancement to their allies the Trojans, and their enemies the Achaean Greeks. Archaeology supports this literary evidence, with extraordinarily rich finds in Thracian royal tombs. These include the earliest gold artefacts in Europe, horse harness trappings dated to 3500 BCE and Bronze Age gold bowls from tomb burials of 1300 BCE. At the time of the Mycenaean civilisation, and that of the Minoans before them, Thrace was a strong and impressive power.

By 1200 BCE, the Mycenaean civilisation of Greece was imploding, but Thracian tribes were expanding into Asia Minor to found the kingdom of Phrygia. In 1050 BCE, the Minoan civilisation in Crete was expiring, and mainland Greece was gripped in a Dark Age, but Phrygia defeated and replaced the Hittites. In south eastern Thrace an advanced and powerful civilisation flourished from the 12th to 6th centuries BCE, and Thrace as a whole continued to prosper from then until the beginning of the 3rd century.

Thrace then was one of the most powerful and populous nations of the ancient world. It constituted a major influence on Greek culture, particularly in relation to religion. This influence was, and still is, a difficult subject to assess precisely. The dominant place Greek and Roman studies possessed in early modern historical thinking impeded Thracian studies until comparatively recently. The fact that Thrace was a culture with an oral rather than written tradition of its own only compounded this neglect. This situation has begun to improve in the post war period, and particularly since the 1970s. Even so, this may be the first attempt to assess the Thracians role in the history of Western magic.

Such a first has implied limitations, but at the same time is too overdue to be neglected. While the majority of studies are unfortunately not in English, Thracology is inestimably more important – to understanding ancient and advancing modern Western occultism – than either Egyptology or the Kabbalah. These are bold words, flouting what 'everybody knows' in favour of something unfamiliar. But it is unfamiliar for all the wrong reasons. The old certainties of classicism have not been questioned by occultists: unhistorical fantasies have been perpetuated in favour of blind traditionalism, or sidestepped in favour of a rootless solipsism. Hence my deconstruction of the old classical picture, itself partly unfamiliar, is an uphill struggle. Regardless of these difficulties, the necessity for such an endeavour is plain enough.

Since Phrygia (located in modern Turkey) plays a substantial part in what follows, it is as well to relate a little concerning it. Its extent was varied in different periods, and to some degree the name has a general significance. Homer locates the Phrygians on the banks of the river Sangarius; here according to other writers, and substantiated by archaeology, were the kingdoms of Midas and Gordius. Under the Romans, Phrygia lay between Mysia and Lydia to the West; Galatia, formerly part of Phrygia, to the East; and Bithynia to the North. Thracian colonists traditionally called the Bryges, from which the name of Phrygia was corrupted, anciently settled the territory. Further waves of Thracian tribes drove them inland, though significant communities remained in the coastal regions between the Hellepont and Propontis, and the mountains known as Ida and Olympus. Here they were in the closest contact with Ionian Greek colonies. At various times the region formed part of the Persian, Macedonian, Alexandrian successor and Roman empires. Phrygia's most famous city was Troy, from which the area bears the name of the Troad. The Phrygians played a significant and important part in the development of Greek culture. Greek music for example, especially flute music, was acquired in part from Phrygia. In addition, the region was closely associated in the Greek mind with the rites of Dionysus or Bacchus, and those of Cybele, Mother of the Gods.

The Hero

Classical literary accounts of the religion and magic of the Thracians generally tend to involve strongly Greek interpretations. There was of course mutual influence between the two, and some adoption of Greek forms by the Thracians is undeniable. Similarly the Roman conquest of Thrace has left a substantial mark on the later monuments and other archaeological remains relevant to Thracian religion. Useful though some of these survivals are when carefully considered, they are very far from being the whole picture.

Towering above these in significance is a less familiar figure, a divine hero on horseback, of whom no less than three thousand representations are known in the region of ancient Thrace. This figure is of the utmost importance to understanding not only Thracian but older Greek religion and magic. He has no known name, as the Thracians were extremely reticent about the names of their deities. In addition it is more than likely that any name he may have possessed would have varied from region to region. Where inscriptions exist in later representations he is identified simply as *Hero*, or *the god Hero*. From this and other indications it is certain no simple mortal warrior is intended by these titles. Although the iconography of the divine rider is influenced by Greek forms, the Hero himself is far more ancient, and pivotal to this entire study.

The god Hero is a complex figure, far more so in many respects than the deities of Classical Greece. However, even though representations of the Hero portray various phases of his myth, the same character is always readily identifiable. His iconography is incredibly consistent, while at the same time the dedicatory inscriptions involve an extremely varied range of functions. His nature plainly involves many roles, in contrast to the highly differentiated Greek gods of the Classical period.

Often his versatility is signified by depicting the Hero with three heads. This may be important when interpreting Hellenistic figures, including those in Italy. In Roman times particular functions are emphasised by superimposing elements specific to the appropriate Greek or Roman god. Sometimes this represents the particular function of Hero being appealed to. On other images it can indicate a quality or feature of his cult most popular in a given region. Even with these superimposed attributes the familiar Thracian iconography is retained. On all occasions his Thracian identity, and thus his intrinsic universality, is never truly in question.

Beginning by simplifying the Hero a little, in advance of what is to follow; two principal contrasting modes can be distinguished. These are the solar and chthonic modes, which in Græco-Roman terms are principally represented by Apollo on the one hand and Dionysus or Dis on the other. A god possessing two such contrasting modes is very rare in the specialising Olympian religion; with the principal exceptions of Hermes, and of Dionysus. Dionysus was one of three deities identified as Thracian among the Greeks, and his martial achievements in conquering India should not be forgotten in preference for his more orgiastic and fructifying nature. In effect the combination of roles of the hero as ancestor of the tribe, as well as its protector and champion explains the Greek perception of Dionysus and Ares being chief male deities among the Thracians. In order to become a male ancestor of course there had to be a mother, the divine mother and lover of the hero, whom the Greeks principally identified with Artemis.

The Great Mother of the Gods

In Greek myth the Great Mother of the Gods is the Cretan Earth Goddess Rhea. She was the source of fruitfulness in the kingdoms of man, beast and vegetation. Hesiod says of her that she was the daughter of Uranus and Gaia or Ge, which is to say of Heaven and Earth. She is also the wife of the god Kronos, and the mother of the majority of the Olympian gods: Hestia, Demeter, Hera, Hades, Poseidon and Zeus. Kronos anticipated his own overthrow by one of his children, and accordingly devoured them as soon they were born. For this reason Rhea, when on the point of giving birth to Zeus, took refuge at Lyctus in Crete, and when he was safely delivered gave Kronos a stone in his place. Homer largely agrees with this account, although he names only the three great sons of Rhea, Zeus, Poseidon and Hades, who divided the world between them.

Hesiod's account correctly identifies Rhea as a Cretan goddess whose worship spread throughout the Greek world, and of particular importance, to Asia Minor. There she was identified with the Great Goddess of the Phrygians, the goddess Cybele. This identification is of crucial importance in understanding Greek myth from the perspective of the 'barbarian interpretation', the key to understanding its origins and much of its underlying meaning. The particular significance of the identification of Cybele and Rhea is undoubtedly that it identifies the Phrygian goddess with the mother of Zeus. Since Cybele is also the mother of the Phrygian kings her relationship with him underpins the link between kingship and the divine. Exactly the same relationship, of son and lover, applies to Thracian kings and the royal cult. The relations of the goddess with both Midas and his son Attis is of the nature of a Phrygian dynastic cult on the Thracian model. That in the Greek legend she is fertilised by Zeus, of whom she is also the mother, is probably explained by the same formula.

Whatever the nature of the Cretan goddess, the identification with Phrygian Cybele, who for our purposes is indistinguishable from the great Goddess of the Thracians, lent to her cult its orgiastic character. Her domain was the mountains and forests, and her attendants were the lions and panthers who dwelled there. She is the Mountain Mother and the Mistress of Beasts. Her link with Dionysus, and with other gods of moisture and fruitfulness, is present throughout the Mystery cults examined in this study. In great part Dionysian wildness is the inheritance of his relationship with the Mother of the Gods.

While scholars insist that the Great Mother of the Gods is a concept of Eastern origin this does not detract from her importance at deep levels of Greek Mystery religion. It does however reinforce the significance of Thracian and Phrygian influence upon it. Significantly while the earliest female idols in Thracian territory are single a later stage comes of double images, one inside the other, as found at Orsoya. The simplest explanation of this is of Mother and Daughter, corresponding to Demeter and Kore or Persephone. That these deities were associated with Thracian influence at Eleusis is not accidental. A few centuries later comes a third kind of image, suggesting the Mother and Daughter have been joined by a son.

The necessity of a son, as part of the mother in ancient theology, is that he does not detract from her omnipotence. This relationship may be seen in the case of Cybele and Attis as well as Persephone and Dionysus. This son and lover is clearly identified in Thracian art as the Hero.

The Daughter – herself a projection of the Mother – represents the fertile virgin with whom the hero is partnered in the heiros gamos. The Orphic conception of Zeus fathering Dionysus upon Persephone derives from this background. The abduction of Persephone by Hades carried a similar meaning. An important myth with a similar theme involves Zeus in the form of a serpent impregnating Rhea with Demeter; then Demeter with Persephone, who in turn produces Dionysus. In Orphic understanding the goddess, (Rhea-Demeter-Persephone) was the protagonist of this triple union. According to Orphic Fragment 145 Rhea became Demeter as the mother of Zeus, who in turn fathers Persephone on her. It continues that she was destined to bear Dionysus to Zeus, and that the son would rule after him as the ultimate ruler of the gods. The Neoplatonists reasonably concluded from this that Rhea, Demeter and Persephone were ultimately one, and so were Zeus, Hades and Dionysus.

These were deep Mysteries, and it is not for a moment suggested they formed part of the daily concerns of religious life for the average Greek. Their significance is fundamentally esoteric, for those whose inner response to the numinous is on an altogether more intense level.

Bendis

A Thracian goddess who certainly influenced the Greeks in the historical period was the goddess Bendis. The Greeks identified her with both Artemis and Hecate through her associations with the Moon and with hunting. Plato makes mention of the mounted torch race that formed a spectacular part of the nocturnal celebrations of her cult. As with Artemis (whose temple at Ephesus had major connection with the cult of Cybele) the role of hunting goddess derives from the extremely ancient cult of Potnia Theron – Mistress of Beasts – that was part of the background of Cybele. It should be noted that the connection of Artemis with the Moon is a late development as is the connection of Apollo with the Sun. The real basis for the ancient identification of Artemis with Bendis – as with the great goddess of Asia Minor – was the connection with streams, forests and the animal kingdom.

Cotys

Another Thracian goddess who influenced the Greeks was Cotys or Cotytto. The Greeks compared her with Persephone and with Demeter; her rites – the Cotyttia – were deemed Dionysian and frowned on by the conservative elite of Athens. Her rites were notorious for debauchery; being celebrated with music and dance. As well as in Athens they were also established in Sicily, where we know that her worshippers carried green boughs hung with cakes and fruit that anyone was permitted to pluck. Interestingly enough they were also accepted in Corinth.

Hieros Gamos and Deification

The roots of sexual mysticism in the Western tradition do not originate in the Tantric tradition of India. Nor, although they are linked with Gnosticism, does it originate within that diverse flowering of late pagan philosophy and religious syncretism. The origins of sexual symbolism and ritual in Western magic lay firmly in the Thracian mysteries; particularly in the rites of deification of Thracian kings in their sacred marriage to the Mother of the Gods. This was perceived as a match of the initiated dynast – who personified the hero – with the virgin daughter, a hypostasis of the Mother herself. This occurred within the life of the king upon earth, and was symbolised in various ways. Among these was a sexual interpretation of ritual acts such as libation, as well as royal marriages. There is a famous story of king Kotys I, arranging a marriage feast for the goddess Athena and then awaiting her in the bridal chamber. This exemplifies ritual marriage between king and goddess in the context of the Thracian dynastic cult. So too it demonstrates how 'barbarian' understanding of Greek traditions retained meaning and context lost in 'civilised' Greece.

Upon death the identification of the king with the chthonic aspect of the hero became complete. Aspects of burial rites show a clear sexual symbolism. Examples of this symbolism are known to and recognised by archaeology; interments face down with legs splayed, or face up with an iron ploughshare upon the groin. Both of these methods of interment symbolise union of the dynast with the Earth goddess. This symbolism may also be implicit in the ploughing of the field of Ares by Jason in Colchis; there the ploughshare is a gift of Hephæstus to the king. So too, as will be seen, Jason's marriage to Medea is replete with connections with the mysteries of Dionysus.

This sexual union in death is largely absent from myth for an excellent reason, it is a Mystery. Although a secret of the Mystery religions, which it was forbidden to reveal, it is nevertheless not concealed entirely. As already mentioned Cybele was identified with Rhea and, through real or perceived ancient links between Phrygian and Cretan mysteries, they shared common origins. Rhea was the wife of Kronos and the mother of his children. In particular the rulers of the three worlds: Sky, Sea and Underworld; Zeus, Poseidon and Hades. It is now time to consider their father.

Kronos

As the role of Kronos as the cruel father of the gods has been mentioned, it is time to examine other apparently contradictory aspects of the god. He was the youngest of the Titans, son of the earth goddess Gaia, and the sky god Ouranos who he famously castrated with a sickle. It was from him also, importantly, that the infant Zeus was hidden in Crete. According to this myth, Zeus subsequently imprisoned him in Tartarus. Another aspect of his mythology appears to be at variance with this, although later versions attempt to reconcile the two by changing his place of incarceration.

His rule over the more favoured parts of the afterlife is the central aspect of the other side of his myth. Far from being a tyrant as portrayed in the myth of the infant Zeus, he is portrayed as the ruler of the Golden

Age, the first age of man. Men then lived and feasted like the gods. Light of heart, neither grief, sickness nor old age touched them and the earth gave freely of her bounty without labour. This rule is mirrored in the afterlife, where Kronos rules over Elysium or the Islands of the Blessed. Puzzled by the contrast, some writers have endeavoured to separate the two themes, claiming the benign version is authentically Indo-European, and the cruel tyrant form originates elsewhere. There are in fact similar Hurrian-Hittite legends, supposed to have influenced Hesiod in his account of the events. However, Hesiod — whose cosmogony is otherwise consistent and logical — mentions both aspects of the myth. Similarly, both sides of the god are present in important rituals. The contradictions, in other words, are an essential part of the god's nature.

One such rite, the Athenian Kronia, which is similar to the better-known Roman Saturnalia, occurred after the harvest. Normal social distinctions were temporarily put aside; masters and slaves feasted together, some accounts even record masters serving the slaves. On the other hand, he is frequently associated with horrific crimes and cult practices. Not all of these are likely to have been real events, but rather a portrayal of his nature. Similarly, foreign deities, in whose cults such practices were real, are consistently identified with him. There may indeed have been influences from Asia Minor and from older cultures, but essentially these contradictions reflect the real nature of the god. In essence, Kronos embodies periods of transition where normality is suspended. These are portrayed in imagery and real events of joyous exaltation on the one hand, and ghastly tales of fearful cruelty on the other.

His Roman form, Saturn, emphasises the benign aspect of the god. While the Hellenistic Greeks came to connect *chronis*, time, with the god Kronos the Romans quite separately connected Saturn with calendars, seasonal events and their feast days. Further indeed, both Saturn and Mars enjoyed higher status and more frequent and prominent cult among the Romans than did their Greek equivalents. This, in my opinion, reflects a comparatively archaic quality to Roman religion, compared with the classical Greek. In other words, older themes buried under Greek classical myth, or lost entirely, are more accessible in their native Roman forms. In the case of Mars – warrior, protector, herdsman and god of boundaries – qualities lost or rejected by the Greeks, perhaps by the Egyptians too in the case of Set, were still celebrated in Roman culture.

Things become clearer when we recall the relation of Kronos with Cretan Zeus. The gods – and the goddesses – do not reduce to one by any necessary rule, but they frequently are modes of each other. The infant Zeus cannot be king of the gods, but there has to be one; this in a sense is Kronos, but in some respects, impossible or otherwise, it is also the adult Zeus. Father Zeus cannot be a monster persecuting himself as an infant; or, as we usually refer to the younger god, Dionysus. Nevertheless, this youngster is destined to rule in his place; and Zeus' avoidance of this in the case of Achilles tells us a good deal. So, though it cannot be so, he also is that monster, though appearing in disguise in the Kronos role. If the young god is not slain, we the worshippers cannot eat him and become one with him. Nevertheless, though he dies, he lives, becomes king of the gods and defeats the terror, the terror that is he. Just as we, who have torn him limb from limb and consumed him, go hunting through the dark, either for the lost boy or his killers.

The slain god, or dead king, who both is and is not the beautiful youthful hero, goes on to unite with the goddess and become Lord of the Underworld, his status undiminished. We see this quite plainly with the post mortem rule of Achilles with Helen or Medea as his queen. So too do we see it in Kronos or Saturn as lord of the Elysian Fields. The deifying power of the Underworld, usually in serpentine form, also cloaks the god in a mask of terror. The terror evoked by the Lord of the Underworld is one we often forget when considering Osiris. We remember the Egyptian god unites with his wife after death; we remember that a dangerous god threatens the infant Horus. We forget that Osiris commands legions of the dead, recalling only that his rule is wise.

Whether considered as the Roman Saturn or the Greek Kronos, his is an exceedingly complex character. In Roman cult his festival was both hugely popular and authentically ancient. Livy attempted to show it originated in 496 BCE, but this is more likely to be the date at which Greek elements entered an existing tradition. His name has been supposed to originate in *satus* referring to sowing (see the famous SATOR magic square), but this is problematic when considering him as lord of the Golden Age predating agriculture. His supposed Etruscan origins fare no better, indeed the former attribution of Phrygian or Cretan connections is more credible. The all-important Capitoline Hill at the centre of Roman religion was originally sacred to him, so we may most usefully consider him an authentic Italian god whose cult later underwent Greek influence. This influence to some extent appears to have emphasised or been adapted to characteristics already present. The laying of the god's statue on a couch for feeding is a general borrowing shared with the other gods. However, Roman celebration of his sacrifice in the Greek fashion, with head uncovered, far from implying deference to the Greeks typifies rather the inversions characteristic of the god.

His feast day was December 17th, and the Saturnalia continued for seven days thereafter, despite attempts of Emperors to shorten it. His statue, kept bound with rope during the rest of the year, was ritually untied on this day. Another feast day, the Sigillaria, fell on the seventh day, interestingly the *Verum* spirit ruling the Winter Solstice bears the name Segal. Social divisions were, within acknowledged limits, either abolished or inverted during Saturnalia. The wearing of felt hats, representing liberation, was customary for all during the celebrations. Slaves celebrated noisily, running shouting through the streets without fear of punishment. They were at liberty to mock their masters, who served them dinner before eating themselves.

It was customary to give gifts on the last day; originally, these were clay heads, likely representing former sacrifices. These gifts were accompanied by written mottoes. The burning of candles was also customary, and these may involve sympathetic magic, as the rebirth of the Sun (Sol Invicta) falls during the same period. As is apparent, both the date and many aspects of these festivities survive in the modern Christmas.

For this limited time, Saturn or Kronos exceeds Zeus in power, while in the order of Ages and in the planetary week he precedes him. He is at once the Lord of Misrule and the chief of the planets, while his eschatological roles underline his centrality to our theme.

GOETIC GALLERY: BARBARICÆ

Cosingas

COSINGAS, MORE CORRECTLY KOSINGAS, was a Thracian king and priest to the Thracian tribes of the Kebrenoi and Sykaiboai. The importance of Thracian royal cults to the development of the Greek Mystery tradition cannot be underestimated, although important features may have been suppressed. For example there was a powerful sexual element in certain Thracian rites, whereas the oracular priestesses of Olympian cults were sworn to chastity. Although officially sanctioned the Bacchic rites, which were of Thracian origin, were the subject of some controversy due – among other things – to the supposed potential for sexual license involved.

On the other hand there were also Thracian ascetics, vegetarian and celibate, accounting in part for the comparisons made with Pythagoreanism. Incidentally, the rites of Eleusis were said to have been founded by a Thracian named Eumolpus, and his descendents were hereditary hierophants. This descent is said to have continued for 1200 years, somewhat astonishingly, since the hierophants were also sworn to celibacy once in office. To avoid sexual feelings during the rituals they were required to anoint their genitals with juice of hemlock.

The significance of Kosingas is remarked upon by Mircea Eliade. According to a writer in the time of Marcus Aurelius (a Macedonian with the alarming name of Polyaenus), Kosingas threatened to ascend to heaven by ladder to speak of the outrageous behaviour of his people to the goddess Hera. This ascent by ladder is typical of shamanic ritual and the association with the Thracians is important. It appears that the Greeks were well aware of such ritual ascents, which may have formed a part of Orphic initiations; occasionally stairs appear to have been substituted. Part of the tribe of the Kebrenoi appears to have been among the Thracian immigrants to Asia Minor. There was a small country and a town named Cebrenia, and a river Cebrenus, in the region of Troy.

Abaris

Abaris the Scythian was given an arrow by Apollo which gave him the power of magical flight wherever he wished and oracular ability. This strongly resembles motifs in Siberian shamanism, where souls are able to ride upon an arrow, an instrument with many connections in shamanic practice. Traditionally he lived entirely without earthly food, and after visiting Greece returned to Hyperborea without eating. He banished pestilences and predicted earthquakes. His healing is referred to alongside that of Zalmoxis in the *Charmides* of Plato: *for if, as he declares, you have this gift of temperance already, and are temperate enough, in that case you have no need of any charms, whether of Zalmoxis or of Abaris the Hyperborean, and I may as well let you have the cure of the head at once; but if you have not yet acquired this quality, I must use the charm before I give you the medicine.* He taught the worship of Hyperborean Apollo and is said to have written religious poems including: a history of the Oracles in the various countries he had visited; an account of Apollo's travels among the Hyperboreans, and the nuptials of the river god Hebrus (a river of Thrace with sands of gold, whose two mouths enter the sea opposite the island of Samothrace, the head of Orpheus was thrown into its waters). He is credited with the foundation of Persephone's temple at Sparta. He is also said to have made the Palladium there, with the bones of Pelops, before the Trojan War. He is mentioned as a Hyperborean magician by Cornelius Agrippa.

Zalmoxis

Zalmoxis was originally the god-king of a royal dynasty of Thrace, known as the Getæ, whose territory was in the lower Danube region. In the Classical era he was described as a man who took Greek customs to the Thracians. This is a typical reversal by what is called the *interpretatio græca*, accounting for the existence among the Thracians of ideas associated with Pythagoras, by giving credit to the Greeks rather than the barbarians. Accordingly he is sometimes called a slave of Pythagoras, whom he in fact predates. According to this story he accompanied his master to

Egypt, before returning to Thrace. On his return he built a banqueting hall in which he taught a doctrine of the immortality of the soul. He also had built an underground chamber into which he retired, like Pythagoras, and he emerged after a three year retirement as if raised from the dead.

To his credit, Herodotus, who provided many of the details, did not believe that Zalmoxis was an associate of Pythagoras, but thought him much earlier whether man or god. His account clearly shows indications of initiatory rituals similar to the Greek Mystery religions, and teachings bearing similarities to those of Pythagoras. The banqueting hall in which he taught also bears similarities to the way of life of the Pythagorean community at Crotona. In an ironic reversal of the interpretatio græca, one version of Pythagoras' own descent into the underworld appears to have borrowed materials from Herodotus' account of Zalmoxis!

The story of a descent into the Underworld, and a triumphant return, are typical features of initiatory rites. Similarly, the survival of the soul after death is typical of the teachings of the Mysteries. This belief appears to have been widespread among Thracian peoples, who believed that after death they would go to Zalmoxis, and subsequently return to life. This cannot but have impressed the Greeks, knowing of the teachings of Pythagoras. The Thracian connections of other ecstatic slain and risen gods and heroes connected with the Mysteries, such as Dionysus and Orpheus, are also important; according to some Zalmoxis is to be identified with Sabazius. Eliade, while accepting shamanic elements entered Greek culture in some fashion, does not count Zalmoxis among the Greek shamans, pointing rather to the strong connections between the materials relating to him with the Mystery religions. At the same time he accepts that Zalmoxis is identifiable as a god of a people among whom shamanism was prevalent. Plato refers to the association of Zalmoxis with the healing arts in his *Charmides*:

> ... such I said, is the nature of the charm, which I learned when serving with the army from one of the physicians of the Thracian king Zalmoxis, who are said to be so skilful that they can even confer immortality. This Thracian told me that in these notions of theirs, which

I was just now mentioning, the Greek physicians are quite right as far as they go; but Zalmoxis, he added, our king, who is also a god, says further, *that just as you ought not to attempt to cure the eyes without the head, or the head without the body, so neither ought you to attempt to cure the body without the soul; and this*, he said, *is the reason why the cure of many diseases is unknown to the physicians of Greece, because they are ignorant of the whole, which ought to be studied also; for the part can never be well unless the whole is well.* For as he declared, all good and evil whether in the body or in human nature, originates in the soul, and overflows from thence, as if from the head into the eyes. And therefore if the head and body are to be well, you must begin by curing the soul; that is the first thing. And the cure, my dear youth, has to be effected by the use of certain charms, and these charms are fair words; and by them temperance is implanted in the soul, and where temperance is, there health is speedily imparted, not only to the head, but to the whole body. And he who taught me the cure and the charm at the same time added a special direction: *Let no one*, he said, *persuade you to cure the head, until he has first given you his soul to be cured by the charm. For this*, he said, *is the great error of our day in the treatment of the human body, that physicians separate the soul from the body.* And he added with emphasis, at the same time making me swear to his words, *Let no one, however rich, or noble, or fair, persuade you to give him the cure, without the charm.* Now I have sworn, and I must keep my oath, and therefore if you will allow me to apply the Thracian charm first to your soul, as the stranger directed, I will afterwards proceed to apply the cure to your head.

In closing this account of Zalmoxis a significant fact of magical historiography, overlooked by traditional ceremonial magicians, deserves an airing here. Cornelius Agrippa – the primary authority of the tradition espoused – reckoned the ancient fame of Zalmoxis as so extensive as to share with Zoroaster the reputation of founder of the magical arts (*Occult Philosophy* 1:11). This places Thracian shamans on an equal footing with the Persian and Chaldean Magi, as regards both influence and power.

Aristeas

Aristeas was an epic poet of the city of Proconnesus. This was a Thracian city on an island in the Sea of Marmara, off the northern coast of ancient Phrygia. It lays north-west of Cyzicus, another island city which was an important stage on the route of the Argonauts. The date of his life is uncertain, though it is said to have been in the age of Croesus king of Lydia (in the 6th century BCE). He is described as a magician whose soul was able to leave his body and return at will; according to Pliny in the form of a raven leaving his mouth. According to Herodotus, Aristeas spoke of having accompanied Apollo, assuming the form of a crow.

One famous story told of Aristeas is that he entered the shop of a fuller in Proconnesus and died. The fuller shut his shop and set out to notify the relatives of the poet. As news of his death spread, a man arrived from Cyzicus declared that he had met and spoken with Aristeas who was on his way to Cyzicus. The fuller returned to his shop, accompanied by many witnesses, but the body was not to be found. He is said to have reappeared to his countrymen seven years after this mysterious death. He was connected with the worship of Apollo, and apparently introduced his cult at the ancient city of Metapontum in Italy after a second disappearance of 240 years (the figure 540 is also found). This city also has a remarkable connection with the life of Pythagoras.

Aristeas was an epic poet of a tradition predating the Homeric form. His work told how, possessed by Apollo, he travelled the greater part of the world. In particular he travelled to the sacred land of the Hyperboreans. Here he met with the Arimazpi, who represent a Scythian tribe. In the poem of Aristeas he depicts the Arimazpi as a very numerous warrior race, who possessed great herds of horses, sheep and cattle. Their bodies were strong, their hair both long and thick. They had one eye in the middle of their foreheads and lived on the banks of a gold bearing river. Their land was renowned for its gold, which it possessed in abundance. The legends tell of gold obtained from the mines by griffins, upon whom the Arimazpi waged constant war to steal the gold, by special knowledge which they alone possessed.

Aside from the single eye and the griffins, this description matches the Scythians and their Thracian brothers very well. Mythically the single eye unites the Arimazpi with the metal working Cyclops. In ancient times the single eye was rationalised as a miner's lamp, which glowing eerily in the dark could resemble an eye. Some modern interpretations suggest a circular tattoo on the forehead, which is credible since both Scythians and Thracians practiced tattooing. Griffins too are an authentic motif of the culture of the steppe peoples, Scythian, Mede and Persian alike. Their presence in the Arimazpi epic is not the invention of an imaginative poet; the magical treasure guarding bird survives in various guises in ancient writings, in folklore and in the grimoires.

Aelianus Claudius, a Roman sophist of Præneste who wrote exquisite Greek, recorded ancient tradition concerning griffins in his writings. He describes a creature with a lion's body, having white wings and powerful talons. Their backs were feathered in black, and the chest red. Ctesias, who recorded many Assyrian and Persian legends, mentions griffins with violet feathers on their backs, possessing a vulture's head and eyes like lightning. They built inaccessible nests on gold rich mountains. There they guarded the gold, from which they made their nests. Isidorus of Sevilla locates griffins in the gold bearing mountains of the Hyperboreans. The blind poet John Milton, who drew upon Classical as well as Biblical lore, speaks of them in his own epic poem; *Paradise Lost*, Book II, line 943:

> As when a Gryfon through the Wilderness
> With winged course o'err Hill or moarie Dale,
> Pursues the Arimaspian, who by stealth
> Had from his wakeful custody purloined
> The guarded Gold.

In ancient Egyptian magic – in which foreign sources were often employed deliberately for magical reasons – the winged lion bodied griffin appears frequently. It is found drawn on wands from the 2nd millennium BCE, and invoked in the later demotic papyri, where it is described as *the griffin of the shrine of heaven.*

In the mining folklore of the Carpathian Mountains the griffin of the Arimazpi has become a magical hen. Traditions of western Transylvania describe a golden hen with golden eggs nested at the top of a mountain. Another Transylvanian tradition speaks of a treasure guarded by a hen sitting on her chicks. The village where this tradition was recorded bore the name of Volcan, commemorating an ancient connection with the god of fire. The grimoires record traditions of a similar type, in particular the text known as the *Black Pullet*. This grimoire has the subtitle of *The hen with the golden eggs*. This magical bird lays golden eggs, and will also find treasure.

Aristeas is mentioned by Cornelius Agrippa under the name Atheus in his psychological chapters, where he compares him and Hermotimus with shamans among the Lapps and Norwegians. Aristeas bears several hallmarks of a shaman; among them are ecstatic trance indistinguishable from death, the power of bilocation, and transformation into a bird.

ARGONAUTICA III:
JASON AND MEDEA

AT THE BEGINNING OF THE THIRD BOOK of the *Argonautica* we are
finally introduced to the principal female role of Apollonius' epic:
Medea of the many spells. It is appropriate that this should occur at
this central stage of the story, for her role is utterly pivotal to it. The opening of this analysis of the third book therefore begins with her. Medea's
mother's identity was a matter of some disagreement among the old writers, although all agreed that her father was Aeetes, King of Colchis, and
that she was the grand-daughter of his father, the Sun god Helios. Hesiod
and Hyginus, who are the more reliable authorities, name her mother as
Idyia, while others mention Ephyre, Asterodia, Antiope or Neaera. She
was the priestess of the great goddess Hecate, who is also credited with
being her mother. She was also the niece of that other famous sorceress
of Greek myth, the enchantress Circe, whose role in the *Odyssey* is almost
as crucial as Medea's in the *Argonautica*. Hecate, Circe and Medea are the
essential female characters in the Græco-Roman mythology of witchcraft.
The close relationship of this trio of enchantresses is both apt and important. Before delving deeper into the nature and deeds of Medea it is
necessary to examine more closely the context in which she appears. Of
particular importance in many respects are her father, King Aeetes of
Colchis, and his intriguingly close relationship with the gods. Aeetes is the
son of the Sun god Helios, whose solar role long predates Apollo's. This
in itself points to the great antiquity of the epic, older even than Homer
which also predates Apollo's association with the Sun. It is necessary to
underline the fact that the lineage of Aeetes exceeded that of mortal heroes, typically sired by a deity upon a mortal. The mother of Aeetes was
the Oceanid or sea-nymph Perseis, daughter of Oceanus; and according to
Hesiod and Hyginus his children, Medea, Chalciope and Apsyrtus, were
fathered upon another Oceanid named Idyia. He and his family have the
appearance of a virtual pantheon, and this goes a long way to explaining
their power and the interest the gods have in them.

One such deity is Hephæstus. At the beginning of this book of the *Argonautica* the goddesses Hera and Athena confer as to how they may assist Jason, and quickly conclude that Aphrodite's assistance is required. Accordingly they visit her palace on Olympus, which Apollonius reminds us was built by Hephæstus. As if by contrast with this event, shortly afterwards Jason and his fellow heroes arrive at the palace of Aeetes. They are immediately awestruck by a wonderful fountain outside it, also wrought by Hephæstus. Nor is this the only gift that Hephæstus has bestowed on the king, as will be seen later.

The kingdom of Aeetes is close by the rock of Prometheus, another fire god whose mythology is closely interwoven with that of Hephæstus. Aeetes is the son of the god of the Sun, and possesses great treasures given him by Hephæstus. All this underlines the status of Aeetes, and also reminds us that his kingdom was an early centre of excellence in the metallurgical arts. From the 15th to 8th century BCE the Colchians developed an expertise in smelting and casting metal long prior to similar developments in Europe. This pre-eminent position depended on the presence throughout the region of the metallurgical caste known to ancient geographers and historians as the Chalybes, and commemorated in myth as the Idæan Dactyls. These same figures, as has been shown at length, were the discoverers of metals, but also the founders of the Mysteries and the very first to be referred to in ancient literature as goetic magicians.

In the late Bronze Age Colchis however was not a hilltop village refuge of a shrinking tribe, but a great and powerful kingdom. Its true place in the history of magic has been overlooked due to the oriental focus of later religious bias. As the place of convergence between the lore of Scythia and the Idæan Dactlys, Colchis is at least as important in this history as any nation of the Middle East. All this considered it makes perfect sense that Colchis should be the home of the pre-eminent sorceress in Classical mythology.

The role of Hephæstus in this third book has already been briefly introduced. Apollonius seems to be taking pains to mention him often at this point in the epic. The palace of Aphrodite which he built is the location of the meeting of Hera, Athena and Aphrodite. It will be recalled that these three goddesses are the contestants for the apple of Eris at the Judgement of Paris. While too complex to enter into here, this motif predates not only Homer's *Iliad*, but also had originally a quite different significance. After Hera and Athena enlist the aid of Aphrodite in their plans she visits her son, Eros, to entice him into causing Medea to fall in love with Jason. To accomplish this she offers him a splendid ball, seemingly a toy but actually a cult object. This she tells him was made for him by Adrestia, the nurse of Zeus when he was a child in the Idæan cave. Its splendour is underlined by her telling him that not even Hephæstus could fashion such a wonder.

A little later the fountain of Aeetes palace is described, and this product of Hephæstus' art is replete with significance. It was composed of four perennial springs, reminiscent of the four rivers of Hades or the paradise of *Genesis*. One of these flowed with milk, another with wine, the third with fragrant oil and the fourth with water. These are of course liquids of libation in the rituals of Greek religion. More intriguing still, the fountain of water produced water that was warm when the Pleiades were rising, but as cold as ice when they set. The Greek word for libation, particularly with wine, was *spendein*; this is plainly derived from the Hittite *sipandi* and represents Bronze Age influences. Such offerings were made to gods, whether celestial or chthonic, and to heroes. In this type of offering the liquid, usually the first part of it alone, is tipped by hand. There is another term, *choe*, which represents libations of the whole contents of the vessel, which is made exclusively to chthonic entities – both gods and the dead – and may be made by hand or tipped from a vessel stood on the ground. This is composed of mixed honey, wine and water.

Additionally, Hephæstus had made Aeetes a pair of bulls with hooves and heads of brass, which breathed great blasts of fire. Besides these he had forged a plough from a single piece of indurated steel. This was apparently a thanks offering to the god Helios, who was supposed to have rescued Hephæstus during the war of the gods and giants. It is interesting to note that this war began at Phlegra in Macedonia, which was not a part of civilised Greece. It was resumed at a place of the same name, in Southern Italy near Cumæ, which was afterwards called Vesuvius. The role of barbaric Macedonia, of the site of the most famous ancient necro-manteion and of a volcano in this legend points to another meaning than the ascendancy of the Olympians. The need of Hephæstus for rescuing in the first place is thus thrown into doubt, the likelihood being that this is part and parcel of the reduction of his former prestige. The relationship between Hephæstus and Helios commemorated in the epic is powerfully suggestive of familial relations between deities relevant to ancient ritual. As will be seen as this study proceeds, the bulls and the plough have an integral role to play, in which just such a ritual appears to be described.

Before this let us return to the meeting of the three goddesses, where Hera queen of the gods expresses with vehement passion her determina-tion to assist Jason. Jason, she points out, faces dire calamity, and she is prepared to do anything in her power to save him even if he sails to Hades to rescue Ixion from his chains. This is a very significant phrase; for the Argonauts are of course embarked on a mission to rescue a soul, and the Argo – or Arrow – is the shamanic vehicle for entering the Underworld.

Meanwhile Jason and his men are in conference on their ship; the plan is formed that Jason and a handful of others will go to the palace of Aeetes to negotiate for the Golden Fleece. Jason takes with him the Wand of Hermes, by which is likely meant a herald's wand, which according to cus-tom grants safe passage to its bearer. On their way they pass willows and osiers, from whose branches hang corpses wrapped in ox hide, for, we are told, the Colchians neither burn nor bury their male dead, but hang them from trees; burying only their women. Thus, Apollonius tells us, earth and air both play equal parts in disposal of the dead. In fact, since tombs have been found in the region, it is likely that these bodies had some other significance. This detail need not detain us apart from adding an eerie note to the approach to the city. During this approach the thoughtful Hera covered the city with a mist, so that the heroes might approach the palace of Aeetes unchallenged. Once they had arrived before the gates the mist dispersed, that they might appreciate the wonders before them: the wide gates, soaring columns, the marble cornice and its bronze supports. Not far distant were lofty vines fed by the fountains Hephæstus had made for the king. Within the gates the palace was as wonderful as without. The courtyard contained several buildings, the court of Aeetes; the quarters of his son, Apsyrtus; those of his daughters Medea and Chalciope, as also of the maidservants.

In normal times Medea would have been at the temple of Hecate, of whom she was the principal priestess, but on this day Hera had made sure she would be present when Jason arrived. Thus Medea is the first to see Jason and his companions appear. It is her cry on first laying eyes on him that alerts the palace to their presence. Before long Jason and Aeetes come face to face and the king learns the object of Jason's visit, and is enraged and mistrustful. Just as King Pelius had set Jason the seemingly impossible task of fetching the fleece, so King Aeetes sets another to prevent it:

> I will give thee the fleece to bear away, if thou dost wish, when I have tried thee. For against brave men I bear no grudge. And the trial of your courage and might shall be a contest which I myself can compass with my hands, deadly though it is. Two bulls with feet of bronze I have that pasture on the plain of Ares, breathing forth flame from their jaws; them do I yoke and drive over the stubborn four-acre field of Ares; and quickly cleaving it with the plough up to the ridge, I cast into the furrows the seed, not the corn of Demeter, but the teeth of a dread serpent that grow up into the forms of armed men; them I slay at once, cutting them down beneath my spear as they rise against me on all sides. In the morning do I yoke the oxen, and at eventide I cease from the harvesting. And thou, if thou wilt accomplish such deeds as these, on that very day thou shalt carry off the fleece; ere that time comes I will not give it, expect it not. For indeed it is unseemly that a brave man should yield to a coward.

The bulls and the plough are of course the works of Hephæstus previously described. The field of Ares, the name the Greeks gave to their god of war, is adjacent to the place where the Golden Fleece hangs on a tree guarded by a great serpent. This is plainly a ritual setting and the ploughing feat is – beneath the Classical overlay – a memory of that rite. The names of Greek gods employed are part of this overlay. In the examination of Hephæstus in the second book of the *Argonautica* it was shown how in ancient Italian traditions Mamers and Mulciber (Mars and Vulcan) were closely related. So here it appears very likely that in the original context gods later represented by Hephæstus and Ares were similarly connected.

Although Roman deities often became indistinguishable from their supposed Greek counterparts the god Mars is a major exception. His name had more ancient forms: Mavors, Mamers and the Etruscan Maris. His earlier form had strong agricultural associations, appropriate to the ploughing of the field of Ares. These agricultural functions are underlined by the spring and early summer timing of his major festivals. The name Mars is connected with words such as margin denoting boundaries, an association which may connect him with archaic forms of Hermes, whose phallic image was 'Pelasgian'. His later exclusively warlike associations connect back to his ancient role as defender of the fields and people. From archaic times he was identified with the pastoral god Sylvanus. He was also the parthenogenic son of Juno, born after she had been impregnated by a flower. This is strongly reminiscent of the birth of Attis in the Greek myth of Cybele, as also the parthenogenic birth of Hephæstus.

This then is the archaic background of the feat of ploughing the field of Ares with the plough and bulls made by Hephæstus. Jason has no choice but to agree to perform this deed at the appointed time. After his devastating interview with Aeetes, Jason and his companions returned to the ship. Medea, feeling all the pangs of love that the arrow of Eros had incited within her, retired to her chamber, full of dread for what awaits Jason. She prayed to Hecate that Jason should succeed, or should he fail, that he should at least know that she cared for him. Needless to say, Medea and Jason are brought together and his task made possible by her potent magic. Before their meeting one of the sons of Phrixus who the Argonauts had rescued earlier in the tale gives a classic description of her power:

There is a maiden, nurtured in the halls of Aeetes, whom the goddess Hecate taught to handle with exceeding skill all the magic herbs that are produced both by the land and the flowing waters. With them is quenched the blast of raging flame, and at once she stays the course of rivers as they rush roaring on, and checks the motions of the stars and of the sacred moon.

At the palace Medea, certain that Jason is doomed and that she cannot live without him, considered suicide. The description of her adept knowledge of herbs is mirrored by her actions at this moment of crisis. Alone and distraught she opened a casket in her chamber that contained herbs potent to heal or to slay. Choosing life with all its perils instead, in the next instant she called her maids to prepare to go to the temple of Hecate. It is no coincidence that these maids are twelve in number, with her the thirteenth; the supposed association of this number with a coven of witches is more likely Classical than biblical. While her maidens were preparing her chariot Medea makes her own preparations:

> Medea meanwhile took from the casket a magic balm called the charm of Prometheus. If a man should anoint his body therewithal, having first appeased the Maiden, the only-begotten, with sacrifice by night, surely that man could not be wounded by the stroke of bronze nor would he flinch from blazing fire; but for that day he would prove superior both in prowess and in might. The plant shot up first-born when the ravening eagle on the rugged flanks of Caucasus let drip to the earth the blood-like ichor of tortured Prometheus. And its flower appeared a cubit above ground in colour like Corycian saffron, rising on twin stalks; but in the earth the root was like newly-cut flesh. The dark juice of it, like the sap of a mountain-oak, she had gathered in a Caspian shell to make the charm withal, when she had first bathed in seven ever-flowing streams, and had called seven times in the gloom of night, clad in dusky garments upon Brimo, nurse of youth, night-wandering Brimo, of the underworld, queen among the dead. And beneath, the dark earth shook and bellowed when the Titanian root was cut; and Prometheus himself groaned, his soul distraught with pain.

There are several points of interest in this passage, not least the connection of the potent plant with the Titan Prometheus. His connection with the temple of the Erinyes was introduced at the end of the comment on the second book of the *Argonautica*. The plant which bears his name, as is shown by this powerful passage, also has obvious underworld connections. Additionally the conjunction of his name and sufferings with the description of the spell has parallels in magical practice. Linkage of ritual actions or components with events in the lives of the gods is known as a historiola, and is common in the Magical Papyri and elsewhere. Another example concerning magical plants, which shares similar geographic and underworld connections, is the origin of the poisonous aconite in the saliva from the jaws of Cerberus.

Such 'mini-myths' are not restricted to plant lore nor to pagan magic, but are also frequent in magic drawing on Christian or Jewish sources. Most commonly spirits are commanded by such and such a name of God, and some great deed of the deity is then cited as reinforcement. Agrippa makes frequent mention of this subject in *The Three Books of Occult Philosophy*; see in particular Book III chapters LXI & LXII. There is though a greater immediacy and vitality in the 'pagan' forms; there the historiola is associated with magical plants, or their analogues in image making and other non-verbal crafts. Through combination of verbal and manual magic – *the song of the pestle and mortar* – the physical world of the passing moment becomes simultaneous with mythic events and persons.

The name in Medea's conjuration, Brimo, is a title of both Hecate and Persephone, who indeed in many respects are one and the same, even if Hecate takes the role of Persephone's companion in Classical mythology. The title of Maiden probably indicates Persephone, but is equally appropriate to them both. The title is also directly related to the Latin root from which comes the spirit name Frimost. The incantation being repeated seven times is also strikingly reminiscent of the conjurations of *The True Grimoire*, while ritual purification in seven streams also has parallels in magical rites far from Colchis. Careful readers will note also that Medea shows herself in this passage and those quoted previously to be a supreme *pharmaceus* or enchanter with drugs. This is not the limit of her powers by any means, any more than the frequent connection of pharmakoi with goetes in ancient literature is merely a grouping together of separate types. Indeed, as this passage illustrates well, conjuration of underworld deities and the gathering and use of powerful plants could be performed by the same individual at one and the same time.

Although not all of the *Argonautica* can be retold here, Medea's departure for the temple contains such a striking analogy it cannot be omitted. Apollonius likens her in her chariot to the goddess Artemis driving her chariot drawn by deer; her maidens he compares to the nymphs who attend the goddess, gathered from glens and streams to follow her; and the townspeople averting their eyes from the royal sorceress as she rides past he likens to the animals that pay homage to the Mistress of Beasts. This comparison is more than poetic language, for Medea is an avatar, an embodiment, of the same power and the homage of the beasts is one of her most truly archaic emblems.

Medea comes to the Temple of Hecate and Jason is brought to the same place, attended half way by the seer Mopsus who turns back so that they may meet alone. Here they declare their love, and Medea reveals the magical means by which he can achieve the task set him by her father. The details of the procedure are full of interest, containing many elements of archaic ritual:

Take heed now, that I may devise help for thee. When at thy coming my father has given thee the deadly teeth from the dragon's jaws for sowing, then watch for the time when the night is parted in twain, then bathe in the stream of the tireless river, and alone, apart from others, clad in dusky raiment, dig a rounded pit; and therein slay a ewe, and sacrifice it whole, heaping high the pyre on the very edge of the pit. And propitiate only-begotten Hecate, daughter of Perses, pouring from a goblet the hive-stored labour of bees. And then, when thou hast heedfully sought the grace of the goddess, retreat from the pyre; and let neither the sound of feet drive thee to turn back, nor the baying of hounds, lest haply thou shouldst maim all the rites and thyself fail to return duly to thy comrades. And at dawn steep this charm in water, strip, and anoint thy body therewith as with oil; and in it there will be boundless prowess and mighty strength, and thou wilt deem thyself a match not for men but for the immortal gods. And besides, let thy spear and shield and sword be sprinkled. Thereupon the spear-heads of the earthborn men shall not pierce thee, nor the flame of the deadly bulls as it rushes forth resistless.

Here is seen the purification by river-water appropriate to the great gods of the Underworld, and an offering not of select parts but of the entire sacrifice as appropriate to a chthonic deity. So too the libation contains no wine, but consists of the more ancient offering of honey. Another significant detail is the departure from the ritual site without looking behind. The sound of feet indicates the approach of the goddess, and the baying of dogs is the sound that heralds her coming. To look back at this point undoes the magic and incurs great danger. Averting the eyes is a common feature of such rituals, the chthonic offering is made looking away, and when leaving the site of the ritual, for example at a crossroads, it is done without looking back.

When Medea has given Jason this advice she asks him to remember her should he succeed and return home alive; asking at the same time about the land of his birth. Jason assures her that he will always remember her, and describes his country. He mentions its legendary founder, Deucalion, the son of the Titan and Lord of Fire Prometheus; he is the first man to build cities and worship the gods with due ceremony. Deucalion is an important figure in a variety of contexts; not least that he is the hero of the Greek equivalent of the Great Flood of the biblical *Genesis*; his ship making landfall at Mount Parnassus rather than Ararat in the region of Colchis. A principal difference in the two accounts is that rather than being chosen to survive by God he is warned by his father Prometheus, the *rebel against the All-Father*. In this way the Greek story is closer to the Sumerian original, wherein Enki warns his favourite of the impending flood sent by the chief deity. The Greeks likely obtained this story from Hittite or Hurrian sources in Asia Minor.

After the Flood Deucalion and his wife Pyrrha repopulate the earth by casting stones behind them; those thrown by Deucalion becoming men, those by Pyyrha women. This came about through Deucalion and his wife asking the goddess Themis for an oracle showing them how to populate their land; given the proximity of Parnassus to Delphi this indicates the period before Apollo became lord of that shrine. In this way Prometheus is responsible for the creation of the race of humanity a second time. A very similar motif to this sowing is involved when the time comes for Jason to face his ordeal at the demand of Aeetes; he has to sow the Dragon's teeth which turn into armed men.

The origins of the serpent's teeth Aeetes possessed are as follows: Cadmus was the brother of Europa, and when she was abducted he was ordered to find her or not return to Phœnicia. Failing to recover her he sought an oracle from Apollo and was bidden to build a city where he saw a young heifer stop and eat. He found the heifer and wishing to thank the gods with a sacrifice sent his companions to a nearby grove to fetch water. The grove, like the field where the Golden Fleece was guarded, belonged to Ares. The waters there were guarded by a great serpent, which we may suspect coiled around one of the trees of the grove. All his companions were slain, and Cadmus came himself to see why they had not returned. Seeing the serpent eating their bodies he fought and slew it with the aid of Athena. Advised by her he sowed half the serpent's teeth, the other half was taken by Athena for Aeetes. As when Jason sowed the teeth, there sprang from the earth armed men; as with Jason also Cadmus cast a stone amongst them causing them to fight each other. Where the story differs is interesting, for there were five survivors, the Sparti or sown men; these assisted him in building his city and became the ancestral heroes of the noble families of Thebes. Their names were: Pelorus, Hyperenor, Oudaeus, Chthonius and Echion.

Echion married a daughter of Cadmus named Agave whose sister Semele was mother of Dionysus. Echion and Agave produced Pentheus, who was later the Theban king whose opposition to Dionysus is the theme of the *Bacchæ*. Echion was also the name of an Argonaut, twin brother of Eurytus and son of Hermes. Eurytus is in turn the name of one of the Giants, who was slain by Dionysus.

Incidentally, Cadmus had to serve as the slave of Ares for eight years to atone for the slaying of the serpent; he then became king of Thebes with the assistance of Athena. All of which confirms that the sowing of the serpent's teeth represents an archaic and chthonic rite of kingship, which is how Aeetes can tell Jason he has often performed the task (without exhausting the supply of teeth). The assistance of Athena for the hero and ancestor of the Theban kings represents the sublimated remnants of a tradition of heiros gamos; as a Thracian King like Kotyos would have understood even if Greeks of his time did not.

The involvement of Dionysus and of twin brothers hardly requires overmuch elaboration. Note however the convergence through the sown men of ancestral snaky heroes and the serpent-legged Giants. The myths of Deucalion and Cadmus clarify the *Argonautica*; revealing that the men springing from the sown serpent's teeth were ancestral heroes, representing the first chiefs of ancient clans. The Greek term for these earthborn men is *autochthons*, a term used of the daimons of the Magical Papyri (see PGM IV 1345 & *The True Grimoire* p. 18).

Striking too – in this kingly rite – is the prominence of Ares, a devalued figure in Olympian myth; this is the warrior aspect of the hero, which is also part of the nature of Dionysus. In the *Bacchæ* – which is set at Thebes and involves the Pentheus already mentioned – we are told that Dionysus has a part in the work of Ares, the madness of war. Dionysus was also celebrated for his victorious and warlike campaign across the world.

The end of the story of Cadmus should be noted before moving on. In later life he and his wife leave Thebes under mysterious circumstances, are transformed into snakes, and find their way to the Elysian Fields. The attentive reader will note this signifies their transformation into chthonic heroes and their privileged place in the Underworld. This is comparable perhaps to Achilles and Medea in the afterlife, reigning on the White Island as blessed ancestral figures.

To return to the *Argonautica*: Jason invoked Hecate as advised by Medea, the ritual and the visitation of the deity is worth quoting here:

> *Jason ... went to a desert spot, like some stealthy thief, with all that was needful; for beforehand in the daytime had he taken thought for everything; and Argus came bringing a ewe and milk from the flock; and them he took from the ship. But when the hero saw a place which was far away from the tread of men, in a clear meadow beneath the open sky, there first of all he bathed his tender body reverently in the sacred river; and round him he placed a dark robe, which Hypsipyle of Lemnos had given him aforetime, a memorial of many a loving embrace.*

The bathing and robing follow a format still found in the later grimoires.

> Then he dug a pit in the ground of a cubit's depth and heaped up billets of wood, and over it he cut the throat of the sheep, and duly placed the carcase above; and he kindled the logs placing fire beneath, and poured over them mingled libations, calling on Hecate Brimo to aid him in the contests.

As mentioned before, this offering is of the chthonic type, the whole victim is offered. No altar is raised, the offering is made in a pit instead; the rite Jason performs illustrates the traditional procedures.

> And when he had called on her he drew back; and she heard him, the dread goddess, from the uttermost depths and came to the sacrifice of Aeson's son; and round her horrible serpents twined themselves among the oak boughs; and there was a gleam of countless torches; and sharply howled around her the hounds of hell.

The manifestation of the goddess plainly follows the later type, when she has become wholly a goddess of magic. Yet for all the subsequent devaluation this is a divine, not a diabolical manifestation.

> All the meadows trembled at her step; and the nymphs that haunt the marsh and the river shrieked, all who dance round that mead of Amarantian Phasis. And fear seized Aeson's son, but not even so did he turn round as his feet bore him forth, till he came back to his comrades; and now early dawn arose and shed her light above snowy Caucasus.

Although the event is full of fear it must be clearly understood that Jason's not turning back is not out of terror, but in accord with traditional ritual protocol. The exact same procedure is enjoined in magical instructions in the Papyri.

As readers are doubtless aware, the Golden Fleece hangs upon a tree, which is guarded by an enormous serpent.

… so huge a serpent keeps guard round and about it, deathless and sleepless, which Earth herself brought forth on the sides of Caucasus, by the rock of Typhon, where Typhon, they say, smitten by the bolt of Zeus, son of Kronos, when he lifted against the god his sturdy hands, dropped from his head hot gore; and in such plight he reached the mountains and plain of Nysa, where to this day he lies whelmed beneath the waters of the Serbonian lake.

According to the Greek mythological account the fleece guarding serpent is the offspring of Typhon, and it is interesting to note how here Typhon's resting place is not beneath Mount Etna, a point which will be returned to anon. For now it is sufficient to note that the serpent and the tree are connected as a motif. In fact a second serpent and tree, guarding not the Fleece but the apples of the Hesperides, is encountered in a later part of the story. Yet a third is a background figure in the epic, the grove guarding serpent whose teeth are sown in the Field of Ares. This serpent too is associated with Ares, to whom the grove belonged.

The serpent coiled around a tree is an important element of Thracian iconography. It has been assumed too often that the serpent is a figure of evil, as in the story of Adam and Eve. While this may be the case in Middle Eastern myth, perpetuated in later Western contexts by St. George and the dragon, there are no grounds for assuming a similar meaning in older Greek and Thracian contexts. In fact all the evidence is counter-indicative to this interpretation. As E.V. Rieu notes in his introduction to *The Voyage of the Argo* the author is plainly not averse to snakes, quite the contrary, he represents them extremely sympathetically. In Thracian depictions of the hero he is frequently hunting and spearing a wild boar. In these images the motif of the serpent and tree is often portrayed, but the hero is never shown attacking it. The most straightforward interpretation of all is plainly that the serpent represents the chthonic form of the hero, or the god with whom in death he is identified. This perhaps explains the curious images on Greek pottery depicting Jason regurgitated from the serpents mouth, a motif never encountered in surviving literary sources.

Powerfully supportive of this interpretation is the fact that a serpent is the most common symbol of 'post-mortem' hero cults.

The famous Letnitsa treasure of pictorial golden panels – on one of which ritual hierogamy of the goddess-daughter and hero-son is portrayed extremely graphically – contains a depiction of a woman bearing a mirror alongside a three headed serpent. That this is not an enemy of the hero but his own chthonic form is strongly implied in Euripides' *Bacchæ*; in a powerful chorus the Mænads invoke Dionysus, inviting him to appear in the form of a bull, a many-headed serpent or a fire-breathing lion. The very next speech in the play makes mention of the serpent Ophis whose sown teeth produced the crop of earth-born men.

The name of Asclepius is probably derived from two Thracian words: *as*, a serpent, and *klepi*, to entwine around a staff. This underlines the links between Thrace and the relatively uncivilised region of Thessaly, where the Greek cult of Asclepius flourished long prior to the establishment of his shrine at Epidaurus. The cult of the late Græco-Roman snake god Glycon combined elements from the cults of Sabazius and Asclepius; far from being an innovation both were in fact ancient forms of the hero-son. That Asclepius was a healer reminds us that this is the meaning of the name Jason (himself a Thessalian hero), and a common epithet of serpentine heroes when invoked at their chthonic shrines.

Asclepius was not merely a healer however, but a restorer of the dead to life. Such renewal of life is a well known symbolic meaning of the serpent shedding and renewing its skin. The hero cults and necromantic tradition are again shown to be inter-linked by this deed of the son of Apollo.

GOETIC GALLERY:
SYMPATHIA

Draw the character on an emerald or ruby, for they have a great sympathy with the spirits, especially those of the Sun, who are the wisest, and are friendlier and better than the others.

The True Grimoire

T HE DOCTRINE OF SYMPATHY originates in the sublime conception of the universe as a single living body, of which God is the soul. *Sympathia* or Sympathy is a central and all pervading concept of Western magic. Its origins may lay in the religious magic of Egypt, and related ideas are present in magical thought the world over. This aside the term itself, and its systemised development in all branches of Western magic, is a product of Greek thought. It was first enunciated by Parmenides, it was the core idea in the thought of Empedocles, it was central to the Stoic school, and was enthusiastically adopted and developed by the Neoplatonists. Its adoption by the latter school is of particular importance for Western magic. In the Neoplatonist development of Theurgy, which profoundly influenced Medieval and Renaissance occult thought, Sympathia was central both theoretically and practically.

The Universe, according to this idea, was one thing. The Greeks recognised that this being was composed of parts, be they termed elements, principles, or roots. All things within the One were composed of differing combinations of these roots, be they numbers, gods, animals, plants or stones, places, climates or anything whatever, their essence was defined by these inherent qualities. In addition, to the degree in which any two things resembled each other through shared qualities, they were attractive to one another, regardless of their relative positions in space. This is stated clearly by both Plotinus and Iamblichus: *the Universe is one being, its parts separated by space, but through possession of one nature are drawn rapidly together.* Such parts may be superior or inferior to each other in nature, without in the least diminishing their attraction for one another.

This conception was originally based on the four elements and the principles of attraction and repulsion, dependent on like and unlike qualities. These four elements of course are not to be confused with what moderns understand by the terms; they are more akin to the states of matter recognised in modern science. Thus the Earth of the Greeks resembles not soil or sand merely, but what scientists call solids; Water signifies qualities inherent in what scientists term liquids; Air gases and Fire plasmas. The elements thus represented the subjective experience of a given thing, its characteristics and behaviour, rather than its objective chemical constituents.

As time went on this classification was systematised: Fire possessed the qualities of heat and dryness, Earth possessed dryness and cold, Water cold and moisture, Air moisture and heat. Fire therefore shared the quality of heat with air, and the quality of dryness with earth. Through the lack of any shared quality fire was antipathetic to water.

On this basis the offerings and ceremonies of religion and magic, as understood by the Greeks, included materials conducive to attracting the gods or other beings it was desired to invoke: *Theurgic art, knowing this and having discovered appropriate vessels conforming to the distinct natures of different gods, often connects together stones, herbs, animals, aromatics, and other sacred, perfect and godlike substances of similar kind; then from these it produces a complete and pure receptacle. For it is not proper to despise all matter, but only that foreign in nature to the deities invoked.*

This application of sympathia, as interpreted by the Neoplatonists, gave Western magic the doctrine of correspondences. The original elemental classification also underwent modification and development. In this development the original elemental classification was extended and diversified into planetary and zodiacal symbols. Nevertheless, the elemental symbolism is the basis of the more complex classifications, which can generally be reduced into these simpler terms.

The development of the original concept of Sympathy is also central to astrological thinking. Planets and Signs possess affinities and antipathies towards one another. The manner in which any configuration manifests itself is determined through these inter-relations. The laws of sympathy and antipathy are the basis of the concept of harmonious or disharmonious combinations in astrology. The particular nature of the planets and elements involved in any combination determines the nature of the outcome.

That astrology should be a sophisticated extrapolation of the concept of divine sympathy is hardly surprising. Despite the presence of star-lore in earlier cultures, Babylonian and Egyptian in particular, astrology is a Hellenistic system. The star-lore of the other cultures was not used to produce astrological charts for individuals, nor was the Zodiac as we know it a feature of any of them. In almost every essential the system of astrology known in the West is a product of the Hellenistic era. The degree to which astrology underlies the whole conception of magic in the grimoires cannot be easily over-emphasised. Astrology is the most irrefutable example of the central place of Greek thought – rather than Judæo-Christian theology – in the system of the grimoires.

Empedocles

Empedocles of Agrigentum in Sicily, flourished 444 BCE. His most famous maxim has been restated in various ways down the centuries: *God is an infinite sphere whose centre is everywhere, and whose circumference is nowhere.* His place in history is assured by his distinguishing the four elements and his explanation of the development of the Universe by the forces of Love and Hate (Sympathy and Antipathy), or as moderns would say, attraction and repulsion.

The laws of sympathy (and antipathy) formed a very substantial part of the magical theory of the ancient world, as indeed of the medieval period and the Renaissance. This kind of magic, termed sympathia, was distinguished from devalued goetia by Plotinus, the father of Neoplatonism; it was also accepted by the medieval Church. The great theorists of Renaissance Hermeticism, Mirandola and Cornelius Agrippa among others, were anxious to be understood as using this permitted magic, not goetia. Yet Diogenes Lærtius reported that Gorgias, the famed sophist and pupil of Empedocles, referred to his master as a goen. In other words, the concept of sympathia originates in Goetia prior to its devaluation.

The description Empedocles gave of the four elements was framed poeti-
cally in semi-mythological terms: *Hear first the four roots of all things: bright
Zeus, life giving Hera, and Aidoneus, and Nestis who moistens the springs of
men with her tears.* The usual interpretation of these equates Zeus with
fire, Hera with air, Aidoneus – a name of Hades – equates with earth,
and Nestis with water; an alternative view, with ancient and modern advocates, prefers Air for Zeus, Earth for Hera, Fire for Aidoneus and water
for Nestis. The name Nestis is unknown from other sources, but appears
to represent Persephone. Firstly by analogy with the first pair mentioned,
she would be the partner of Hades, also the name means without eating, and tearful Persephone fasted in the Underworld. This identification
is also accepted in academic studies of Empedocles; particularly Peter
Kingsley, who combines the insights of a qualified academic and an unre-
pentant mystic. The description continues in terms more suited to what
was once known as Natural Philosophy or as we call it, Science: *And these
[elements] never cease changing place continually, now being all united by
Love into one, now each borne apart by the hatred engendered of Strife, until
they are brought together in the unity of the all, and become subject to it. Thus
inasmuch as one has been wont to arise out of many and again with the separation of the one the many arise, so things are continually coming into being and
there is no fixed age for them; and farther inasmuch as they [the elements]
never cease changing place continually, so they always exist within an immov-
able circle.* In this he appears to have anticipated later Megarian philosophers' ideas of an eternal, imperishable cosmos: *For these [elements] are
equal, all of them, and of like ancient race; and one holds one office, another
another, and each has its own nature ... For nothing is added to them, nor yet
does anything pass away from them; for if they were all continually perish-
ing they would no longer exist ... And whither should they perish, since no
place is empty of them ... For from these [elements] come all things that are
or have been or shall be; from these there grew up trees and men and women,
wild beasts and birds and water-nourished fishes, and the very gods, long-lived,
highest in honour.* It is tempting to see these elements, personified as heavenly and chthonic gods and goddesses, as another grouping equivalent to
the first-born race of the Kabirs.

Empedocles was said to be the disciple of a Pythagorean philosopher named Telauges, reputed to be the son of Pythagoras. It may be more likely that Telauges was a consecrated successor of Pythagoras, making Empedocles the successor of an occult Pythagorean lineage. Curiously however, accounts of the life and death of Empedocles draw on a 'letter of Telauges', who is also referred to as Jelanges, son of Pythagoras. This letter was written to Philolaus, himself a famed Pythagorean philosopher of 374 BCE, who proposed a revolving Earth in a heliocentric Solar system, and may have written the *Golden Verses* attributed to Pythagoras. This Telauges cannot be the master of Empedocles. Whatever the case, Empedocles taught the doctrine of transmigration associated with Pythagoras, and other Pythagorean concepts, and was evidently considered highly by later Pythagoreans. His writings included an account of the bodies he had previously occupied: *...I was born once a boy, and a maiden, and a plant, and a bird, and a darting fish in the sea.* These transformations – like those of Pythagoras – resemble the symbols of a Mystery cult. He termed the transmigrating soul, which possessed the power of attaining divinity, the dæmon. Dodds suggests an identity between this indwelling spirit and the soul of the shaman which can be separated from the body during life, and migrate from one incarnation to another. The original form of this concept is not that all souls transmigrate, but that in this way a magician inherits power from his former existences. An Indian origin for this Pythagorean teaching has often been brought forward, but there is no evidence for it, and a more localised origin is far more likely. A description by Empedocles of an unnamed man, who tradition takes to be Pythagoras, supports this idea of accumulated knowledge and power: *And there was among them a man of unusual knowledge, and master especially of all sorts of wise deeds, who in truth possessed greatest wealth of mind for whenever he reached out with all his mind, easily he beheld each one of all the things that are, even for ten and twenty generations of men.*

His pupil Gorgias is reputed to have referred to Empedocles as a *goen* without implying disapproval. It is beyond doubt that his reputation as a divine magician is entirely in keeping with his own view of himself:

> O friends, in this great city that climbs the yellow slope
> Of Agrigentum's citadel, who make good works your scope,
> Who offer to the stranger a haven quiet and fair,
> All hail! Among you honoured I walk with lofty air.
> With garlands, blooming garlands you crown my noble brow.
> A mortal man no longer, a deathless godhead now.
> Where e'er I go, the people crowd round and worship pay,
> And thousands follow seeking to learn the better way.
> Some crave prophetic visions, some smit with anguish sore
> Would fain hear words of comfort and suffer pain no more.

His role as a magician is well illustrated from his writings:

> Cures for all evils whatever there are, protection against old age shalt
> thou learn, since for thee alone will I accomplish all these things. Thou
> shalt break the power of untiring gales which rising against the earth
> blow down the crops and destroy them; and again, whenever thou wilt,
> thou shalt bring back their blasts; and bring unseasonable drought out
> of dark storm for men, and out of summer drought bring streams
> pouring from heaven to nurture the trees; and thou shalt lead out from
> Hades the spirit of a man that is dead.

He taught that by understanding the elemental powers, rain or drought could be conjured by magical songs. His disciples were informed that he could teach them to make the wind blow or cease, the rain to fall or the sun to shine, to banish sickness and old age, and to revive the dead. Significantly this revival is described as a rescuing journey to the Underworld.

Not surprisingly, his reputation among later writers on magic and the cabala is considerable: he is mentioned several times by Cornelius Agrippa in the *Three Books of Occult Philosophy*, and cited as one of his authorities by the famous astrologer-magician Michael Scot. His famous maxim comparing God to an infinite circle is quoted by the Abbot Trithemius; he is several times referred to by Giordano Bruno and Pico della Mirandola, and cited by Reuchlin in his *De Arte Cabalistica*.

The relationship of philosophy and magic in Greece was completely mis-represented by the mechanistic rationalism of nineteenth century thought, creating a false image which is slowly dispersing. Some modern authors have attempted to rationalise the reputation of Empedocles by portray-ing him as a former magician turned scientist; others, such as Bertrand Russell, see him as a scientist who in old age sought solace in magical re-ligion. These convolutions – which seek to retain what they approve and account for what they do not – are both unnecessary and unsupportable from Empedocles' writings. He evidently combined many roles in himself simultaneously. As a goen (perhaps the last to bear the title honourably), he was at one and the same time poet, seer, healer, naturalist, philosopher, preacher and counsellor. A type he clearly describes and identifies with in the *Purifications*: *they* [are] *prophets, hymn-writers, physicians and chieftains among men dwelling on the earth; and from this they grow to be gods, receiv-ing the greatest honours, sharing the same hearth with the other immortals, their table companions, free from human woes, beyond the power of death and harm.*

His poetry was so esteemed that it was recited at the Olympic Games, alongside that of Homer and Hesiod. He was a great opponent of tyr-anny, and several times refused the sovereignty of his native city. He taught rhetoric in Sicily, and alleviated mental anxieties and physical pain with music. He famously forestalled a would-be murderer by the power of music: *When a certain youth ... rushed with a drawn sword on* [Judge] *Anchitus, the host of Empedocles, because ... he had publicly condemned his father to death ... Empedocles changed the intention of the youth by singing to his lyre that verse of Homer* [Odyssey 4. 793–4]:

> *Nepenthe without gall, o'er every ill,*
> *Oblivion spreads;*

He thus snatched his host Anchitus from death, and the youth from his crime of homicide. (*Life of Pythagoras*, Iamblichus, translated by Thomas Taylor). This music magic is typical of the goen and the founders of the Mysteries.

The Many Deaths of Empedocles

So great was his power that Empedocles claimed to have attained the level of divinity while in life. Accounts of his death, and his age on dying are extremely contradictory; with the same mixture of rationalising and mythic symbolism as accounts of his life. However, the oldest stories credit him with bodily translation from the level of humanity to that of divinity. There is a tradition that Empedocles was – like Pythagoras – an incarnation of the archer god Apollo.

Literary materials regarding Empedocles vary from the rationalistic to the mystical or mythological. The impression is inescapable that all are incomplete attempts to make sense of older traditions that were not well understood to either kind of author. Modern academics are naturally cautious in assessing such material. Such caution led to Charles Kahn rejecting the description of Empedocles as a shaman on the grounds we possess no account of Empedocles journeying to the Underworld and returning from the dead. Academic caution is commendable and necessary, and the use of the term shaman in the Greek context is not necessarily helpful. Nevertheless, one is entitled to wonder about the extensive variations in accounts of Empedocles death. There is more than a trace of symbolism involved with these varied accounts, whether related to Greek shamans or to the Mysteries.

> Heraclides, relating…how Empedocles got great glory for sending away a dead woman restored to life, says that [afterwards] he celebrated a sacrifice and that some of his friends, including Pausanias were invited. After the banquet they lay down, some going a little way off, and some laying under the trees close by in the field, and some wherever they happened to choose. Empedocles himself remained in the place where he had been sitting. When day broke, and they arose, he alone was not to be found. When he was sought for, and the servants were questioned, they said they did not know. One of them said that at midnight he had heard a loud voice calling Empedocles, and that he got up and saw a great light in heaven, but nothing else. As they were

all amazed at what had happened Pausanias sent some people to look for him. Afterwards he was commanded not to busy himself about the matter, as what had happened was deserving of thankfulness, and that it was fitting that they sacrifice to Empedocles as to one who had become a god.

Diogenes Lærtius: Life of Empedocles

Lærtius does not tell us who commanded Pausanias in this way, but the tenor of the message strongly suggests it was an Oracle. He then relates that: *Hippobotus says that he rose up and went away as if he were going to climb Mount Etna; and that when he arrived at the crater of fire he leaped in, and disappeared, wishing to establish a belief that he had become a god. But afterwards the truth was detected by one of his brazen slippers having been dropped ... Pausanias, however, contradicts this statement.* Many writers have pointed out that this description derives from a hostile and rationalising retelling of older traditions. It is significant that Demeter, while searching for Persephone, who was abducted in Sicily, lit her torches from the fires of Etna. Also significant is the fact that the single sandal is an emblem of Hecate, whose relation to these goddesses is extremely close.

Diodurus of Ephesus also relates this death by fire; however the Letter of Telauges says he slipped and fell into the sea. Another version given by Laertius, this time quoting Demetrius of Traezen, says that *as the lines of Homer* [presumably *Odyssey* II. 275] *say:*

> He now, self murdered, from a beam depends,
> And his mad soul to dark Hades descends.

Lærtius also recounts a tradition that he died after falling from a chariot on a journey to a festival in Messene. That he broke his thigh in the fall and died of his injuries, and had a tomb at Megara. To what kind of festival was he travelling, was it perhaps in honour of Pelops; in whose legend a death by drowning and another from a fall from a chariot are features? The variations in accounts of Empedocles death include dying in Sicily, and in the Peloponessus (the Greek mainland south of the Isthmus).

Those describing the fall stipulate a Peloponnesian location. This region of Greece had strong connections with Sicily through colonisation, there being a Messene and a Megara in Sicily named after these Peloponnesian cities.

The Greek Megara already possessed a famous tomb, of Megareus son of Poseidon; and any such tomb would have been the site of an oracle. Apollo was worshipped at Megara in the form of a stone pyramid, a form with strong Thracian parallels. Empedocles was perfectly qualified to be associated with an oracular hero's tomb, whether in life as a resident soothsayer or subsequently as the demon of an oracle. Some such oracles – like that of Trophonios – involved journeys to and from the Underworld to obtain one's answers. Whatever the case, literary tradition credits Empedocles, who gave the four elements to occult philosophy, with four deaths: by burning, by hanging suspended in the air, by drowning and by crashing to earth. Although these traditions regarding his death do not originate with Empedocles himself – any more than the death of Moses in the Books of Moses originates with Moses – they are not to be put aside as meaningless. They reflect beliefs and traditions with which he was involved. Empedocles might respond to cautious academics that, despite their reservations, he had his own understanding with Hades.

ELEMENT	RITUAL DEATH	DEITY	ALT. DEITY
Fire	Volcano	Zeus	Hades
Air	Hanging	Hera	Zeus
Earth	Chariot fall	Hades	Hera
Water	Drowning	Nestis	Nestis

ELEMENT	DIRECTION	SIGN	NAME	ALT. NAMES	ELEMENTAL SPECIES
Fire	East	Aries	Bael	Oriens, Magoa	Salamanders
Earth	South	Capricorn	Amaymon		Gnomes
Air	West	Libra	Paymon		Sylphs
Water	North	Cancer	Ariton	Egin, Gaap	Undines

MATERS DE MYSTERIA

'se gu melai – the kiss of Isis is honeyed

Melissa

SARAH ILES JOHNSTON in her *Restless Dead* traces the appearance of the Orphic *goes* to known changes to traditional funereal rites, imposed by the emergent city-states. This change is parallel to transformations in hero cults, from numerous familial hero cults to single civic ones. Various restrictions were now placed on funeral rites, involving numbers of mourners in particular, as well as expense and duration and so on. Alongside the capacity of ostentatious funerals to incite or provoke reaction outside the family group, a key factor in this is the capacity of traditional rites – presided over by females – to incite blood feuds. The words goes and goetia derive from the root *goos*; the howling or lamenting of these female mourners. A key element of the change is indicated by the masculine *-es* or *-etes* suffixed to the feminine *go-* root. This peculiar change in the language occurs as a new male specialist emerges, who is significantly linked to the simultaneous emergence of Orphism. His art involves funeral rites in the new context. Both the laying and raising of ghosts, of influence on the Underworld generally, are associated with him.

Having identified this critical phase in the development of Western magic as a literary tradition, involving the Orphic books, the magical papyri and the grimoires, it is important not to oversimplify, particularly to assume that this is where the magical element in these rites first appears. It is certainly important to discern that the emergent male practitioner is an individual, neither marginalised initially nor at the same time a civic official.

This study seeks to partially regenerate the older stratum by extrapolation from elements of the new. So given the above provisos, this is a pivotal point in our discussion, the precise point from which chthonic religion shows us a new body with an old shadow.

The male Orphic spiritual entrepreneur with his magical manual, his alleged Persian influences and so forth is controversial and important; a Greek shaman at the very root of the magical grimoires. Behind him stands, as it were, a dark alter ego: female, Bacchic, representing and indeed embodying traditions now deemed inimical to the stability of the polis. Orphism reformed or transformed Dionysian traditions, traditions in which females – the frenzied mænads – had formerly been prominent. From this point on real mænadism became increasingly rare, fading to an occasional enactment of ancient custom; finally mænads became merely an artistic convention, flesh and blood women replaced by purely mythic figures. The resemblance of the Dionysian mænads to the avenging Furies commemorates the role of women as major participants in household cults centred on hearth and tomb, and the agrarian magic of the village. Such women and their ritual roles were in many respects the archetypal predecessors for later state magic. Thus, the figures of Medea and Melissa, among others, precede goetia on the Persian male model.

The name Melissa came to be applied to a priestess of Delphi, but the origins of the name far predate the Delphic usage. The name was also a title of priestesses of Artemis, Rhea and Cybele, among others. It is a feature of goddess cults with links to Asia Minor and to Crete, reflecting the Minoan and Hittite influences on certain aspects of Greek religion. Offerings of honey were an unvarying part of rites of the gods at Cretan Knossos. The Dictean cave where the infant Zeus was raised was the home of bees who fed him with honey. Here Melissa was the daughter of Melissus, king of Crete; her sister was Amalthea and together they fed the infant Zeus with the milk of goats (others say that Amalthea was a goat). Melissa is said to be the first to discover honey; some imagine she was turned into a bee, since this is the meaning of the name, another is honey. There is an immense amount of lore from earliest times connected

47

with the bee and with honey. Much of this lore connects with the name Melissa; here we have space only for a portion of it.

Despite the numerous variants of this myth, two elements recur in all: his guards, and being fed upon honey either by bees or by nymphs called bees. Zeus was guarded by the Curetes or Corybantes; as counterparts or companions of the Dactyls these figures represent the males with whom the term goetia was anciently connected. In myth, the chain of important female figures named Melissa begins here. Historically and archeologically also they are connected with the same rites and Mysteries from a very early date. Examining some of the women who bore the name provides additional insights.

One such figure in the 7th century BCE was the wife of Periander – the tyrant of Corinth 625–585 BCE – who he apparently slew during pregnancy. Later he sent messengers to consult the oracle of the dead upon the Acheron regarding a pledge which had been given into his charge by a stranger but could not be found. Melissa appeared, but refused to tell where the pledge was: *she was cold*, she said, *since she had no clothes; those garments buried with her were of no use, since they had not been burnt.* She gave as proof of truth to Periander a cryptic saying: *the oven was cold when he baked his loaves in it.* When this message was brought to him, Periander recognised the meaning of her proof: that he had secretly slept with her corpse.

He immediately made a proclamation that all the wives of Corinth should assemble in the temple of Hera. So the women dressed themselves in their finest clothes, and came there, as if to a religious festival. Then, with the help of his guards, he stripped them all, making no difference between free women and slaves; and, taking their clothes to a pit, he called on the name of Melissa, and burnt the whole heap. This done, he sent a second time to the oracle; and Melissa's ghost told him where he would find the stranger's pledge.

The details of this story are well known from Diogenes Lærtius and other authors, such as Herodotus. It is likely that a degree of rationalisation has taken place, since Periander lived many centuries before these writers, who struggled in interpreting religious and magical aspects of their past. What is certain is that Periander founded Dionysian rites in Corinth, and that the city maintained close links with the necromantic oracle of Thesprotia; for large finds of Corinthian pottery have been excavated there. Daniel Ogden in *Greek and Roman Necromancy* suggests the evidence points to a major cult of Melissa, perhaps as the presiding genius of the oracle. It has been suggested that Periander's actions at the temple of Hera were misunderstood or misrepresented by later authors; rather than a simple act of personal tyranny, what they really represent is the establishing or reforming of a cult. This is very possible: even Herodotus – who was on occasion influenced by political feeling – wrote two centuries after the event, while Plutarch wrote in the first century AD. Periander is without doubt a most complex and exotic figure. He was defined by the Archaic period and must have been near inscrutable to the rationalising classical intelligentsia. He is no less opaque to modern sensibilities: accused of sending boys from Corcyra to be castrated in Lydia, he was also accounted by most ancient authors to be one of the Seven Sages of Greece.

Corinth had substantial and ancient links with the East, having no Mycenaean past. The cult of Hera in Corinthian territory was ancient; the oldest and most sacred temples of Greek culture all belonged to this goddess, and these included a major temple at Perachora, which dated to at least the 8th century. Periander's gathering of fine clothes for a funereal offering to Melissa appears to have taken place at the sanctioned outpost of this temple in Corinth itself. If this was a rite, it bears comparison with Roman rituals of Fortuna Virilis where female ritual nakedness was the norm. It is interesting to note that Corinth was visited by Apollonius of Tyana, a Pythagorean reformer. He is alleged to have there tormented a female vampire named Lamia who appeared in the form of a Phoenician lady, who may represent Melissa.

Corinth also founded the Sicilian city of Syracuse, and maintained close links with their colony. Corinthians then had strong links with cult sites of Persephone, who was equally at home in Sicily or Thesprotia. It has been suggested that Melissa's story is a demythologising of Persephone, and it certainly possesses mythic qualities; but perhaps the evidence suggests a more complex relationship. Servius, in a commentary on *Aeneid* I.

430 wrote of a woman of Corinth named Melissa who refused to initiate others into the Mysteries after her admission into them. She was torn to pieces and Demeter caused bees to spring from her body. This suggests a context involving both Mystery rites and necromantic oracles. Perhaps Periander's relationship with Melissa included something akin to the periodic marriage of the wife of the Basileus to Dionysus, whose mother in Orphic theology was also Persephone. The death of either one of these Melissas also bears comparison with the death of Dirce in Thebes, where the slain queen became a patron of mysterious rites. The context for these traditions suggests ritualised abduction by 'Hades' and marriage to 'Dionysus', in which the descent into the underworld is performed by 'Melissa'.

Helios was honoured to an unusual degree in Corinth, unusual that is on the Greek mainland, as distinct from Rhodes. Medea is said to have come there as an exile, and after her separation from Jason fled the place in a chariot drawn by dragons, which belonged to Helios, the founder of her line. Medea's marriage to Jason had taken place in the cave of the daughter of Aristæus, Makris, who had there fed the infant Dionysus on honey, indicating that she too was a Melissa. Given the connection of honey, caves and ancient rites, the account given by Pausanius of the discovery of the oracle of Trophonius is also worthy of note:

> This oracle was formerly unknown to the Boeotians, they discovered it on the following occasion. No rain had fallen for more than a year, so they dispatched envoys to Delphi from every city. When asked for a remedy for the drought, the Pythian priestess bade them go to Trophonius at Lebadea, and get the cure from him. But when they came to Lebadea, and could not find the oracle, Saon, the oldest of the envoys, saw a swarm of bees, and he advised them that they should follow the bees wherever they went. Straightway he observed the bees flying into the earth and followed them to the oracle.

The antiquity of Boeotian traditions is well established, and the role of Delphi in this tale may be a little suspect. The city of Lebadea was situated near Mount Helicon, the pre-Delphic abode of the Muses; it sent a contingent to the Trojan War. Aspledon, a son of Poseidon and the nymph Midea, founded the city. His mother's name is that of a town in Boeotia, but also of another in Lycia. This country was the winter resort of the god in Delphic times, and a 'primitive' Apollo flourished there well in advance of Delphi.

Medea as Scarlet Woman

Earlier in this study, I pointed out that the Holy Books of Thelema and those of other modern magical movements have their precedents in the Orphic literature. Regarding the most prominent of the former, it is notorious that while the *Book of the Law* makes frequent mention of the Scarlet Woman, it nowhere refers to her as Babalon or by any other name. It is likely enough that the Scarlet Woman has borne more than one name over the ages. What is certain however is that while Babalon is extremely appropriate when drawing on the Biblical tradition, there is an equally compelling alternative in the Classical heritage. The main claim of Babalon is as the personification of the wicked city identified with the Scarlet Woman of *Revelations*. However, the description of the Scarlet Woman in the *Book of the Law* has definite characteristics that have no link to this identification.

III: 43 *Let the Scarlet Woman beware! If pity and compassion and tenderness visit her heart; if she leave my work to toy with old sweetnesses; then shall my vengeance be known. I will slay me her child: I will alienate her heart: I will cast her out from men: as a shrinking and despised harlot shall she crawl through dusk wet streets and die cold and an-hungered.*

III: 44 *But let her raise herself in pride! Let her follow me in my way! Let her work the work of wickedness! Let her kill her heart! Let her be loud and adulterous! Let her be covered with jewels, and rich garments, and let her be shameless before all men!*

III: 45 *Then will I lift her to pinnacles of power: then will I breed from her a child mightier than all the kings of the earth: I will fill her with joy: with my force shall she see and strike and the worship of Nu: she shall achieve Hadit.*

Before examining these, it bears saying that the clauses of warning and of reward (43 and 44) are similar in many details: if she does not 'kill' her heart, then it will be 'alienated', and so forth. Nevertheless, Medea avoided all the limits upon her sex: neither her father nor partner – not even her children that by some accounts she slew – prevented her ascent to 'pinnacles of power'. Did she achieve Hadit, derived from an Egyptian title of the Sun god? As a famed descendent of Helios it is scarcely necessary to ask, while if Nu represents more conventional ideas of the goddess, Medea's solar nature distinguishes her from them. Depicted in Greek literature and art as an outspoken and headstrong woman, decked in barbaric finery, she in no way resembles the modest and veiled chattels of Classical Greek civilisation.

As a skilled pharmakos she has a claim on the cup of Circe, which intoxicates and transforms; if the work demanded of her be magic, she never deserted but rather personifies it. Her bridal night with a hero in the cave of initiation, her bed decked with the sacred fleece, is another claim to the title Scarlet Woman. Her story indeed casts the dire warnings and admonitions back in the face of the Beast. Jason's efforts to play the conventional role of a respectable gentleman saw him fall from the path, without in any way limiting her. The laurels of his achievement – on which he wished to sit – were his only and wholly through her power.

PAPYRUS PARALLELS

THE FOLLOWING RITUAL FROM THE PAPYRI has close correspondences with folk magic and the grimoires. In the text that follows, some of the parallels are indicated with italic type. For comparative purposes I've included *The Cabala of the Black Pullet.*

Apollonius of Tyana's old serving woman: Take Typhon's skull [that of an ass] and write the following characters on it with the blood of a black dog: ......SABERRA. Then, going to a suitable place, by a river, the sea, or at a *fork of a road*, in the *middle of the night* put the skull on the ground, place it under your left foot, and speak as follows:

ERITHYIA [or more likely EILEITHYIA] MEROPĒ GERGIRŌ CHĒTHIRA ANAPEROUCH ... LYRŌPHIA GĒGETHIRA LOLYN GOUGŌGĒ AMBRACHA BI ... AEBILĒ MARITHAIA MPROUCHE ABĒL ETHIRAŌ AP ... ŌCHORIĒLA MŌRĒTHIRA PHECHIRŌ ŌSRI PHOIRA AMERI ... PHĒ. OUTHĒRA GERGERGIŌ TITHEMYMĒ MĒRAPSĒCHIR AŌRIL.

Come, appear, O goddess called Mistress of the House [Nepthys].

After you say this, you will behold sitting on an ***ass*** a woman of extraordinary loveliness, possessing a heavenly beauty, indescribably fair and youthful. As soon as you see her, make obeisance and say: *I thank you, lady for appearing to me. Judge me worthy of you. May your Majesty be well disposed to me. And accomplish whatever task I impose on you.*
   The goddess will reply to you: *what do you have in mind?*
   You say, *I have need of you for domestic service.*
   At that, she will get off the ass, shed her beauty, and will be an old woman. And the old woman will say to you, *I will serve and attend you.*

After she tells you this, the goddess will again put on her own beauty, which she had just taken off, and she will ask to be released.

But you say to the goddess, *No lady, I will use you until I get her.*

As soon as the goddess hears this, she will go up to the old lady, and will take her molar tooth and a tooth from the ass and give both to you; and after that it will be impossible for the old woman to leave you, unless you want to release her. From that time forth, you will receive a bounty of great benefits, for everything that your soul desires will be accomplished by her. She will guard all your possessions and in particular will find out for you whatever anyone is thinking about you [or whatever anyone is plotting against you].

Indeed she will tell you everything and will never desert you: such is her store of good will toward you. But if ever you wish, there is a way to release her (but never do this!). Take her tooth and the ass's tooth, make a bonfire, and throw them into the fire, and with a shriek the old woman will flee without a trace. Do not be prone to release her, since it will be impossible for you to replace her.

But do release the goddess, when you are sure the old woman will serve you, by speaking as follows: MENERPHER PHIĒ PRACHĒRA LYLŌRI MĒLICHARĒ NĒCHIRA. When the old woman hears this, the goddess will mount the ass and depart.

The phylactery to be used throughout the rite: the skull of the ass. Fasten the ass's tooth with silver and the old lady's tooth with gold, and wear them always; for if you do this it will be impossible for the old woman to leave you. This rite has been tested.

The closest parallels for this rite are perhaps the *Spell of Invisibility* in *Verum* and the *Cabala of the Black Pullet*, though others will doubtless occur to readers familiar with the grimoires and folk magic traditions.

54

The Cabala of the Black Pullet,
also called The Secret of the Black Hen

The famous secret of the Black Pullet, a secret which one cannot count on resulting from any Cabala, which had been lost for a long time, and has been found again, we translate hereafter:

Take a black pullet which has never lain eggs and that a single rooster has not approached; do in turn, in taking it, not make it cry out, and for that you must go at eleven o'clock at night, while it is asleep, take it by the neck, so that you'll most especially prevent it from crying out: you return along a large road, to the right place **where two routes cross**; there, **at the stroke of midnight**, make a circle with a rod of cypress, place yourself in he middle and split the hen in two pronouncing these words three times:

Eloim, Essaim, frugativi et appelavi.
[Eloim Essaim, come peacefully and speak with me?]

Turn then to face East, kneel and say an oration; that done, you make The Grand Appellation; then the impure spirit will appear to you dressed in a scarlet galena robe, with a yellow jacket and watery green colour breeches. Its head which will resemble that of a dog with **donkey** ears, will be surmounted by two horns; its legs and feet will be as those of a cow. He will ask you your orders; you will give it these as you well judge, since it will not be able to refuse to obey you, and you will be able to render yourself very rich, and consequently the happiest of men.

The idea of asking a demon for a familiar – more properly a parhedros or magical assistant – simultaneously connected with but separate from itself is exemplified by the relation between Nepthys and the old serving woman. The rite taking place at a fork in the road obviously has many parallels, and points to the correspondences between medieval and New World magical traditions and those of the more distant past. Even the closing words of the rite from the papyri, *this rite has been tested*, would not be out of place in a medieval grimoire, see for examples *Albertus Magnus's Book of Secrets* and others.

Hecate and the Dactyls in the Papyri

In PGM LXX. 4–25 is a ritual plainly drawing on a background of Mystery cult practice. The ritual has been the subject of a paper by the editor Hans Dieter Betz, his analysis of the rite places it in the late 3rd or early 4th centuryAD, and he sees in it elements of a catabasis ritual from the Mystery cults. This initiation involved both Hecate and the Idaean Dactyls, as at Samothrace. As appropriate for a catabasis ritual, the rite involved a descent into a cave. This of course is comparable to that of Trophonios, of necromantic oracles and even the grotto of Mithras &c.

The ritual in the Papyri however is a charm against fear of punishment in the Underworld. This alone alerts us to its eschatological background. There are many interesting details in the ritual, not least two authentic protective magical gestures from the period. Two brief formulae precede the rite (PGM LXIX. 1–3 & PGM LXX. 1–4) wherein similar protective formulae are contained. The first advocates saying PHNOUNEBEĒ twice, then: *give me your strength,* IŌ ABRASAX, *give me your strength, for I am* ABRASAX, the entire formulæ is to be repeated seven times, while holding your thumbs. The second, which may be fragmentary, introduces itself as a charm for favour or protection by undoing a hostile spell, further describing itself as a phylactery and a charm for victory. While similar in purpose the words recited differ from the above: AA EMPTŌKOM BASYM, *protect me.* The ritual in question then follows, and in the introduction the ritualist is instructed to identify themselves with Ereshkigal (in this period seen as identical with Hecate, as becomes apparent) who is *the one holding her thumbs,* referring to the same gesture used above. The magician or initiate uses this formula when confronted in the underworld by a chthonic spirit.

If 'he' (the spirit) approaches after the performance of the above formulæ and gesture, then the magician performs another magical gesture, taking hold of their right heel. An additional formula follows, being a recital of Hecate's symbols: virgin, bitch, serpent, wreath, key, herald's wand, golden sandal. These are plainly symbols from a Mystery rite, and recur throughout the Papyri.

The part of principal interest to Betz, and very relevant to us, involves a further recitation. This includes a variant of the Ephesian letters and a declaration that the ritualist has been initiated, has descended into the underground chamber of the Dactyls and seen the sacred things (the symbols of Hecate aforementioned). The location envisaged for this adventure is a crossroads, which while it may also represent an earthly place, is nevertheless synonymous with that in the geography of Hades. The instructions that follow are specific, having performed this, turn around and flee (that is, do not look back as you depart). The context has changed and similarly the gender of a potentially dangerous spirit changes. It is in such places, the text avows, that *she* appears and it is clear that *she* is Hecate.

There follows an additional and presumably related application; reciting this formula late at night, concerning whatever you wish, the rite will cause it to be shown you in dream. A more serious application then follows; recite it while scattering sesame seeds should an underworld entity lead you away for death and it will preserve you. This occasion could equally be when visiting the underworld as a 'shaman', or in the post mortem state as an initiate possessing special knowledge.

These formulæ all regard manipulation of the underworld, even though the applications apparently differ. A further ritual then follows, and again Hecate theology is clearly discernible; shape a cake from best quality bran, sandalwood and the sharpest vinegar, write the name of your intended victim on it. While doing this the operator looks into a magical light while saying the name of Hecate (likely this indicates the recitation of the appropriate formula: PHORBA PHORBA BRIMŌ AZZIEBYA), adding a request to deprive the target of sleep. Although such instruction is missing, it is clear enough that the intention is that the cake forms a ritual deposit at a crossroads. Its resemblance to a cake for Cerberus, as well as the general context of the material collated, makes this a clear inference. Further protective formulae follow, one of which involves speaking through two knives, reminiscent of the magical use of swords in Balkan rituals with a similar Mystery cult background.

This collection of protective formulae is extremely interesting and underlines various facts. The ASKEI KATASKEI formula is, as we would expect, attributed to the Dactyls; unusually the author also refers to it as the Orphic formula. This, in my opinion, does not and cannot imply that this is an invocation of Orpheus; an interpretation made by Georg Luck in *Arcana Mundi*. Rather it simply conforms to the ancient idea that the rites of the Dactyls came under the tutelage of Orpheus, or as we might say, the Orphic movement.

On a practical level, it is plain that both this formula and the recital of the symbols of Hecate – from an authentic initiation ritual – are here magical devices for protection in a variety of underworld contexts. So too, the leaving of the site without looking back conforms to both the myth of Orpheus, and the magical preparations made by Jason for obtaining the Golden Fleece. Plainly, these are authentic and widely known gestures and practices, worthy of our attention in the modern context.

The symbols previously listed occur in a variety of contexts in the papyri, of which one is particularly interesting (PGM VII. 756–94). Throughout these fascinating texts a female and lunar form appears, balancing the male solar-pantheistic deity (Abraxas, Helios Aion &c.). In this particular rite appears a list of 14 sounds and 28 symbols. Their number implies multiples of the seven vowels of the Greek alphabet and of the seven planets corresponding. Of the 28 symbols 21 are animals, the last seven reproduce the symbols above mentioned. The terms of the incantation reveals that the deity addressed is essentially lunar-pantheistic, only IAO who made her is higher in nature; she is *mistress of the whole world*. The 28 symbols are effectively correspondences of the Lunar Mansions, which I have taken the liberty of attributing to the conventional Mansions of the grimoire tradition, with some additions. As the last seven symbols differ from the remainder insofar as they are not animal symbols, I have also collated animal symbols from other related rites of the Papyri to supplement them. The attribution is a convention facilitating work with the individual mansions. The reader need have no fear that I have made errors in this attribution. Lunar animals are essentially interchangeable, there is no correct order; four groups of seven such animals would do equally well, following the precedent of other lunar rites.

The association of the Mansions with Arab astrology is a misnomer; the Arabs are here, as elsewhere, the heirs of the Hellenistic synthesis. The question remains, from where did the Greeks obtain them? Earlier scholarship has shown that they are not Chaldean in origin. The most likely source appears to be India, which had a lunar astrology from the period of the *Vedas*. From there they were adapted to Hellenistic astrology and thus to the modern Western schema. Tropical astrology with its zero Aries point is not the only system for working with the Mansions, but for the purposes of this synthesis, it is the most straightforward; it dovetails with the grimoires and with modern astrology in a coherent fashion. I therefore make no apologies for not working from the Indian sidereal system, which while valid in its sphere lacks the syncretic qualities I consider desirable.

Astrological Magick and the Gods

CHALDEAN	OLYMPIC	ROMAN	GOETIC SUBTEXT
Ninib	Kronos	Saturn	Dionysus-Kthonios
Marduk	Zeus	Jupiter	
Nergal	Ares	Mars	
Shamash	Helios	Sol	Dis-Pater
Ishtar	Aphrodite	Venus	
Nabu	Hermes	Mercury	
Sin	Selene	Luna	Persephone

Lunar Correspondences integrating elements of the Magical Papyri, True Grimoire and Quimbanda

Lunar Mansion Cusps (Critical Degrees)	Animals & Symbols from the Papyri	Spirits of The True Grimoire	Quimbanda correspondences of Verum Spirits
0 Aries	Ox	Lucifer	Exu Lucifer
12 Aries	Vulture	Satanachia	Exu Marabo
25 Aries	Bull	Agliarept	Exu Mangueira
8 Taurus	Scarab	Tarchimache	Exu Tranca-Ruas
21 Taurus	Falcon	Fleruty	Exu Tiriri
4 Gemini	Crab	Belzebuth	Exu Mor
17 Gemini	Dog	Sargatanas	Exu Veludo
0 Cancer	Wolf	Nebiros	Exu Dos Rios
12 Cancer	Serpent	Astaroth	Exu Rei De Sete Encruzilhadas
25 Cancer	Horse	Scirlin	Exu Calunga
8 Leo	She-goat	Claunech	Exu da Pedra Negra
21 Leo	Asp (or Royal Uraeus)	Musisin	Exu da Capa Preta

4 Virgo	Young Horned Goat	Bechaud	Exu dos Ventos
17 Virgo	He-goat	Frimost	Exu Quebra-Galho
0 Libra	Cynocephalus Baboon	Klepoth	Exu Pomba Gira, Pomba Gira Rainha da Praia.
12 Libra	Cat	Khil	Exu Sete Cachoeiras
25 Libra	Lion	Mersilde	Exu das Sete Cruzes
8 Scorpio	Leopard	Clisthert	Exu Tronqueira
21 Scorpio	Fieldmouse	Sirchade	Exu das Sete Poeiras
4 Sagittarius	Deer	Hiepact	Exu das Matas
17 Sagittarius	Polymorph (Dragoness)	Humots	Exu das Sete Pedras
0 Capricorn	Virgin (Mare)	Segal	Exu Gira-Mundo
12 Capricorn	Torch (Bitch)	Frucissiere	Exu dos Cemiterios
25 Capricorn	Lightning (She Wolf)	Guland	Exu Morcego
8 Aquarius	Garland (Cow)	Surgat	Exu das Sete Portas
21 Aquarius	Caduceus (Camel)	Morail	Exu da Sombra
4 Pisces	Child (Dove)	Frutimier	Exu Tranca-Tudo
17 Pisces	Key (Sphynx)	Huictigaras	Exu Maraba

IMPLICATIONS FOR
MODERN PRACTICE

Solar Magic

THE NATURE OF THE HERO according to the barbarian interpretation is plainly dual, embracing both the Underworld and the Sun. To use Greek terms the nature of the hero is helio-chthonic. The aptness of this identification for our purposes is reflected in the fact that the Abraxas of the Magical Papyri combines Helios and Typhon; the same texts also frequently name them individually. This has several implications concerning modern magick, as well as liturgical adaptations of *The True Grimoire*. The ritual of *The True Grimoire* includes the performance of prayers for success at stated times. These times suggest analogies with rites in modern magical systems; these include both *Abramelin* and *Liber Samekh*, which relate to the attainment of Knowledge and Conversation of the Holy Guardian Angel. The Holy Guardian Angel is referred to Tiferet in modern generic Qabalah, which in turn is related to the Sun. In addition, and of particular interest in relation to *Samekh* in this context, are the four daily adorations of the Sun collected in *Liber Resh vel Helios*, intended for the daily use of the Thelemic magician, but equally of use to modern practitioners of Græco-Egyptian magic:

Verum	*Resh vel Helios*	*Abramelin*	*Samekh*
Dawn	Dawn	Dawn	Dawn
3 hours after	···	···	···
Noon	Noon	Noon	Noon
Sunset	Sunset	Evening	Sunset
on retiring	Midnight	···	Midnight

Very similar timings occur in the Magical Papyri in the context of visionary magic with a lamp (see PDM XIV 153): *you recite the spells of praising Ra at dawn in his rising and you bring the lamp when lighted opposite the sun and recite to it the spells as below four times.* The visionary experience then takes place at midday; see also PDM XIV 295–308 and 475–480 and passim.

Purification Rites

A major part of Orphic ritual, and of the Orphic life, involved purifications; the purpose of these was principally, even wholly eschatological. That is, these were preparations for death. As seen in the accounts of the divine men Empedocles, Pythagoras and others, such rituals not only assured the initiate of an agreeable afterlife, but were part of a process of self deification which – or so we must assume on the basis of available evidence – was to culminate in the post mortem state. As related in Book Four, the religious rituals of the Greeks routinely used purifications with water, comparable to modern magical procedures. The Balkan rites discussed there likely reproduce those of a Thracian mystery cult similar to those of Orphic societies.

My own goetic work employs adaptations of Thelemic ritual known as *Pyramidos*, particularly its opening and closing. An important aspect of this ritual is that it can be broken down into sub-rituals, which are indeed rituals in their own right. In this respect, among others, the rite is deeply instructive. Comparing it to the Orphic idea delineated above, we become aware that purification rites are not mere preparations for the 'big stuff';they are essential processes worth pursuing alone. While the principal reason for this is their eschatological significance, the same process has more day-to-day implications. This capacity is present in Hoodoo and other New World traditions, but temporarily lost sight of in Western magic. They are powerfully protective, and can be employed to rid oneself of malign influences and so forth, often without any other procedures being necessary. Such influences, in antique magic and many still extant are primarily associated with the dead, whether encountered accidentally or deliberately deployed. This underlines the reciprocal relationship of eschatological concerns in all forms of magic.

Self-deification – the Magician as Hero

There are many strands to what I perceive as the importance of reinstating the hero as a spiritual entity in Western magic. One of these is realigning the current with its analogues in other cultures that possess living magical traditions that acknowledge the dead. Recognising the evolved dead as important and venerable spiritual entities demands such a place. So too, though after another manner, the lesser ranks of the dead require our consideration. When we assess the roots of goetia, which are the roots of modern magic in the West, their current neglect is an absurdity. Fallen angels simply cannot compare with the dead as a natural focus of attention; they represent nothing like as great a part of our evolution and life experience. It is apparent that the roots of the tradition, reaching into the present if it were but acknowledged, do indeed make this emphasis; our response should be perfectly clear.

The hero in particular has several natural roles to play, beyond mere lip service to tradition, which the prominence of said angels principally relies on. In fact, heroes are not merely artefacts of ancient Greek or Thracian culture. While their presence may be unsuspected or unidentified, heroes are nevertheless still present at the centre of grimoire magic. This is, to be clear, the magical hero or hero as magician. Grimoire magic is associated with the names of several such heroes, with whom, consciously or not, magicians identify themselves. Three such heroes are strongly associated with grimoire magic, namely Solomon, Moses and Enoch. These are, mythically speaking, the authors of magical texts, who first uttered the incantations and wielded the instruments that these texts prescribe. In effect, the magician is acting with their authority. We are, as it were, stepping into their shoes; in short, identifying with them. Such an illustrious predecessor and role model is, simply put, a magical hero.

An example that particularly illustrates the implicit identification of the magician with a magical hero occurs in the *Grand Grimoire*. This text contains a scripted dialogue with a spirit, which the magician is to replicate when conjuring. The name of the spirit appears beside the words they will speak, the name of Solomon beside those the magician speaks:

Lucifuge Rofocale: *I am here, what do you want of me? Why do you disturb my repose? Smite me no more with that terrible wand.*

Solomon: *Hadst thou appeared when I first called thee. I should have not smitten thee. Know that if thou dost not accede to my request, I am determined to torment thee forever.*

And so on.

Without in the least recommending this procedure, clearly the magician is ritually following in the footsteps of Solomon. While implicit rather than explicit, nothing could be plainer than that the magician is identifying with a hero, the ultimate role model, and that the magic is empowered by so doing. Nor do we have to look very far for examples where this same identification is completely explicit. The ritual of the Headless One, from which derives Crowley's *Liber Samekh*, is one way or other among the most famous rituals in modern occultism. This rite, which originates in the Magical Papyri, involves the magician identifying explicitly with another hero magician of the grimoire tradition:

Thee I invoke, the Headless One,
Thee that didst create the earth and the heavens...
Thou art Asar un Nefer whom no man hath seen at any time
Thou art Iabas Thou art Iapos...
I am Moses your prophet unto whom Thou didst commit thy
   mysteries celebrated by Israel.

Aleister Crowley advised the magician to replace the name Moses with their Adeptus Minor motto, and Israel with his or her 'magical race'. However, in the original context of the ritual the point still stands. In fact, in terms equally appropriate to that context, Crowley's advice essentially means the magician may adapt it only when his or her own self-deification process reaches a suitable point. That is, when they have become – or are becoming – a magical hero in their own right.

Remaining with Crowley for a moment, he was of course the recipient of an inspired or channelled magical text. Adorations from an Egyptian stele, translated in versified form, are an important part of this text; they and the stele form a concise statement of its cosmogony. Both are in widespread use among Thelemites and other magicians. Some of the passages of these adorations are equally explicit concerning the role of a magical hero; in this case, an Egyptian priest named Ankh-af-na-khonsu. Whoever makes these adorations identifies himself or herself with this priest and claims his authority:

I am the Lord of Thebes, and I
The inspired forth-speaker of Mentu;
For me unveils the veiled sky,
The self-slain Ankh-af-na-khonsu
Whose words are truth. I invoke, I greet
Thy presence, O Ra-Hoor-Khuit!

Unity uttermost showed!
I adore the might of Thy breath,
Supreme and terrible God,
Who makest the gods and death
To tremble before Thee –
I, I adore thee!

Appear on the throne of Ra!
Open the ways of the Khu!
Lighten the ways of the Ka!
The ways of the Khabs run through
To stir me or still me!
Aum! let it fill me!

The light is mine; its rays consume
Me: I have made a secret door
Into the House of Ra and Tum,
Of Khephra and of Ahathoor.
I am thy Theban, O Mentu,
The prophet Ankh-af-na-khonsu!

By Bes-na-Maut my breast I beat;
By wise Ta-Nech I weave my spell.
Show thy star-splendour, O Nuit!
Bid me within thine House to dwell,
O winged snake of light, Hadit!
Abide with me, Ra-Hoor-Khuit!

As can be seen, adorants identify themselves with the prophet in the first and fourth verses; in the opening lines of the fifth verse, they name the parents of the prophet as if they were their own. There is no rubric advising the adorant to insert his or her own name or those of their own parents in this rite. It is a straightforward matter of identification with a magical hero, in which the names of the parents form additional reinforcement; such reinforcement incidentally forms a frequent part of many rituals of the Papyri. These examples are sufficient to establish that heroes remain a presence in the magic of the grimoires and elsewhere. This should not be surprising, although the practical implications may require some assimilation. For, when properly understood, the goetic path not only involves calling upon and identifying with heroes, but ultimately becoming one.

VOLCANIC CONJURATIONS

*There are many other mountains all over the earth that are on fire, and yet
we should never be done with it if we assigned to them all giants and gods
like Hephæstus.*

Life of Apollonius of Tyana

I**N INTRODUCING THIS CURIOUS CHAPTER,** an obscure passage of *The
Fourth Book of Occult Philosophy* contained in *A Discourse of the Nature
of Spirits*, by Geo. Pictorius Villinganus, deserves our close attention.
Interestingly enough the *Discourse* is framed as a dialogue between the
Dioscuri, Castor and Pollux:

> Aristotle speaking of miracles, mentioned a certain mountain in
> Norway, named Hechelberg, environed about with the Sea, that con-
> tinually sent forth such lamentable voices, like the yelling & howling
> of infernal devils, insomuch that the noise & clamour of their terrible
> roaring might be heard almost a mile; and the flocking together of great
> Ravens and Vultures near it, did prohibit any access thereunto. And he
> reporteth that in Lyppora near about the Aeolian islands, there was a
> certain Hill from whence in the night there was heard Cymbals, and
> sounds of tinkling instruments of brass, with certain secret & hidden
> screechings, laughings and roarings of Spirits. But even now, Castor,
> thou didst make mention of Zazelus, whom also thou didst assert to
> have been called Eurynomus by Pausania; I desire thee to shew me
> something more largely concerning this Spirit.

The mountain is of course Iceland's most famous landmark, the volcano,
Mount Hecla. It is referred to as Norwegian as Iceland was formerly a
Norwegian possession, where a tolerant attitude was extended to pagan
beliefs from the tenth century. The mention of cymbals and other instruments is reminiscent of the Corybantes, which while apparently a fanciful
resemblance will become less so as this chapter proceeds.

Having thus far introduced the subject of spirits associated with volcanoes in the grimoires, it is time to take the matter further. The following material is drawn from the grimoire materials included in the augmented 1665 edition(s) of Reginald Scot's *Discoverie of Witchcraft*. As with the material from Cellini's autobiography, the relevant material is quoted in full; my comments are interspersed for the purposes of highlighting relevant themes:

> ### A form of conjuring Luridan the Familiar,
> #### otherwise called Belelah
>
> Luridan is a Familiar Domeſtick Spirit of the North, who is now become a servant to Balkin, Lord and King of the Northern Mountains, he calls himself the Aſtral Genius of Pomonia, an island among the Orcades beyond Scotland. But he is not particularly resident there; for in the dayes of Solomon and David, he was in Jerusalem, or Salem, being then under the name of Belilah; after that he came over with Julius Caesar, and remained some hundreds of years in Cambria, or Wales, inſtructing their Prophetical Poets in British Rhimes, being then surnamed Urthin-Wadd Elgin, from whence he betook himself unto this island, Anno 1500 and continued there for 50 years, after which he resigned his Dominion to Balkin, and hath continued ever since an attendant to this Prince.

A notable feature of the passage quoted above is the manner in which it derives a mythological context for the spirits concerned, based on local – that is British – traditions. They are seen as residents in the country despite their former 'Solomonic' residence in the Middle East. The connection with the Romans is also interesting, suggesting some antiquity – real or imagined – for the traditions with which the imported lore has been merged. What is most noteworthy of all is the connection with Welsh Bardic lore, this is important given the connection of poetry and magic in both Greek and Celtic cultures. As can readily be seen none of this is a fanciful elaboration of the text, being clearly stated within it.

He is a Spirit of the Air in the order of Glauron, and is said to pro-
create as mortals do; He is often sent by his Maſter upon errands to
Lapland, Finland, and Strik-finia; as also to the moſt Northern parts
of Russia, bordering on the Northern frozen Ocean: his office (being
called by Magicians) is to demolish ſtrong holds of Enemies, deſtroy-
ing every night what they build the day before; to extinguish fires, and
make their Gunshot that it hath no power to be enkindled; for his
nature is to be at enmity with fire: and under his Maſter with many
Legions he wageth continual warrs with the fiery Spirits that inhabit
the Mountain Hecla in Ise-land, where they endeavour to extinguish
these fiery flames, and the inhabiting Spirits defend the flames from
his Maſter and his Legions.

The mention of Mount Hecla in the *Fourth Book* is undoubtedly the inspiration behind this passage; the legends themselves are genuine and obviously served the need of the author to semi-localise his spirits. Olaus
Magnus wrote extensively about magic in Sweden and Norway in 1555
and in consequence the North gained a major reputation as the stronghold of magic in Europe. The magical elements of Scandinavian culture
were certainly known in the British Isles; and this magical text itself is
said to have been composed by a Norwegian magician named Vaganustus.
There is also a persistent tradition that Norwegian magicians were resident in England in the reign of Elizabeth I.

In this conteſt they do often totally extirpate and deſtroy one another,
killing and crushing when they meet in mighty and violent Troops in
the Air upon the Sea; and at such time many of the fiery ſpirits are de-
ſtroyed, when the Enemy hath brought them off the Mountain to fight
upon the water; on the contrary, when the battle is on the Mountain itself, the Spirits of the Air are often worſted, and then great mournings
and doleful noises are heard both in Iseland and Russia, and Norway
for many days after.

But to proceed to the form of conjuring this aforesaid Spirit, the Magician muſt draw a Circle in a Moonshine night in some solitary Valley; the Circle muſt be 16 foot over, and another Circle a foot distance within the same, being both drawn with chalk, and the Exorciſt being girded about with two Snakes skins tyed together, and having many Snakes skins tyed to his cap, and hanging down before and behinde, muſt also with Chalk draw the form of a fiery Mountain at one side of the Circle on this manner;

The astonishing costume of the magician deserves our attention; it is matched by similar descriptions elsewhere in the *Discoverie*. There is certainly something more than a little shamanic about these garments; the inspiration of this description cannot but have originated with Scandinavian shamans.

And round about the Mountain these following names muſt be wrote, Glauron, Opotok, Balkin, Opotok, Urthin, Opotok, Swaknar, Nalah, Opotok, ✠ ✠ ✠. After the Mountain is drawn, he muſt consecrate the same in these following words, Ofron, Anepheraton, Baron Barathron, Nah halge tour hecla, In the name of the Father, Son and Holy Ghoſt, Amen. ✠ ✠ ✠. After the Magician hath consecrated the Mountain, he muſt write betwixt the circles these following words; Urthin ✠ Malc hii ✠ ✠ Kiddal Kattron ✠ Agla ✠ Glaura ✠ Eashamo ✠ Phowah ✠ Elohim ✠ Immanuel ✠ Amen. [a triangle and cross follow, three times repeated alternately]. Which done, he muſt begin to Invocate the Spirit on this following manner.

Conjuration of Luridan

O ye Powers of the East, Athanaton; of the West, Orgon; of the South, Boralim; of the North, Glauron; I charge and command you by the dreadful Names here mentioned, and the Consecration of this terrible Mountain, to present your selves one of every sort before this Circle by the power of Immanuel, and his holy Name. After this hath with fervency been thrice repeated, the Exorcist will hear great noises of Swords and fighting, Horses neighing, and Trumpets sounding, and at last there will appear four little Dwarfs or Pigmies naked before the Circle, their speech will be antient Irish; which afterwards being confined to a Triangle, they will interpret; the substance thereof will be from where they came last, and what wonderful things they can do; Then the Magician must ask them, if they know one Luridan a familiar; they will answer Hamah ni trulloh Balkin, he is Secretary or servant unto Balkin, and after the Exorcist hath charged them to bring the said Luridan unto him, they will immediately bring him like a little Dwarf with a crooked nose, and present him before the Magician in the triangle; then the Magician shall bind and tye him with the bond of obligation, and with his own blood, without any contract of conditions to be performed, that he will attend him constantly at his thrice repeating Luridan, Luridan, Luridan, And be ever ready to go whether he will, to the Turks, or to the uttermost parts of the Earth, which he can do in an hour, and destroy all their Magazines.

The mention of dwarves speaking the Irish language is another instance of the interweaving of folkloric and Solomonic themes. Fairy-lore themes are particularly prevalent in many English grimoires; this feature resembles in a curious way aspects of European Jewish demonology in Germany and elsewhere on the continent. Plainly the author is aware of the antiquity and pre-Christian nature of the type of spirits involved, although happy enough apparently to adapt Christian magic to their employment.

After the Magician hath so bound him, he shall receive from the Spirit a scrole written in this manner:

Which is the Indenture to serve him for a year and a day; and then the Magician shall dismiss him for that time in the form of a dismission.

The use of the term indenture is worthy of note. Unlike the term pact, it bears no necessary implication of a reciprocal arrangement; however, as will be plain from the text below, these spirits also required to be pleased. This is the end of the ritual as given in Scot, but an additional note follows in Chapter IV of the next book, the spelling, capitalisation and italicised sections are as in the original:

> … we will leave the waters and insist a little on the nature of *Igneous* or *Fiery Spirits* that inhabit the Mountains in Hecla, Aetna, Propo Champ, and Poconzi; Where the Courts, and Castles, of these puissant Champions are kept. The opinion of some is, *That they are not Astral, but Infernal Spirits, and Damned Souls, that for a term of years are confined to these burning Mountains for their Iniquities*: Which opinion although it be granted, yet we may assert, That for the most part the apparitions, sounds, noises, clangours, and clamours, that are heard about the Mountain *Hecla* in *Iseland* and other places, are the effects of separated Starry beings, who are neither capable of good or evill, but are of a middle vegetative nature, and at the dissolution of the *Media Natura* shall be again reduced into their primary Aether.

Aside from its insight into the minds of theologians and others of the period, there is a greater significance to this passage. This is its plain and direct connection of lore associated with Hecla, as in Scot, and Etna, associated with Hephæstus or Vulcan in the mythic background of the present book.

Nor is the association of pagan entities and these spirits out of place, as may plainly be seen in a passage preceding the above by a page or two:

> 7. … the Terrestrial Spirits… are of several degrees according to the places which they occupy, as Woods, Mountains, Caves, Fens, Mines, Ruins, Desolate places, and Antient Buildings, call'd by the Antient

heathens after various names, as *Nymphs, Satyrs, Lamiae, Dryades, Sylvanes, Cobali* &c. And more particularly the Faeries, who do principally inhabit the Mountains, and Caverns of the Earth, whose nature is to make strange Apparitions on the Earth in Meadows, or on Mountains being like Men, and Women, Soldiers, Kings, and Ladyes Children, and Horsemen cloathed in green...

9. Certainly the *Lares* and *Penates,* or household Gods of the antient Heathens were no other than such like Spirits who for several years would keep their residence in one house till upon some displeasure offered, or offenses done by any of the sayd Family, they departed and were never afterwards heard of. There are plenty of such examples to be found in *Olaus Magnus,* and *Hector Boethius* in his *History of Scotland,* relating wonderful passages of *Robin-goodfellows,* and such as have been familiar amongst mankind.

As if to make his meaning plainer to us, his latter day readers, he immediately follows this passage with the assertion that Luridan was a familiar spirit of this kind, and that Balkin, who as he remarks resembled a Satyr, was no more nor less than a Lord and father of the Northern Faeries around Caithness and its islands. He asserts also that the spirits associated with the phenomena of Mount Hecla were of the same kind. If one thing emerges from all this it is the fact following. When the grimoires were being composed magicians already appreciated that the so called evil spirits of the theologians were to be identified with the faeries of the common folk and many entities of antique pagan lore. Indeed, while the magicians and their clients cannot be called pagans as such – save in isolated places like Iceland, and in the Baltic – the familiar spirits were nonetheless remnants of the household gods of the pagans, and persisted far longer than the major gods of the old pantheons.

Another conjuration from the same source, also making use of the image of a volcano, follows next.

Conjuration of Balkin

How to conjure the Spirit Balkin the Master of Luridan

As in the former Chapter, the Exorcist is instructed to draw the form of the Mountain Hecla within the circle, so in this form of Conjuration he must do the same, adding these names to be written around the Mountain; Rahuniel, Seraphiel, Hyniel, Rayel, Fraciel, These are the names of Olympick Angels, governing the North, and ruling over every airy Spirit that belongs unto the Northern Climate; so that the authority of these names must be used in the calling up of this Spirit, because he is a great Lord, and very lofty, neither will he appear without strong and powerful Invocations.

The angels named closely resemble those from the *Heptameron*; they equate with *Angels of the fifth heaven ruling on Tuesday*, being those which are called from the North: Rahumel, Hyniel, Rayel, Seraphiel, Mathiel and Fraciel. This supports the derivation of the Hecla theme from the *Fourth Book*, in which the *Heptameron* was first translated into English.

Therefore the Magician must make upon Virgin Parchement the two Seals of the Earth, and provide himself a Girdle made of a Bears skin with a rough side next his body, and these names wrote about it in the outerside, ✚ Alpha ✚ Coronzon, Yah, Taniah, Adonay ✚ Soncas ✚ Damael ✚ Angeli fortes ✚ pur pur ✚ Elibra, Elohim ✚ Omega ✚ per flammam ignis ✚ per vitam Coronzon ✚ Amen. ✚.

The characters of the angels of the seven daies, with their names:
of figures, seales and periapts

The Seals of the Earth

This passage is rich in interesting and important details. Firstly, the Seals of the Earth illustrated in the older part of *Discoverie*; these serve essentially the same protective role in rites of evocation as some of the pentacles in the better known *Key of Solomon*. These seals and – even more so – the two other talismans from Scot's compendium reproduced below, appear to be older and more primitive than the latter pentacles of Solomon, although not so much as the figures illustrating the oldest Greek text of the *Key*.

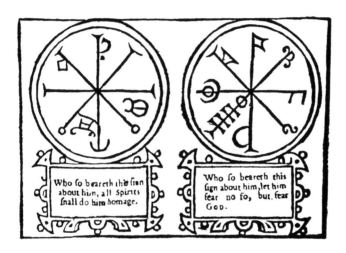

Who fo beareth thɛ fign about him, all Spirits fhall do him homage.

Who fo beareth this fign about him, let him fear no fo, but. fear God.

Next there is the description of the magical belt, which influenced the compiler of the *Goetia of Solomon* along with the names of spirits translated from Weir which were first widely published in English in Scot's text. On the belt and in the rite appears the name Coronzon, often assumed mistakenly to have originated in the Enochian system of Doctor Dee. Here however there is no trace of influence running from Dee to the grimoire, and by far the more likely implication is that the influence runs the other way.

Dee's diary was published in 1659 by Meric Casaubon, whereas this material was added to the *Discoverie* in the augmented edition of 1665 but contains older material. This includes elements of the *Heptameron*, first published in English ten years previously. The Seals of the Earth however appear to be a part of the original text of *Discoverie* as it appeared in 1584. This places it prior to Casaubon's publication by over a century. Indeed April 1584 is the same year that Coronzon appears in Dee's diary; and in order for Scot to publish the Seals of the Earth that year they must have pre-dated both his publication and Dee's diary entry.

Examination of the Dee material shows that Coronzon is not an integral part of the Enochian system. His name is not derived from any Enochian tablet, it occurs in a passage of Dee's diary, and despite being mentioned by the Angel Gabriel this likely reflects Dee and Kelly's acquaintance with this grimoire or others related to it. Coronzon may even derive from corrupt spellings of Kronos in sources such as the *Picatrix*, or perhaps a Byzantine proto-Key. In any case, in the context of this grimoire Coronzon is a name invoked to protect the operator, there is nothing inherently devilish about it.

In addition, the name Soncas which appears on the bear's skin girdle is also derived from the *Heptameron* angels of Tuesday, this time from among the western angels. Resuming our text where we left it:

> Also he muſt provide a black Prieſtly Robe to reach to his ankles, and a new Sword with Agla on one side, and On upon the other; having likewise been very continent and chaſt for three days before the execution of his design: and when the appointed night approacheth, he muſt take with him an earthen pan with fire therein, and a little Viol with some of his own blood, as also some of the Gum or Rozin that comes from the Firr-tree.

The inscription of the sword matches the description in the *Heptameron*. The use of fir resin as incense is a pleasing touch, and again shows the adaptation of the Solomonic materials to local conditions.

And coming from the appointed place in some solitary Valley, the circle must be drawn with chalk, as the former, one circle within another, and these powerful names in the circumference, Otheos on Pathon ✠ Breschit, Hashamaim, Waharetz Wahayah ✠ Tohu ✠ va Bohu [pentagram] ✠ ✠ ✠ [pentagram] magnus es tu ben Elohim qui super alas ventorum equitaris ✠.

The first part of the inscription of the Circle is manifestly derived from the Hebrew text of the first verse of *Genesis: In the Beginning God created the Heavens and the Earth.*

This Circumscription is accounted amongst Magicians of all the most powerful and prevalent.

After this Circle, Mountain, Fire, Turpentine, Girdle, Garments, Sword and Blood must be consecrated according to the foregoing forms of Consecration, adding also this to the end of the consecration.

Mighty art thou O Adonay, Elohim, Ya, Ya Aie, Aie, Acimoy, who hath created the light of the day, and the darkness of the night, unto whom every knee bows in Heaven and on Earth, who hast created the Tohu and the Bohu, that is stupor and numbness in a thing to be admired, and mighty are thy magnificent Angels Damael and Guael whose influence can make the winds to bow, and every airy Spirit stoop; let thy right hand sanctifie these consecrated utensils, exterminating every noxious thing from their bodies, and the circumference of this Circle. Amen. Calerna, Shalom, Shalom, Agla on Sassur, Tafrac, Angeli fortes. In Nomine Patris, Filii, & Spiritus Sancti. Amen, Amen, Amen.

As before the Angels mentioned appear identical with those of the *Heptameron*; Dameal and Guael, Angels of the fifth heaven ruling on Tuesday, who are among those called from the East.

After that, he shall sweep the circle with a Foxes tayl, and sprinkle the same round with his blood, dipping also the Sword, or anointing it with the same, and brandishing the same in his right hand, he shall begin to conjure the Spirit on this following manner.

> *I Exorcise and Conjure thee thou great and powerful Balkin, Lord of Glauron, Lord of Luridan, and of fifteen hundred Legions, Lord of the Northern Mountains, and of every Beaſt that dwells thereon by the holy and wonderful Names of the Almighty Jehovah, Athanatos* ✠ *Aionos* ✠ *Dominus sempiternus* ✠ *Alethios* ✠ *Saday* ✠ *Jehovah, Kedesh, El gabor* ✠ ✠ *Deus fortissimos* ✠ *Anapheraton, Amorule, Ameron* ✠ ✠ ✠ *Panthon* ✠ *Craton* ✠ *Muridon* ✠ *Jay, Jehovah, Elohim pentasseron* ✠ ✠ *trinus et unus* ✠ ✠ ✠ [pentagram] *I Invocate and Command thee thou aforesaid Spirit, by the powers of Angels and Archangels, Cherubim and Seraphim, by the mighty price Coronzon, by the blood of Abel, by the righteousness of Seth, and the prayers of Noah, by the voyces of Thunder and dreadful day of Judgement; by all these powerful and royal words above said, that without delay or malitious intent, thou do come before me here at the circumference of this consecrated Circle, to answer my proposals and desires without any manner of terrible form either of thy self, or attendants; but only obediently, fairly, and with good intent, to present thy self before me, this Circle being my defence, through his power who is Almighty, and hath sanctified the same, In the Name of the Father, Son, and Holy Ghoſt. Amen.*

It is very interesting to note that in the course of making this conjuration the magician makes the sign of a pentagram in the air. This is over three hundred years before the Golden Dawn instituted their Ritual of the Pentagram in which the same gesture appears, and in which it had been thought to originate.

> After the Magician hath thrice repeated this Conjuration, let him immediately set the fire before him, and put the Rozin thereon to fumigate at the appearance of the conjured Spirits, and at the inſtant of their appearance he shall hold the Censer of fire in his left hand, and the Sword in his right, ſtill turning round as the Spirits do.

For a little space after the Invocation is repeated, he shall hear the noise of Thunders, and perceive before him in the Valley a mighty storm of Lightning and Rain; after a while the same will cease, and an innumerable company of Dwarfs or Pigmies will appear mounted on Chamelions to march towards the Circle surrounding the same.

Next comes Balkin with his Attendants; he will appear like the god Bacchus upon a little Goat, and the rest that follow will march after him afoot.

Given the relations between Hephæstus and Dionysus already discussed, the appearance of Bacchus in the context of a volcanic conjuration is intriguingly apt.

As soon as they come near the Circle, they will breath out of their mouths a mist, or fog, which will even obscure the light of the Moon, and darken the Magician, that he cannot behold them nor himself; yet let him not be discomfited, or afraid, for that fog will be quickly over; and the Spirits will run round the Circle after Balkin their Lord, who rides upon a Goat; they will continue to surround the Circle, till the Magician begin the form of obligation or binding their Leader or King in this form, with the Sword in his right hand, the Fire and Rozin burning before him.

Note the position of the fire, as in the conjurations in the Coliseum and the later French grimoires. It is all the more striking that the volcano image occupies essentially the same position as the brazier in the *Grand Grimoire* and *Grimorium Verum*. It is tempting to see in the burning resin a vivification of the volcano image; as if it were simulating the fumes of the fiery mountain. Certainly, the importance of the magical fire in goetic ritual assumes a greater symbolic importance, given the connection of the original Goes with fire as well as mountains and volcanoes and their associated divinities. Nor is it extending this too far to indicate the connection of the sword with magical weapons made by the Dactyls and other workers with fire upon and within such mountains.

I conjure and bind thee Balkin, who art appeared before me, by the Father, by the Son, and by the Holy Ghost, by all the holy Consecrations I have made, by the powerful Names of Heaven, and of Earth, and of Hell, that I have used and uttered in calling upon thee, by the Seals which thou here beholdest, and the Sword which I present [show] unto thee, by this sanctified Girdle, and all the sanctified and potent things aforesaid, That here thou remain peaceably, and of thy present shape before the Northern quarter of this Circle, without injury to me in body, soul, or fortune; but on the contrary, to answer faithfully unto my demands, and not hence to remove, till I have licenced thee to depart, In the Name of the Father, Son, and Holy Spirit. Amen.

When he is thus obliged, he will alight from this Goat, and cause his Attendants to remove further into the Valley, then he will stand peaceably before the Circle to answer the Magician.

After this the Magician shall begin to demand into his own possession a Familiar to build or pull down any Castle or strong hold in a night; and that this Familiar bring with him the Girdle of Conquest, or Victory, that the Magician being girded with the same may overcome all enemies whatsoever.

And further, the Spirit is able to inform him of all questions concerning Thunder and Lightning, the Motions of the Heavens, the Comets and Apparitions in the air, Pestilence and Famine, noxious and malevolent blasts, as also of the Inhabitants of the Northern Pole, and the wonders undiscovered throughout the whole world.

The association of spirits and magicians with the North was elaborated in the work of Olaus Magnus already mentioned.

Likewise if the Exorcist inquire concerning the habitations of starry Spirits, he will readily answer him, describing their orders, food, life, and pastime truly and exactly.

After the Magician hath satisfied himself with inquiries, and curious questions unto the Spirit, there will come from amongst the company a little Spirit of a span long, like a little Ethiop, which the great King Balkin will deliver unto the Exorcist to continue as a Familiar with him as long as his life shall last. This familiar the possessor may name as it pleaseth him.

The three last, who had this Spirit into possession, were three Northern Magicians, the first Honduros a Norwegian, who called it Philenar, and commanded it at his pleasure with a little Bell.

After him Benno his eldest Son injoyn'd the same under the same name. And Swarkzar a Polonian Priest was the last who enjoy'd it under the Name of Muncula; all which names were imposed upon it, according to the pleasure of the Masters; and therefore the naming of this familiar is left to the discretion of the Exorcist.

Polonia is a Latin name for Poland, again indicating Northern connections, real or imagined, for the material reproduced here.

Now when the Master hath taken this familiar into his custody and service, the Spirit Balkin will desire to depart, being wearied if the action continue longer then an hour. Therefore the Magician must be careful to dismiss him in this following form:

Because thou hast diligently answered my demands, and been ready to come at my first call, I do here licence thee to depart unto thy proper place, without injury or danger to man or Beast; depart, I say, and be ever ready at my call, being duly exorcised and conjured by sacred Rites of Magick; I charge thee to withdraw with quiet and peace; and peace be continued betwixt me and thee, In the Name of the Father, Son, and Holy Ghost. Amen.

Then the Spirits company will begin to march about their Prince, and in a formal Troop will march along the Valley, whilst the Magician repeateth Pater Noster, &c. until the Spirits be quite out of sight and vanished.

This is a compleat form of conjuring the aforesaid Spirit, according to the Rules of Vaganostus the Norwegian.

ARGONAUTICA IV:
HOMEWARD BOUND

IN THIS SECTION OF THE ARGONAUTICA the heroes having left Greece behind them at the beginning, now depart also from Thrace and the Black Sea. They travel across and out of mainland Europe by river, and the major climactic part of the adventure takes place in Libya or Africa. This mirrors our journey, where our route re-examines the impact of ancient magic on European grimoires, and the relations of our magic to the Arab world.

The Argonauts fled from Colchis with the Golden Fleece; with a huge Colchian fleet in pursuit. The route of the Argonauts and their pursuers involves all manner of geographical impossibilities; some of the details may be based on old accounts of amber trade routes involving journeys overland and upon rivers. In the *Argonautica* the land routes have been omitted and the rivers and oceans have been assumed to intersect conveniently for a naval pursuit, which they do not. Accordingly the action moves from the Black Sea to the Adriatic, where the next important events occur.

A horrific murder marks the next major stage of the epic, although the details and location vary considerably from one source to another. The oldest tradition has it that the brother of Medea, Apsyrtus, accompanied the Argonauts and that either Medea or Jason slew him and strewed his dismembered corpse in their wake, that Aeetes, obliged to collect them for proper burial, would be delayed. Apollonius departs from this tradition, making Apsyrtus the leader of the Colchian fleet, who, on agreeing to parley is betrayed and murdered by Jason at a Temple of Artemis on a sacred island. Neither version distracts from the main point, which is that Jason and Medea were rendered impure through blood guilt.

Jason, in the account of Apollonius: *cut off the extremities of the dead man, and thrice licked up some blood and thrice spat the pollution from his teeth, as it is right for the slayer to do, to atone for a treacherous murder.*

They then buried Medea's brother on the island, which, when some of their Colchian pursuers settled there, was called Apsorus in his memory. Despite the apparent rightness of the hideous ritual of expiation, Jason and Medea's crime – a complex case of murder, fratricide and sacrilege – was marked by the Furies for punishment. This was a serious obstacle to their completion of the quest's dangers and troubles awaited them until the intervention of another seminal figure in the mythology of ancient magic.

Meanwhile a fight with the crew of Apsyrtus' ship followed the murder. Afterwards Peleus the son of Aeacus and father of Achilles, both major underworld figures, advised flight. The Argonauts took counsel among themselves and perceived that the Colchians would lose heart and be divided by the loss of their prince. Accordingly they sailed on to the mouth of the Eridanus, a famous river commemorated in a constellation. It was near here that the Heliades, sisters of Phæthon, were transformed into poplars, and their amber tears were carried off by the waters of the river. The Colchians were accustomed to compare Apsyrtus to Phæthon, the son of Helios, and call him by this name. Medea and Jason's crime has all the appearance of a ritual slaying equated with the mythic death of the other.

The river Eridanus is often identified with the River Po in modern Italy, but Apollonius' description points to the other side of the Adriatic, the vast complex of islands on the shores of ancient Illyria, modern Croatia. The Argonauts now laid low awhile on the Isle of Amber; as before their story is interwoven with legendary accounts of journeys on the ancient amber trade route. Since the Neolithic era the amber trade had traversed Europe, with amber from Jutland arriving by a combination of land and river routes at the Adriatic for dispersal throughout the Mediterranean. As noted in *The True Grimoire* there is every reason to suspect that traditions concerning amber, rather than ambergris, are an influence on some of the goetic texts.

Here then the Argonauts took refuge, awaiting the dispersal of the Colchian fleet. Their pursuers had been told not to return empty handed and sought new homes for themselves, on the islands and in Illyria, rather than return to face the wrath of Aeetes. This may point to an identification of magical traditions associated with Colchis and the local traditions of Illyrian tribes. A Colchian settlement is said to have been founded near the tomb of Cadmus, the grandfather of Dionysus, who gave Aeetes the dragon's teeth. Curiously the later Byzantine empire relocated Paulician heretics from the region of ancient Colchis, first in Thrace and then in Bosnia, where ancient funeral rites survived until the Middle Ages. Symbols from the cult of the Thracian hero survived on gravestones of this community.

When the Argonauts departed the Isle of Amber, they had difficulty making headway due to the numerous islets ahead of them. They took refuge at an obscure place referred to as the Hyllean coast. Here they bestowed on the friendly locals a sacred tripod, which if buried would preserve the land from any invader. Mention is made of a king Hyllus who had recently died, whose father had once visited the Isle of Macris, the nurse of Dionysus, to obtain absolution for a frightful murder. The Argonauts were unaware that they could make no further progress on their journey until such absolution had been made for the death of Apsyrtus.

Accordingly, the Argonauts departed and sailed far to the south. Here Apollonius conceals his geographical knowledge; in order to preserve the authority of the inviolable but un-geographical *Odyssey*. Accordingly he has the Argonauts leave the string of Liburnian islands which the Colchians had occupied behind them. They then continued on past Corcyra, Melite and Cerossus and see the island of Nymphæa. This he tells us is the home of the goddess Calypso; she had entertained Odysseus and her name may commemorate a connection with the Chalybes. Then Hera, knowing what ills laid in wait if they were not absolved of their crime, intervened with a wind that blew them all the way back to the Isle of Amber. As they ran before the wind the beam of the oracular oak from Dodona which Athena had built into the ship spoke out. It announced in direful tones the anger of Zeus, and that they were doomed to wander endlessly over tempestuous seas until Circe purged them of their guilt. It bade Castor and Polydeuces – who men invoked as guardians from peril at sea – to beg the gods for access to the Italian Sea, where they would find her.

From this point Apollonius is describing unknown territory beyond such geographical knowledge as he or perhaps any Greek possessed. He describes how the ship forged its way up the river Eridanus, and confronted a spectacular scene. What greets them is the outfall of a huge, steaming lake where the son of the Sun-god Helios, Phæthon, had fallen blazing from heaven. So too a nauseating stench arose from his gigantic remains, this is strongly reminiscent of the body of Python buried at Delphi, his very name is said to mean rotting. While not proven it is worthy of note that some commentators have suggested a connection also between Python and the awesome figure of Typhon, another buried god.

His still burning body was the cause of perpetual clouds of vapour. Birds flying over the waters could not make the other side and plunged flightless into the lake. Necromantic oracles situated at underworld lakes were frequently described as 'birdless', while magical vapours are frequently associated with necromantic caves and oracles, not least Delphi but also various caves of Charon or Pluto. On the banks of the river were the daughters of Helios, encased in trees, bewailing their brother's fate and crying tears of amber. It is a haunting scene as Apollonius describes it; the stench from the half consumed god, the loud lamenting of his sisters, are a physical presence in the story. The emphasis is utterly understandable, and an examination of the context is clearly required.

Phæthon

The legend of Phæthon the son of Helios and the nymph Clymene has been little examined by occultists, although his fall from heaven and other elements of his myth connect him with important Luciferean themes. His name figures fairly largely in the *Argonautica*, in the first place as a pet-name for Apsyrtus, son of Aeetes, both of whom are also related to Helios, and secondarily in his own right as a mythological figure alluded to at various points. As a rotting corpse emitting magical vapours, he resembles the similarly named Python at Delphi. He is also at the same time an oracular hero and a mystery god comparable to Dionysus. Additionally, as a murder victim denied marriage and children his was a type of ghost suitable for evocation in necromantic rites.

There are variant forms of his myth; one is of a handsome youth beloved by the goddess Aphrodite, who rewarded him with the care of one of her temples in Syria. In this form he is an ancestor of Adonis, another important figure who is a doomed beautiful youth. This Phæthon is the son of Eos, the Titan goddess of the dawn who was sister to Helios and Selene. Although a variant myth this still places him in the family of Helios, and of Titanic race. His father in this myth is Cephalus, a mortal man.

The more usual form in which he is son of Helios and Clymene is more important here. Clymene, a sea nymph, must be considered; for the variants of her myth are important. In some she is the mother of Prometheus, in others his wife, while also said to be the wife of Helios. It appears to me to be idle to attempt to distinguish the Clymene of these myths from one another as while other Clymenes are to be found, the Clymene in these particular variants is plainly identified as an Oceanid. Part of this confusion may instead be due to the nymph Rhode, from which Rhodes takes its name also, being given the name of her daughter Clymene. In this case it is Rhode who is mother of Phæthon and bride of the Sun. The proximity of Rhodes to Syria underlines the connections of both forms of the myth to Middle Eastern cults. The inter-relation of Prometheus and Helios through Clymene is very interesting in either case. Both are major figures in the *Argonautica*, and Hephæstus is important in relation to each of them. Given the connection of both with fire, it should be born in mind that the fire-working magicians, the Telchines, also originate on the island of Rhodes.

A curious figure arises in the myth as a friend of Phæthon; this is Epaphus the son of Zeus and Io. Epaphus was born on the river Nile and became the king of Egypt married to a daughter of the Nile named Memphis, after whom he named the city he built. He was in turn the father of a daughter named Libya from which Africa took its name. Evidently a fusion of Greek mythology with Egyptian geography is at play here.

According to the myth, Phæthon became vain and was taunted by Epaphus with accusations of mortal parentage. Insulted he came to his father Helios – who it will be recalled was a Sun-god long before Apollo claimed that privileged status – to beg a favour proving his divinity. The generosity of the father was such that he granted the favour before Phæthon named it. His son then asked the right to drive the chariot of Helios through the heavens. Helios foreseeing inevitable disaster tried to dissuade him, speaking of the danger and the impropriety if he undertook the task. The monstrous forms of the zodiacal signs to be encountered on the journey are an important feature of the warning. Phæthon however would not be dissuaded and Helios had sworn the inviolable oath of the gods upon the Styx. Consequently Phæthon took the reins of the chariot and made the attempt, but the horses would not be guided by him and strayed too near the earth, causing blasting heat and threatening a universal conflagration. Zeus, seeing the danger, struck Phæthon dead with a thunderbolt so that he plunged into the river Eridanus.

On the banks of the river the sisters of Phæthon, called the Heliades or Phæthontiades, mourned his loss. Their tears flowed so inconsolably that Zeus or the gods in their compassion turned them into poplar trees on the bank, and their tears became amber carried by the river to the sea. There are differing versions of their names: Lampetie, Phæthusa and Lampethusa; or according to Hyginus: Merope, Helie, Aegle, Lampetie, Phoebe, Aetheria and Dioxippe; Germanicus mentions nine, as if in comparison to the Muses: Merope, Helie, Aegle, Aegiale, Phoebe, Petre, Charie, Arethusa and Dioxippe. The title of Heliades belongs particularly to Phæthusa, Lampetie and Phoebe. Some details of their attributes are given in Apollonius' description, suggesting images reminiscent of the Church sibyls: Phæthusa bearing a silver crook, Lampetie a staff of shining copper.

Another mourner at the riverside was the Ligurian king Cycnus, a kinsman of Phæthon. His mourning was so plaintive and his voice – given him by Apollo – was so sweet that he was transformed into a swan. It is from this myth that we derive the phrase *swan song*, said to be sung before a swan dies, *evoking in a mournful tone*. The chariot of Helios, the Heliades and Cycnus are all commemorated in constellations.

These mythological details are the most widely received but their basis is in much older ritual. The fact is that other authors use Phæthon as a title of the Sun, its interpretation being shining (a similar term is also used of Jupiter). The fall from the chariot is reminiscent of incidents in the myth of Pelops, and of course Empedocles. The foremost cult centre of Helios was at Rhodes, where was anciently celebrated a spectacular sacrifice of a chariot and four horses which were caused to plunge into the sea. Walter Burkert is inclined to link this with the myth of Phæthon, and it is difficult to disagree with him. The names Hyperion (*he who goes before*) and Phæthon (*bright*, or *shining*) were originally epithets of Helios himself; they became separate personalities in later Greek myth, becoming his father and son respectively.

While not mentioned by Homer or Hesiod, later writers describe the night-time passage of Helios from West to East in a golden cup, a form of boat fashioned by Hephæstus, whose relationship with Helios is quite marked in the *Argonautica*. This passage through the night is strikingly similar to Egyptian ideas regarding the boat of Ra. This nocturnal sun is a sign too that Helios is not without a chthonic role, comparable with the solar-chthonic heroes of Thracian cults, while the 'cup' – his boat of the night – resembles the libation bowl central to Thracian and Orphic ritual. The chariot and horses, surely an ancient part of the non-Olympian cult, are also not described by Homer, and first appear in the *Homeric Hymns*. The horses are named in later sources as Pyrios, Euos, Aethon and Phlegon, or as Euos, Aethiops, Bronte and Sterope. The latter two names are very close to two of the Cyclops, assistants of Hephæstus: Brontes, Arges and Steropes. This is far from being the only linkage we have seen between these two gods. The sacrifices to Helios included white rams, boars, bulls, goats and lambs, but particularly white horses and honey.

The Argonauts emerged from their inland river journey at the mouth of the Rhone. Apollonius assures us that this journey was made possible by Castor and Polydeuces, and gives this as the reason for their being honoured with altars and rituals; even though, as he tells us, this was not the only journey where their role of saviours of mariners was demonstrated. This of course was a fulfilment of the oracle the oaken beam from Dodona had made. It is likely their role here is a deliberate prelude to the expiation of guilt by the sorceress Circe; the twins as it were, are lighting the ritual fire. For this reason another glance at the Dioscuri (first examined in Book Four), is a fitting preliminary to this event.

The Dioscuri

The antiquity of the Dioscuri in Indo-European tradition is demonstrated by their precise analogues in the *Rig Veda*, the Asvin; who are horsemen, heroes and protectors. While their father in Greek myth is Zeus, the Vedic Asvin are children of the Sun; who at Rhodes, Corinth and Colchis was called Helios. The Dioscuri as such were pre-eminently worshipped in Sparta, and later Rome where they were known as the Gemini or Castores, but they were widely honoured elsewhere. In addition very similar figures, under different names, were honoured in other states, Messenia had the warrior brothers, Idas and Lynceus, who were Argonauts like the Dioscuri.

The Theban twins, also sons of Zeus and associated with horses, were named Zethos and Amphion. According to the classical myth, Zeus had fathered them on Antiope, who was imprisoned by the orders of her husband's second wife, Dirce. She escaped when near her term, and fled to Mount Cithaeron, where according to Nonnus she gave birth to the twins at a crossroads. They were subsequently raised by a shepherd and kept ignorant of their parentage. Amphion was given a lyre by Hermes (compare Marsyas) and practiced song and music while his brother spent his time hunting and guarding the flocks. They learned the truth of their birth and returned to Thebes, where the ruler Lycus, had given Antiope to his wife Dirce, a daughter of Helios, who treated their mother cruelly. The brothers killed them both, Dirce they slew by tying her to the horns of a bull, a fate she had planned for Antiope. According to some accounts they then threw her in a spring which afterwards bore her name. They then fortified Thebes, Amphion playing his lyre enchanted the stones so that they moved of their own accord (compare Orpheus). After these feats Amphion was married to Niobe, a nymph with various associations with Cybele the Mountain Mother.

Notable in this myth, which contains numerous subtexts, is the rescue of their mother by the twins; comparable to the rescue by the Dioscuri of their sister Helen. Their birth at a crossroads, a detail preserved by Nonnus in his epic *Dionysiaca*, probably represents the Roman integration of the Dioscuri with the Lares. A funerary votive relief from Lebadeia, home of the Oracle of Trophonios, is worth mentioning in this connection. Probably from the early Hellenistic period, it shows an initiate of her cult being presented to Cybele (identified by a flanking lion and throne). He is led by the hand by Persephone, who bears a key; immediately behind her stands Dionysus, then Pan. Behind these is a female figure bearing two torches, this figure is likely to represent Hecate. Behind her is a mature male figure bearing a horn of plenty and flanked by snakes; he is either Trophonios or Zeus Meilichios, if indeed a distinction was drawn between them in the local cult. Finally appear three Curetes with their shields and behind them the Dioscuri in pointed caps. The family of the deceased are represented as far smaller, and stand in front of the Dioscuri; it is interesting to note that the deceased, an initiate, is represented equal in size to the gods, having achieved the status of a hero with their own funerary cult. The whole illustrates that in the Greek mind these varied chthonic gods were interconnected in the rites and Mysteries of the time.

Long before this period the myth of Zethos and Amphion was already powerfully linked to the Dionysian theme; Dirce is said to have been a devotee of Dionysus, and he avenged her by driving Antiope mad, and caused a spring to appear at the site of Dirce's death. There were apparently two springs associated with her, one flowed past Thebes, the other was on Mount Cithaeron. It is not without relevance that Polydeuces' name means *much sweet wine*; the name is a clear reference to ritual usage, reminiscent of male initiations on Lemnos. In addition of course figures such as the Curetes were connected to the birth of Dionysus and the celebration of his Mysteries.

It is important to note that Dirce, whose name means double or cleft, is thought to be the same as Dercetis or Derceto. This is an alternative name of the Syrian goddess Atargatis, whose cult resembled or connected with those of Astarte and Astaroth. She was often represented as a beautiful woman above the waist, while the lower part had the form of a fish. There was also a spring in Spain, whose waters were said to be uncommonly cold, which bore the name Derce. The spring of Dirce was doubtless important in the rituals of ancient Thebes long prior to the classical myth accounting for them. We should not suppose that any historical 'wicked stepmother' gave it its name. It would be highly unwise also to interpret the myth in terms of religious conflict of the Orphic versus Dionysian type, or in any other historical fashion. The whole basis of the myth involved ritual.

The rituals of the Dioscuri and similar figures were intimately connected with initiations involving secret societies of warriors, both Greek and Roman, particularly cavalry. The Roman *equites* (knights) held equestrian parades in honour of the Dioscuri, and practiced secret initiations. The rites of the Dioscuri were often nocturnal, the leader of the Theban cavalry was the only person to know the whereabouts of Dirce's grave. Upon retirement he met secretly with his successor at night and they performed sacrifices in her honour without the use of fire, and removed all trace of their actions before dawn.

Young Spartan warriors also performed nocturnal rites, offering a dog in the temple of Phoebe, a female figure from the myth of the Dioscuri, as Dirce is in the Theban myth of Zethos and Amphion. The Theban practice however is most instructive, the outgoing officer equates fairly naturally with Castor, and the younger man with Polydeuces. The connection of the superior twin with music and the younger with greater activity also makes sense in terms of a hierarchal structure within a secret society of warriors. The imparting of knowledge to the young men by elders in such a society through sacred songs is completely natural in such a context. It is significant too that with the passage of time in such societies the youth becomes at a later stage the elder, so that the twin polarities are united in him.

This is illustrated also in astrological symbolism where the Dioscuri are represented in the constellation Gemini, of which the two brightest stars bear their names. Castor rises with the 19th degree of Cancer and Pollux with the 22nd degree. The word Gemini, meaning twins, was one of their titles among the Romans, who also referred to them as the Castores. The employment of these stars in ritual magic bears very close relation to their mythology. Of the two brothers Polydeuces was immortal and his brother mortal; when Castor was slain Polydeuces was given the choice of living always as an immortal on Olympus or giving half his immortality to his brother so they could divide their time between Olympus and Hades. Polydeuces chose the latter, and the two thereafter alternated between the realm of the dead and the realm of the gods. The rising and setting of these stars has similar significance to the Morning and Evening Stars.

Interestingly, although Polydeuces was the immortal twin, his star, Pollux, is seen as malefic and connected with evening and the dark. By the same token Castor is seen as benefic and connected with the morning and the light. Astrological magicians desiring the benefits of Castor's influence invoke him when his star is rising, but only while Pollux is still below the horizon (in the underworld). When the influence of Polydeuces is required he is invoked in the evening, after the star of his brother has set, that is when it has entered the underworld. His nature, when badly aspected, connected to Ascendant or Midheaven or to the luminaries, is considered brutal, tyrannical, cruel and violent; his brother by the same token confers good nature and elevated morals and manners. The background of the observational star lore described above reflects the Chaldean connections of Greek astrology, for in Babylon the two stars were also seen as a pair, *the herdsman and the warrior,* just as the Phoenicians first saw them as protectors at sea. Despite their Vedic origins, the Dioscuri as we inherit them are a composite of Greek and Middle Eastern tradition.

An important feature of their cult was that they were honoured as immortals with the same burned offerings as Olympians, and also with the libations proper to heroes and the dead. Votive reliefs to the Dioscuri often employed symbols of twinhood. Besides the dokana these could consist of two amphorae, shields, or snakes. The Spartans saw the pear tree as sacred to Castor and Polydeuces, and hung such votive images in its branches.

Classical invocations of Castor and Pollux were unique in involving a table laden with food at the home of the individual or family making the offering. This was called the *theoxenia* or god-entertaining rite, and was proper to the Dioscuri alone. A table was spread, a couch with two cushions prepared and two amphoræ, thought to have been filled with panspermia, a mixture of many grains, placed for them. Votive reliefs show the twins riding through the air to the feast; others show twin snakes curling around the amphorae. After a suitable interval the human participants feast in their honour. In return the Dioscuri protected the celebrants.

Such offerings could be made at the public hearth of a city, but this simply mirrored the domestic cult. In this way the Dioscuri resemble various household gods to be discussed in a later chapter. The cult of the Dioscuri or Castores survived long after the official sanctioning of Christianity, and the Church endeavoured to substitute saints in their place. Of particular interest in this respect are Saints Cosmas and Damian, who were substituted for them in their capacity of healers. In Santeria these saints are the masks of the Ibeyi, divine twins who are children of Chango, an important Orisha who wields thunder in the form of an axe, curiously reminiscent of the thunderbolt wielding Zeus who was the father of the Dioscuri. Interestingly, a favoured offering for the Ibeyi, who are also healers, is to hold a children's party in their honour, reminiscent of the theoxenia.

To summarise then, the Dioscuri represent officers of archaic secret societies central to many themes in the history of goetia and ecstatic religion. They are connected with chthonic and nocturnal rites; being guides and protectors in the Mysteries and in the perils of everyday life. They came to be associated with the crossroads, an archetypal site for the practice of magic; an association which is completely natural to twin figures who are representatives at once of the celestial and the chthonic realms, of light and darkness, death and immortality. They are, finally, associated in myth and ritual with goddesses central to the Mysteries such as Cybele and Demeter, and – through Dirce – with Astaroth, whose importance in ritual magic requires no underlining.

Aea and Circe

To return to the narrative of the Argonauts; having emerged from their riverine adventures with the assistance of the Dioscuri, shortly thereafter the Argo came to the island of Aea. This island is variously placed, and like the island of Nymphae is called the home of Calypso in ancient writings. So too the name represents the island of Circe, and is connected with her Colchian origins as sister of Aeetes. The Argonauts bring the Argo into the harbour, where:

> … from the ship they cast hawsers to the shore near at hand. And here they found Circe bathing her head in the salt sea-spray, for sorely had she been scared by visions of the night. Her chambers and all the walls of her palace seemed to be running with blood, and flame was devouring all the magic herbs with which she used to bewitch strangers who came thence; and she herself quenched the glowing flame with a murderer's blood, drawing it up in her hands; and she ceased from deadly fear. Wherefore when morning came she rose, and with sea-spray was bathing her hair and her garments.

Circe is engaged on their arrival in a traditional purification rite performed in the aftermath of a nightmare. While unaware of it, she is clearly haunted by the horrors of the crime she is to expiate on behalf of Medea and Jason – perhaps even haunted by the ghost of her kinsman Apsyrtus. Our first glimpse of her in the epic reminds us immediately that she is a powerful sorceress, and like Medea is a pharmakos who works her magic with powerful drugs. While repellent substances were employed in magic, *murderers blood* is an example of literary elaboration; the precedent of some of the noxious ingredients enumerated by the witches in the Scottish play. Circe's purifications of course might also be performed prior to expiation rituals such as she is soon to perform. Next, we are told of the strange retinue that accompanies her, substituting for the men turned into animals in Homer's account of her:

And beasts, not resembling the beasts of the wild, nor yet like men in body, but with a medley of limbs, went in a throng, as sheep from the fold in multitudes follow the shepherd. Such creatures, compacted of various limbs, did Earth herself produce from the primeval slime when she had not yet grown solid beneath a rainless sky nor yet had received a drop of moisture from the rays of the scorching sun; but time combined these forms and marshalled them in their ranks; in such wise these monsters shapeless of form followed her.

These are demonic familiars of a sort, and have their analogues in Kabbalistic thought, regarding earlier unsuccessful creations. When men were transformed into animals in the *Odyssey*, it was by Circe's magic. These shambling monstrosities however were produced by earth before Hephæstus or Prometheus created humanity. Does making these monsters the work of an Earth goddess diminish Circe in any way, while simultaneously outdoing Homer? Apollonius' sensibilities would likely not permit either, so he must be intending something else. These monsters follow Circe, while Homer's transformed men approached Odysseus. So in fact, this interlude enhances Circe's authority. The poet may also be suggesting that her authority derives from the goddess whose creation these monsters are; that Circe, like Medea, is a priestess of ancient and terrible Mysteries.

And exceeding wonder seized the heroes, and at once, as each gazed on the form and face of Circe, they readily guessed that she was the sister of Aeetes.

Now when she had dismissed the fears of her nightly visions, straightway she fared backwards, and in her subtlety she bade the heroes follow, charming them on with her hand. Thereupon the host remained steadfast at the bidding of Jason, who went forth drawing with him only the Colchian maid. And both followed the selfsame path till they reached the hall of Circe, and she in amaze at their coming bade them sit on brightly burnished seats. And they, quiet and silent, sped to the hearth and sat there, as is the wont of wretched suppliants.

This act of taking refuge at the hearth reaches deep into the roots of the traditions explored here. As will be seen later in this sixth book, many household gods and spirits were associated with the hearth. In fact the two centres of domestic Greek religion were the hearth and the grave, and the customs relating to these are both important in the history of goetic magic. These domestic traditions are the root and core of the later development of religious practice on a civic and national level. The earliest temples were hearth houses and date to the 8th century, the treasury temples with which we are familiar from the classical period were a later development. Even after this shrines such as Delphi remained the hearth of Greece, the source of sacred fire to renew those elsewhere after times of crisis and war. The sanctity of the hearth explains many features of Greek tradition, including its role as sanctuary for suppliants as here in the home of Circe. This sanctuary could be claimed by strangers as well as kinsfolk. So too the virginity of the goddess Hestia, and of the Vestal virgins, lays in the necessity of ritual purity applied to the fire. A death in the house required the extinguishing of the fire and its renewal from a sacred source. So too the immoveable nature of the hearth explains why Hestia plays little role in Greek mythology despite being one of the Twelve Olympians. Her image never took part in processions, and generally retained a more primitive form, in which separated legs, and even feet, were generally absent.

Medea hid her face in both her hands, but Jason fixed in the ground the mighty hilted sword with which he had slain Aeetes' son; nor did they raise their eyes to meet her look. And straightway Circe became aware of the doom of a suppliant and the guilt of murder. Wherefore in reverence to the ordinance of Zeus the god of suppliants, who is a vengeful god yet succours the guilty, she began to offer the sacrifice with which ruthless suppliants are cleansed from guilt when they approach the altar. First, to atone for the murder still unexpiated, she held above their heads the young of a sow whose dugs yet swelled from the fruit of the womb, and, severing its neck, sprinkled their hands with the blood; and again she made propitiation with other drink offerings, calling on Zeus the Cleanser, the protector of murder-stained suppliants.

Regardless of the appeal to the ordinances of Zeus, the expiatory offering of a sow is in all respects a chthonic ritual. Washing the hands of the
suppliants in this sacred blood is an act of salvation, of washing away sin,
as much magical as religious. Circe not only expiates the crime of murder
– all the more awful in that Medea played a part in the murder of her
own brother – she also effectively lays the ghost, and not dissimilar rites
could equally call them forth. The ghost of Phæthon is of course one who
died by violence, who were doomed to have no rest unless or until being
conjured professionally. He embodies the spirit to be conjured, just as this
action defines Circe as a necromancer. In this role, she is a death goddess,
a very Persephone or Astaroth, the patron of the art and its tutor. As well
she might be, since the performance of just such rituals by female mourners begot goetia in the first place.

All the necessary associations can be grasped in an instant by the visual
sense. See her in soiled and rended vestments; her hair loose and in disar-
ray like a bed of snakes. A Lamia, she has the eyes of Medusa, either in
her face or in her hands. She wields rods: be they whips or wands or fiery
torches; such a woman's eyes are all these things before we resort to hazel
or elder. Her shrieks can invoke vengeance, because as a Fury she embodies it. She is at once the Sibyl conjuring, and the bride of Hades invoked.

Meeting her was a critical point of the journey of Odysseus, and so it
is here for Argonauts, and such drama is appropriate to her first scene in
our narrative. Her immediate duties done, naturally she remains on stage
here and:

> … her attendants the Naiades, who ministered all things to her, bore
> forth from the palace all the refuse of ritual in a mass.

They may have taken it to a crossroads for disposal, perhaps buried it in
the mountains, or cast it into a stream. Naturally Apollonius does not detain us with such details. As a commentator I, like the Naiades, have lesser
tasks to perform than addressing an epic poem to the sophisticated gen-
tlemen of the Alexandrian library. So I shall tell you about the Naiades,
as befits my station.

The Naiades, nymphs of fountains, springs, rivers and wells, were lesser deities in their own right. They dwelled in and around the water sources associated with them, and are essentially indistinguishable from the Undines of later occultism. They are generally depicted as young and beautiful virgins, frequently leaning upon an urn from which water flows. Receiving great veneration, and regarded as the source of oracles, possession and ritual ecstasy, their sacrifices consisted of lambs and goats, attended by libations of wine, honey and oil. Simpler offerings were also made, of milk, fruit and flowers.

That Circe is attended by these lesser deities is deeply significant; while it prefigures the attendance of familiar spirits upon the archetypal witch – as the female attendants of Medea prefigure the coven – there is no doubt that it also powerfully underlines Circe's status as a goddess. It is as such that Homer describes her in the *Odyssey*. There he depicts her dwelling in a stone built house in the middle of a clearing, surrounded by dense forest. Instead of the earth born monsters described by Apollonius, Homer describes this house as surrounded by wolves and lions. These were not savage but fawned upon any men who approached, for they were men themselves, transformed by Circe's magic.

Circe's magical work continues in their absence:

> And within, Circe, standing by the hearth, kept burning atonement-cakes without wine, praying the while that she might stay from their wrath the terrible Furies, and that Zeus himself might be propitious and gentle to them both, whether with hands stained by the blood of a stranger or, as kinsfolk, by the blood of a kinsman, they should implore his grace.

The wineless offering is a well established chthonic rite, associated with both the Furies and with older forms of Dionysus, or indeed Aristæus. The cakes too are a frequent part of rites of the dead, or of Hecate and Cerberus, with parallels in Vedic times. These offerings were likely performed with averted gaze.

Such ritual actions at the hearth were part of the household cults that preceded those of the polis. The hearth was the centre of the household, and the sacred laws of hospitality also revolved around it. Guests, be they strangers or more familiar persons, effectively claimed sanctuary at the hearth as sacred place. The hearth was the place of Hestia, Vesta to the Romans, who was central first to the home, only later to the city-state or Empire. The male head of the household is both priest and the paradigm of Father Zeus, whose role in relation to suppliants in these prayers reflects the relations of the householder to the guest. This was by no means his only name however, gods of fire had equal claim.

Here Circe acts as priestess of her own home; her mythic form a fire goddess, her earthly form an important female of a household cult. This role reminds us that Hera – the Mother – is Jason's patron in the epic. The Mother of the gods is a very complex figure, likely subsuming many disparate regional traditions. Although the pastiche of her in Homer discourages excess effort at rehabilitation in this study, she certainly has a place here. Circe may be enacting these rituals in her honour, or as her representative. If so let us imagine an archaic form of Hera Akrea, with her ancient Corinthian temple linking her to the same traditions as Helios, Medea and Melissa.

The essential expiatory rite performed, Circe is able to seat her guests in chairs of honour, and ask for news and an account of their adventures. For the first time Medea lifts her gaze (the time for averting the gaze and for raising the head, for silence and for speech, are required body language, custom and ritual), and Apollonius speaks of the power residing in the eyes of Children of the Sun, emitting golden rays of flashing light. Later in their adventures Medea wields the famous evil eye, perhaps for the first time in the literary record; the connection of this malign power with that of the Sun is worthy of note.

Medea gives a limited account of their adventures, the quest of the Argonauts and her flight with them from Colchis, omitting to mention the murder. The offence given to Aeetes is admitted, the murder of Apsyrtus not spoken but guessed; Circe – having acquitted the duty expected of host and kinswoman already – will permit them to stay no longer.

Wanderers still, Hera has not forgotten them. Her next intervention on Jason's behalf comprehensively links our themes. Introducing these as swiftly as may be; Hera despatches her messenger, winged Iris, to summon Thetis to her presence. This Iris does, and having sent Thetis to Hera does not escort her but travels to the coast where Hephæstus' anvils are pounded by the hammers of the fire god and his Cyclops assistants. Iris bids him silence them awhile and travels on to the home of the king of the winds, these too are bidden cease, save for a soft air from the west to bear the Argonauts towards the island of King Alcinous.

Thetis meanwhile attends Hera's call, and Hera speaks to her, of her attempted seduction by Zeus, and how Thetis had withstood him from regard for Hera. Zeus' only abandoned this desire when informed of the secret that Thetis was destined by fate to bear a son of greater than his father. A child of promise, whose coming had been the secret Prometheus withheld in defiance of Zeus throughout his torture. Aeschylus' *Prometheus Bound* gives us a truly Luciferian epiphany in expressing the grandeur and nobility of Prometheus' defiance.

According to the regular story Zeus, fearing dethronement as he had dethroned Chronos, desisted from pursuit of Thetis, who bore Achilles to mortal Peleus. At this point of the epic, in the chronology of myth, Achilles was being reared by Chiron the centaur, while Peleus was among the Argonauts. So too Hera foretells that when Achilles comes to the Elysian Fields, he shall there marry Medea. It is difficult not to see in this outcome a fulfilment of the fate of Zeus to be dethroned by a *son greater than his father*. The Father, Hades or Zeus, carries off the maiden; it is a youthful hero, whether Achilles or Jason or a Thracian divine king on the Dionysian model, who wins the hand of the daughter – a Helen, Medea or Melissa – exemplified by Persephone. Such an outcome is itself to be expected, and Apollonius withholds their union from us only a little longer.

Thetis next did as instructed by Hera and visited her mortal husband Peleus, the father of Achilles with a message for the Argonauts. She had left him in a rage a few years before; he had woken in the night and disturbed her passing their son through fire, prior to anointing his limbs with ambrosia. By this process she would have conferred immortality upon him; instead, enraged at Peleus crying out, she abandoned their home and returned to the sea. Remorseful and dazed at seeing Thetis again, when she had gone Peleus passed her instructions to his comrades.

The gentle wind Hera had arranged for them bore them swiftly on, until they came near the island of Anthemoessa (west of Naples: Ischia or Capri).

The Sirens

On the island of Anthemoessa lived the Sirens, monstrous birds with the heads of women whose singing lures mariners to their doom. According to Apollonius, these were the daughters of the river god Achelous, borne to him by the Muse Terpsichore. Although there are several variants of their parentage, one in particular is worth examining. As daughters of the sea god Phorcys, they are sisters of the Graeae and the Gorgons, and of the serpent and nymphs who guarded the golden apples of the Hesperides.

We first met the Sirens when discussing the transposing of the Underworld journey to the starry sky in the *Vision of Er*. Under apparent Pythagorean influence, Plato made them guardians of the Eight Spheres: those of the Fixed Stars and the Seven Planets. In this context the 'music of the spheres' is their song. Now, at one time, there were two Sirens with the delightfully 'barbaric' names of Aglaopheme (*lovely speech*) or Himorepa (*gentle voice*) and Thelxiepia (*enchanting speech*). Later accounts increase this to three, some adding Peisinoe (*persuasive*) to the two above; Apollodorus mentions Peisinoe playing the lyre, Aglaopheme – who he calls Aglaope – singing and Thelxiepia accompanying them on the flute; an alternate listing gives: Parthenope (*maiden voice*), Ligeia (*shrill*) and Leucosia (*white*). There is also a group of four: Thelxiepeia, Aglaopheme, Peisinoe and Molpe (*song*). This gives us a list of eight names, as if awaiting attribution to the spheres of Plato's apocalypse by a contemporary mythographer. In which case I am happy to oblige:

Sphere	Siren
Fixed Stars	Leucosia
Saturn	Himorepa
Jupiter	Molpe
Mars	Ligeia
Sun	Peisinoe
Venus	Aglaope
Mercury	Thelxiepia
Moon	Parthenope

Apollonius records the tradition that the Sirens had formerly been hand-maidens of Persephone, prior to her abduction. Their connection with singing predates their transformation, for as our writer informs us, they used to sing to Persephone in chorus. According to myth, Demeter transformed them into birds. This was either in punishment for the loss of Persephone, or to aid in the search for her. The birdlike form was very frequent in funerary monuments, and even among grave goods. This suggests a benign psychopompic role outside of myth. There is a natural association of these ideas with the magical singing of dirges. When combined with winged beings presiding over the Spheres, an imaginative magician might see the outlines of an ascent ritual.

The resemblance of the Sirens to the small birdlike human figures commonly used to represent ghosts in Greek art is more than coincidental. In fact, both ghosts and Sirens share iconographic details with the Erinyes or Furies. While their original form was birdlike with a human head, the oldest examples are bearded; but throughout mythology and in most representations they are female. Later this appearance gives way to women with fish tails, resembling a mermaid. In this form she is immediately recognisable in the Voodoo loa, La Sirène, an aquatic form of Freda, the

Voodoo Venus. The resemblance of the fish-tailed goddess Atargatis to this later form of siren is likely fortuitous but links the image usefully to Dirce and Astaroth for modern iconographic purposes. Indeed, a demon named Vepar, the 42nd demon of the *Goetia,* is a demon in mermaid form; the table of rulerships in my *True Grimoire* attributes this spirit to Astaroth's rule.

Persephone

Whereas the daughter was initially a projection of the Great Mother of the Gods, in Classical myth and the influential Rites of Eleusis Persephone was the daughter of the chthonic goddess Demeter and of Zeus the Sky-Father. In Homer her name appears as Persephonia, the form Persephone appears first in Hesiod. The latter, it is relevant to remind the reader, was a notable devotee of Hecate. Other forms of the name are: Persephassa, Phersephassa, Persephatta, Phersephatta, Pherephatta and Phersephonia. The Roman form was Proserpina and some features of her cult in Italy, and particularly in Sicily, are prior to the Classical influence.

The name or rather title, Kore, meaning the daughter (of Demeter) was adopted in Attica after the founding of the Eleusian Mysteries; the two were frequently referred to as Mother and Daughter (the Greek for mother being Meter). However, in the Homeric epics there is no trace whatever of her being considered the daughter of Demeter. Nor is there any trace of her being considered in any sense a kindly goddess. Homer describes her simply as the wife of Hades, and she bears epithets which mean *exceedingly awesome* or *dreaded* (Epaine) and *venerable* (Agayn, Agne).

The myth of her abduction by Hades first appears in Hesiod, while for Homer her abode already was in the underworld and she had no connection with the regeneration of vegetation in Spring. That the abduction may have been feigned as part of a marriage ritual is a not unlikely suggestion. Ovid's *Metamorphoses* gives the following lines to the water nymph Arethusa who witnessed the event and told Demeter what she had seen; they well describe the transition from maiden to Hades' Queen:

> All the depths
> Of earth I traverse: – where her caverns lie
> Darkest and nethermost I pass, and here
> Uprising, look once more upon the Stars,
> And in my course I saw her! Yea, these eyes,
> As past the Stygian realm my waters rolled,
> Proserpina beheld! Still sad she seemed,
> And still her cheek some trace of terror wore,
> But all a Queen, and, in that dismal world,
> Greatest in place and majesty, – the wife
> Of that tremendous God who rules in Hell.

Her symbols in this context are the torch or crossed torches, and her diadem; these appear in representations of her whether enthroned beside Hades or alone. However, as with Homer's relative silence regarding Dionysus, omission of other elements regarding Persephone should probably not be over-emphasised as they have been in the past. Since they bear all the signs of great antiquity it is more likely that these elements are ignored in aristocratic epics. Nevertheless her agrarian role is not of particular importance for this discussion, so will be no further enlarged upon. As the Queen of the Underworld it was believed no-one could die unless Persephone or her minister Atropos cut off a hair of their head, which myth may originate as an explanation of the custom of cutting hair from the body and strewing it outside the door as an offering to the goddess.

A point concerning her that is of direct, even central relevance to our study is her role as first mother of Dionysus. In this Orphic version of his myth Dionysus was slain by the Titans, who were then destroyed by the thunderbolts of his father Zeus. Humanity was formed from the sooty smoke arising from their bodies, and thus inherited the guilt of the Titans as a form of original sin. This guilt was expiated by the ascetic practices of Orphism, and also by the famous Initiation of the Dead which was the rite Plato mentioned in his important reference to Goetia. By such means the forgiveness of Persephone for her son's murder was earned for the dead, and a place in the Isles of the Blessed obtained. With the Titanic guilt expiated the initiates partook wholly in the divine nature of Dionysus, permitting them to proclaim *I am a child of Earth and Starry Heaven*; a phrase which appears on the gold funerary leaves buried with Orphic initiates, and echoes the *Hymn to Demeter* of the Eleusian Mysteries.

Having passed the Sirens, the Argonauts faced worse dangers at the Wandering Rocks. Hera had foreseen this and her intervention saves them, arranging for Nereids to carry the ship safely past. Hephæstus – whose forge lies nearby the scene – witnesses their adventure; he rested on the haft of his great hammer to observe the momentous occasion. It can be no accident that Apollonius introduces him so regularly into the tale.

The adventure of the Wandering Rocks is another nod to the geography of the *Odyssey*. Here the Argonauts, like Odysseus before them, confront the monsters Scylla and Charybdis, personifications of dangerous rocks and a deadly whirlpool. The myth of Scylla is particularly interesting, due particularly to the presence in it of both Typhon and of Circe, and bears repeating here. Scylla was once a beautiful nymph, though strange to say a daughter of Typhon (or as others say, of Phorcys, as described in the account of the Sirens). The sea god Glaucus loved her, and when she resisted him, he sought the aid of Circe; whose fame with herbs and incantations was universal. Circe however fell in love with him herself, and tried to banish Scylla from his mind, without success. Circe then punished her rival by enchanting the fountain where she bathed with magical herbs. Scylla was transformed into a frightful monster; below her waist sprang a mass of doglike creatures, which barked incessantly and stood upon twelve legs. Above sprang further monstrous transformations, six different heads, each with three rows of teeth. Appalled, she hurled herself into the sea; there she was instantly transformed into deadly rocks beside the whirlpool of Chaybdis.

Fronting the Ionian gulf there lies an island in the Ceraunian sea, rich in soil, with a harbour on both sides. Beneath which lies the sickle, as legend saith – grant me grace, O Muses, not willingly do I tell this tale of olden days – wherewith Cronos pitilessly mutilated his father. Others call it the reaping-hook of Demeter, goddess of the nether world. For Demeter once dwelt in that island, and taught the Titans to reap the ears of corn, all for the love of Macris. Whence it is called Drepane (Sickle Island), the sacred nurse of the Phaeacians; and thus the Phaeacians themselves are by birth of the blood of Uranus. To them came Argo, held fast by many toils, borne by the breezes from the Thrinacian sea; and Alcinous and his people with kindly sacrifice gladly welcomed their coming.

In the same passage that Apollonius asks the Muses' indulgence for his unwilling recounting of the tale of old time, we encounter Macris, the nurse of Dionysus. This concatenation of attitudes and themes is not merely incidental. The sickle of Kronos is a familiar motif, while less well known is attribution of the same instrument to chthonic goddesses such as Demeter, *goddess of the netherworld*. In Book Four, I mentioned the manufacture of this weapon by the Telchines, its association with Artemis Orthia, and its historical use by the Chalybes, associated with Cybele in her pre-Classical guise. It is also interesting to note that the Chalybes were, so to speak, castrators rather than castratos. While a sophisticated Hellene like our author obviously feels ambivalent regarding some barbaric traditions, he is simultaneously passionate about the Mysteries they represent, albeit in Orphic guise.

An important aspect of the Mysteries is undoubtedly the mystical marriage, which has a mythic prototype in the marriage of Jason & Medea. Here, on the island of Phaeacia, is where it takes place. Some of their Colchian pursuers arriving on the island, they are in grave danger; but both parties are guests of Alcinous and he has authority in the matter. In the story, his wife Arete takes pity on Medea and influences his decision. He tells the Colchians that if Medea is still a virgin they may take her back to her father, but that otherwise he must find for Jason as her husband. This is in fact a fix, as Medea is informed of this decision in advance and arrangements for the marriage are made in haste. Since the marriage rather than the ancient rights of fathers and husbands is what concerns us, it is to that subject we now turn. I shall let the epic poet describe the scene:

And straightway they mingled a bowl to the blessed ones, as is right, and reverently led sheep to the altar, and for that very night prepared for the maiden the bridal couch in the sacred cave, where once dwelt Macris, the daughter of Aristaeus, lord of honey, who discovered the works of bees and the fatness of the olive, the fruit of labour ... There at that time did they spread a mighty couch; and thereon they laid the glittering fleece of gold, that so the marriage might be made honoured and the theme of song. And for them nymphs gathered flowers of varied hue and bore them thither in their white bosoms; and a splendour as of flame played round them all, such a light gleamed from the golden tufts ... That cave is to this day called the sacred cave of Medea, where they spread the fine and fragrant linen and brought these two together.

While in the context of the story in modern eyes this is reminiscent of a marriage of convenience to avert deportation, the cave and other details evidently give it a deeper significance at the same time. An important feature of the Dionysian rites was a mystical marriage; the most freely discussed occurrence of the motif in all Greek religion, yet curiously the only one not referred to as hieros gamos. In Athens and Attica, where Mycenaean survivals are not unlikely, the wife of the archon was married to the god for the occasion. The title of king (*basileus*) and queen was retained in these rites despite democratic rule in Athens. In the Mycenaean Linear B texts the title of basileus is not a title of a ruler, but of a guild master, and in particular the master of the guild of smiths. It is tempting to see in this a connection between Dionysian cults and the religio-political status of smiths in Hittite culture. The *fiery epiphanies* of Dionysus in the *Bacchæ* of Euripides lend circumstantial weight to such an identification.

In any case, Medea and Jason here are certainly taking magico-religious roles; they are living embodiments of a god and goddess united in a deeply significant manner, whether productive of fertility or with some later metaphorical significance overlaid. On one model, the superior partner here is a female deity. Such a marriage affirmed the status of a Thracian style hero-king, who was subsequently deified in the afterlife. On another, the female partner is the mortal wife of an equally mortal basileus, simultaneously married to a god, Dionysus. However, there is in many respects little real difference between the two. What is important is that the divine status of Medea, and the cult significance of much of the story, is plainly underlined. The Colchians accept the fait accompli and the story moves on, but other significant details arise before our heroes depart:

> And still the altars which Medea built on the spot sacred to Apollo, god of shepherds, receive yearly sacrifices in honour of the Fates and the Nymphs. And when the Minyae departed many gifts of friendship did Alcinous bestow, and many Arete; moreover she gave Medea twelve Phaeacian handmaids from the palace, to bear her company.

The significance of the pastoral Apollo is evident, and the sacrifice to Fates and Nymphs has relevance to our theme. The twelve maidens, who clearly substitute for Medea's former attendants as priestess of Hecate, are an artificial way of maintaining a canonical presence. A resemblance to a coven of witches is an obvious inference, but in this ancient context what would they represent? The number of the Olympians is a ready association, and the maidens may embody a solar or lunar zodiac surrounding the goddess in pantheistic mode.

> And on the seventh day they left Drepane; and at dawn came a fresh breeze from Zeus. And onward they sped borne along by the wind's breath. Howbeit not yet was it ordained for the heroes to set foot on Achaea, until they had toiled even in the furthest bounds of Libya.

The Argonauts were close to home when, travelling up the western coast of Northern Greece, fate intervened. A northerly gale blew them off course, sweeping the Argo southwards into the gulf of Libyan Syrtis from which no ship can escape. A high tide beached the ship in a ghostly mist-swept desert landscape, devoid of water or human habitation. The helmsman Ancaeus made clear their desperate plight, no escape by sea was possible from that place, and yet surviving there was equally impossible. The Argonauts despaired and laid down some distance apart, gathering their cloaks over their heads to await a miserable death. Meanwhile the maids of Medea gathered around her and began a piteous dirge. Yet all was not lost:

> ... the heroine-nymphs, warders of Libya, had pity on them, they who once found Athena, what time she leapt in gleaming armour from her father's head, and bathed her by Triton's waters.

Apollonius does not tell us if these nymphs matched Medea's attendants in number. However, he did introduce this stage of the journey with them; and has now mentioned them again immediately before the Libyan warders appear. These nymphs are of course likely to resemble Libyan priestesses, and are associated in the Greek mind with the goddess Athena. If there is such a connection it is likely to be of great age, and Athena would have been quite different from the unassailable political goddess of Athens. There may even be a connection between Athena and the Libyan sibyl as well as older goddesses of whom Lamia is likely a recollection. The later connections of Libya and Greece concern the founding of Cyrene, which is an element in the Argonauts tale. The Oracle of Ammon at Siwa, which is connected with the Libyan Sibyl motif, is also relevant. The goatskin garb of the Libyan nymphs also connects them with orgiastic cults such as those of Dionysus. This is particularly significant considering the symbolism of the oracular advice they give to Jason on this occasion.

> It was noon-tide and the fiercest rays of the sun were scorching Libya; they stood near Jason, and lightly drew the cloak from his head. And the hero cast down his eyes and looked aside, in reverence for the goddesses, and as he lay bewildered all alone they addressed him openly with gentle words: *Ill-starred one, why art thou so smitten with despair? We know how ye went in quest of the Golden Fleece; we know every task ye have faced, all the mighty deeds ye wrought in your wanderings over land and sea. We are the solitary ones, goddesses of the land, speaking with human voice, the heroines, Libya's warders and daughters.*

The use of the word heroines is significant here; heroes in classical Greek cults were indeed wardens of the city to which the cult of an individual hero was attached. Like heroes too, nymphs were essentially chthonic figures who could inspire oracles and cause possession states and ritual frenzy. Perhaps too we should consider the role of Athena in assisting the Argonauts, her connection with these Libyan nymphs may have influenced Apollonius at this stage of his epic.

> Up then; be not thus afflicted in thy misery, and rouse thy comrades. And when Amphitrite has straightway unyoked Poseidon's swift-wheeled chariot, then do ye pay to your mother a recompense for all her travail when she bare you so long in her womb; and so ye may return to the divine land of Achaea. Thus they spake, and with the voice vanished at once, where they stood. But Jason sat upon the earth as he gazed around, and thus cried: Be gracious, noble goddesses of the desert, yet the saying about our return I understand not clearly. Surely I will gather together my comrades and tell them; perhaps between us we can divine a clue of our escape, for the counsel of many is better.

The oracular pronouncement of the Libyan nymphs introduces the next stage of the adventure. Jason roused his comrades with the news of his vision, a good omen if only they could decipher its meaning. Amphitrite is of course the name of an ocean goddess, wife of Poseidon. The reference to her unyoking the chariot of the sea god does not long remain cryptic, for a huge horse springs from the sea and gallops off across the sands. Among the Argonauts is the hero Peleus, the son of famous Aeacus who was made a judge in the Underworld. Peleus is also the father of Achilles by another sea goddess, Thetis, and thus one of the most senior members of the crew. With such a pedigree he was ideally suited to interpret the oracle:

> I deem that Poseidon's chariot has even now been loosed by the hands of his dear wife, and I divine that our mother is none else than our ship herself; for surely she bore us in her womb and groans unceasingly with grievous

travailing. But with unshaken strength and untiring shoulders will we lift
her up and bear her within this country of sandy wastes, where yon swift-
footed steed has sped before. For he will not plunge beneath the earth; and
his hoof-prints, I am certain, will point us to some bay above the sea.

The Argonauts accordingly picked up their ship and carried her across
the sands on their shoulders. The underlying significance of this is to be
sought in Dionysian ritual. From the sixth century there was a ritual of
Dionysus in which a ship was rolled upon wheels or carried in procession. This Burkert connects with a legend of Dionysus known from the
Homeric Hymns. One form of the legend upon which this rite is based
has Dionysus hire a ship at Icaria to take him to Naxos, but the crew are
pirates and decide to sell their passenger as a slave in Asia. The god then
changed the mast and oars into serpents and transformed himself into a
lion, ivy burst forth on all sides of the ship and the playing of flutes filled
the air. The sailors leapt over the side and were transformed into dolphins,
with the exception of the helmsman Acoetes who had protested at their
plans. Another version of the tale has the pirates kidnap the drowsing
youth from the shore at Chios or Icaria. Acoetes was terrified at the awesome power of the god unleashed against his comrades, but Dionysus
reassured him and together they sailed to Naxos as planned. Some accounts of the persecution of Dionysus by King Pentheus suggest that the
prisoner he takes is not the god, but the faithful helmsman. This is all the
more likely as the helmsman in the ritual is the priest of Dionysus, and
doubtless personifies him in some respect.

Dionysus was the chief deity of Naxos, which was apparently founded
by Carian settlers. The mythological significance of Naxos in the legend
of Dionysus is considerable. Dionysus celebrated his triumphant return
from India on the island, a campaign that involved his departure to and
return from foreign parts, a key element of the god's myth. It was at Naxos
also that Dionysus rescued Ariadne after she had assisted Theseus slaying
the Minotaur, and been abandoned on the island. This makes Dionysus
the son-in-law of Minos, another of the Judges of the Underworld, as well
as a son of Persephone; this certainly stresses his chthonic connections.

Ariadne also resembles Medea; in that she is a helper-maiden who assists a foreign hero against her father the king. Medea's stature is greater in direct proportion to the lesser ability of Jason in comparison to Theseus and Homeric heroes. Unlike Ariadne and other helper-maidens she is far from a helpless damsel in distress; as a passionate barbarian Medea broke all the accepted bounds of temperate and civilised society, rejecting at every turn the secondary roles that it laid down for women.

The next important event in the tale is the death of Mopsus; a mythical seer and the object, as we have seen, of an oracular hero cult. The second of the Argonauts to die here, a *dread serpent* bit him, to which creature – connected as it is with chthonic heroes and oracles – Apollonius scrupulously avoids attaching blame:

> …too sluggish of his own will to strike at an unwilling foe, nor yet would he dart full face at one that would shrink back. But into whatever of all living beings that life-giving earth sustains that serpent once injects his black venom, his path to Hades becomes not so much as a cubit's length…

So deadly in fact, that recovery was impossible:

> …not even if Pæeon, if it is right for me to say this openly, should tend him, when its teeth have only grazed the skin.

Pæeon incidentally was a physician who treated wounds suffered by the gods themselves in the Trojan War. Doctors accordingly sometimes received the title Paeonii, and healing herbs *paeoniae herbæ*. It is perhaps best not to speculate on this occasion why saying this was potentially impious.

> For when over Libya flew godlike Perseus Eurymedon for by that name his mother called him – bearing to the king the Gorgon's head newly severed, all the drops of dark blood that fell to the earth, produced a brood of those serpents.

Our author attributes venomous serpents in the Libyan sands to the spilt blood of Medusa. This is reminiscent of the mythic origin of aconite in the saliva of Cerberus. Such a historiola could potentially lend a poison the name *blood of Medusa* in a ritual context.

> ... quickly and in haste they dug a deep grave with mattocks of bronze; and they tore their hair, the heroes and the maidens, bewailing the dead man's piteous suffering; and when he had received due burial rites, thrice they marched round the tomb in full armour, and heaped above him a mound of earth.

The wailing of the maidens is of course the exact ancient funereal practice from which goetia takes its name. The ritual dance in full armour is obviously reminiscent of the dance of the Corybantes. In addition, the placing of the grave of the seer in Libya may well be a claim to some oracular shrine, though not I think that of Jupiter Ammon. Immediately after this the heroes embark, but can find no outlet to the sea:

> Then straightway Orpheus bade them bring forth from the ship Apollo's great tripod and offer it to the gods of the land as propitiation for their return. So they went forth and set Apollo's gift on the shore; then before them stood, in the form of a youth, wide ruling god Triton, and he lifted a clod from the earth and offered it as a stranger's gift, and thus spake: *Take it, friends, for no stranger's gift of great worth have I here by me now to place in the hands of those who beseech me. But if ye are searching for a passage through this sea, as often is the need of men passing through a strange land, I will declare it. For my sire Poseidon has made me to be well versed in this sea. And I rule the shore if haply in your distant land you have ever heard of Eurypylus, born in Libya, the home of wild beasts.*

The clod of earth, a seemingly lowly gift, is a token of hospitality in keeping with ancient custom. It bears far greater significance than appears, for it represents a claim to the territory sanctioned by a god. This is a mythic event legitimising the presence in Libya of Greek cities, in particular the city of Cyrene, with its links to Aristæus. The sea god Triton, answering the magic of Orpheus' offering, comes in disguise as a noble youth named Eurypylus. According to Pindar this youth was the son of Poseidon *the earth-embracer, immortal Ennosides.* A scholiast on Apollonius, which has several times done us service, names his mother as Celaeno. She was a daughter of Atlas who after death the gods placed among the stars as one of the Pleiades. Although a minor character in some respects, he is a valuable connecting thread in our tapestry, worthy of a digression here.

Eurypylus

The hero Eurypylus, whose parentage we have briefly described, was either a prince or king in the region of the future city of Cyrene. He had other roles in Greek myth, having in one place this story, in that place another, but the important features have a good deal in common. The account of Pausanias gives many of the more important details. When the Greek had taken Troy and were dividing the spoils among themselves:

> Eurypylus ... got a chest, in which there was a statue of Dionysus, the work some say of Hephaestus, and a gift of Zeus to Dardanus. But there are two other traditions about this chest, one that Aeneas left it behind him when he fled... the other that it was thrown away by Cassandra as a misfortune to any Greek who found it. However this may be, Eurypylus opened the chest and saw the statue, and was driven out of his mind by the sight. And most of the time he remained mad, though he came to himself a little at times.

The fated gift of Zeus is very reminiscent of Pandora's Box, with its own Hephæstean and Promethean links. It also brings together a familiar cast: Dionysus, Hephæstus, Dardanos the Cabir, Cassandra the Sibyl and so on. As for Eurypylus, afflicted with madness by the god, he did not return to Thessaly, but wandered far, coming eventually to Delphi:

… and he went to Delphi and consulted the oracle about his disorder. And they say the oracle told him, where he should find people offering a strange sacrifice, to dedicate his chest and there dwell. And the wind drove Eurypylus' ships to the sea near Aroe, and when he went ashore he saw a lad and maiden being led to the altar of Artemis Triclaria.

This was in the region of Achaia, and the handsome couple were a sacrifice offered to the goddess in expiation for an ancient crime. A youth named Melanippus had fallen in love with Comaetho, a priestess of the temple, and she with him. Being refused leave to marry:

Melanippus and Comaetho satisfied their ardent love in the very temple of Artemis, and afterwards made the temple habitually their bridal-chamber. And forthwith the wrath of Artemis came on the people of the country, their land yielded no fruit, and unusual sicknesses came upon the people, and the mortality was much greater than usual.

And when they had recourse to the oracle at Delphi, the Pythian Priestess laid the blame on Melanippus and Comaetho, and the oracle ordered them to sacrifice to Artemis annually the most handsome maiden and lad… Now all these lads and maidens had done nothing against the goddess but had to die for Melanippus and Comsetho, and they and their relations suffered most piteously…

Prior to the arrival of Eurypylus:

The oracle at Delphi had foretold that a foreign king would come to their country, and that he would bring with him a foreign god, and that he would stop this sacrifice to Artemis Triclaria…

And he [Eurpylus] saw at once that the oracle referred to this sacrifice, the people of the place also remembered the oracle, seeing a king whom they had never before seen, and as to the chest they suspected that there was some god in it. And so Eurypylus was cured of his disorder, and this human sacrifice was stopped.

The new worship of Dionysus, which represents a religious reform of which the above is the foundation myth, combines with that of Artemis in the following manner:

Nine men, who are chosen by the people for their worth, look after his worship, and the same number of women. And one night during the festival the priest takes the chest outside the temple. That night has special rites. All the lads in the district go down to the [river] Milichus [the mild, elsewhere a title of chthonic Zeus in ophidian form] with crowns on their heads made of ears of corn: for so used they in old time to dress up those whom they were leading to sacrifice to Artemis. But in our day they lay these crowns of ears of corn near the statue of the goddess, and after bathing in the river, and again putting on crowns this time of ivy, they go to the temple of Dionysus Aesymnetes [the Lord, or Ruler]. Such are their rites on this night.

The figure of Eurypylus is thus the essential link between the local rites of Artemis and Dionysus His tomb was in the shrine of the goddess, but his hero cult formed part of the worship of Dionysus. Incidentally, the same city possessed a temple of Cybele, with a concealed statue of Attis and a public one of the goddess.

Other very ancient rites persisted in this region, and Pausanias is worth quoting again. His account of another rite of Artemis shows how the priestess essentially personified the goddess in ritual, illustrating the archaic inter-changeability of ritual personnel and the deities served.

And every year the people of Patrae hold the festival called Laphria to Artemis, in which they observe their national mode of sacrifice. Round the altar they put wood yet green in a circle, and pile it up about 15 cubits high. And the driest wood lies within this circle on the altar. And they contrive at the time of the festival a smooth ascent to the altar, piling up earth so as to form a kind of steps. First they have a most splendid procession to Artemis, in which the virgin priestess rides last in a chariot drawn by stags, and on the following day they perform the sacrificial rites, which both publicly and privately are celebrated with much zeal. For they place alive on the altar birds good to eat and all other kinds of victims, as wild boars and stags and does, and moreover the young of wolves and bears, and some wild animals fully grown, and they place also upon the altar the fruit of any trees that they plant. And then they set fire to the wood. And I have seen a bear or some other animal at the first smell of the fire trying to force a way outside, some even actually doing so by sheer strength. But they thrust them back again into the blazing pile. Nor do they record any that were ever injured by the animals on these occasions.

Here too, at Patræ, was a myth of Eurypylus and a chest made by the fire god. The incidence of a barbarous and ancient rite involving wild animals is deserving of scrutiny. Artemis, in common with other archaic goddess-es, is a Potnia Theron or mistress of wild beasts. So too, Eurypylus intro-duced himself to the Argonauts as *born in Libya, the home of wild beasts*. The linkage he supplies between Artemis and Dionysus is also significant. Artemis is a virgin huntress, as is the nymph Cyrene; Aristaeus, who was worshipped here alongside her, is a god of the hunt and of honey, closely linked to Dionysus. That Eurypylus' story connects with human sacrifice is most striking in another respect. A passage of Virgil's *Aeneid*, which supplies more details of the Wooden Horse of Troy than does Homer, involves a soothsayer named Eurypylus. He was sent by the Greeks to consult Apollo how they might find safe journey home, and returned with an injunction to human sacrifice. Given these facts, the death in Libya of Mopsus may involve more than appears. He was also a soothsayer, and his death occurred just when the Argonauts were themselves troubled by fears concerning their return home.

The god Triton then, under the form of Eurypylus, appeared to the Argonauts and offered a significant gift of Libyan soil.

Thus he spake, and readily Euphemus held out his hands towards the clod, and thus addressed him in reply: *If haply, hero, thou knowest aught of Peloponnesus and the sea of Minos, tell us truly, who ask it of you. For*

*not of our will have we come hither, but by the stress of heavy storms have
we touched the borders of this land, and have borne our ship aloft on our
shoulders to the waters of this lake over the mainland, grievously burdened;
and we know not where a passage shows itself for our course to the land of
Pelops.*

So he spake; and Triton stretched out his hand and showed afar the
sea and the lake's deep mouth, and then addressed them: *That is the
outlet to the sea, where the deep water lies unmoved and dark; on each side
roll white breakers with shining crests; and the way between for your passage out is narrow. And that sea stretches away in mist to the divine land of
Pelops beyond Crete; but hold to the right, when ye have entered the swell
of the sea from the lake, and steer your course hugging the land, as long as it
trends to the north; but when the coast bends, falling away in the other direction, then your course is safely laid for you if ye go straight forward from
the projecting cape. But go in joy, and as for labour let there be no grieving
that limbs in youthful vigour should still toil.*

This Euphemos was also a son of Poseidon, and of Europa daughter of
great Tityos. This parentage of course also connects him to the family of
the Judges of Hades. He had fathered a son on Lemnos, destined to found
a city in Libya, bringing our voyage from first landfall to the last great
stage of the journey. He made a significant marriage too, according to a
scholiast on Pindar; to Sterope, a daughter of Helios.

Shown how to escape to the open sea by the god Triton, who disappeared into the waves with the tripod, the heroes brought forth a sacrificial sheep that Jason slew. The god reappeared in his true form, like a
man from the waist up, but with two great spined tails ending in crescent
flukes. He grasped the ship and drew it to the sea, before sinking back into
the waves. They heroes built altars on the shore and set sail at dawn, soon:

> …rugged Carpathus far away welcomed them; and thence they were
> to cross to Crete, which rises in the sea above other islands.

But here, while still at sea, they were confronted by a last great peril:

...Talos, the man of bronze, as he broke off rocks from the hard cliff, stayed them from fastening hawsers to the shore, when they came to the roadstead of Dicte's haven. He was of the stock of bronze, of the men sprung from ash-trees, the last left among the sons of the gods; and the [Zeus] son of Kronos gave him to Europa to be the warder of Crete and to stride round the island thrice a day with his feet of bronze. Now in all the rest of his body and limbs was he fashioned of bronze and invulnerable; but beneath the sinew by his ankle was a blood-red vein; and this, with its issues of life and death, was covered by a thin skin. So the heroes, though outworn with toil, quickly backed their ship from the land in sore dismay.

This bronze giant is undoubtedly a composite figure, partly inspired by the Colossus of Rhodes, well known to Apollonius; he represents both a giant, a magical automaton and the god Helios. Hurling rocks at the ship from the shore, they were unable to come close:

And now far from Crete would they have been borne in wretched plight, distressed both by thirst and pain, had not Medea addressed them as they turned away: *Hearken to me. For I deem that I alone can subdue for you that man, whoever he be, even though his frame be of bronze throughout, unless his life too is everlasting. But be ready to keep your ship here beyond the cast of his stones, till he yield the victory to me.* Thus she spake; and they drew the ship out of range, resting on their oars, waiting to see what plan unlooked for she would bring to pass; and she, holding the fold of her purple robe over her cheeks on each side, mounted on the deck; and Aeson's son took her hand in his and guided her way along the thwarts. And with songs did she propitiate and invoke the Death-spirits, devourers of life, the swift hounds of Hades, who, hovering through all the air, swoop down on the living. Kneeling in supplication, thrice she called on them with songs, and thrice with prayers; and, shaping her soul to mischief, with her hostile glance she bewitched the eyes of Talos, the man of bronze; and her teeth gnashed bitter wrath against him, and she sent forth baneful phantoms in the frenzy of her rage.

Medea's slaying of Talos is variously described, but while spirits are invoked, so too a power in the mind and eyes of the witch is a feature of them all. This is indeed the first literary account of the evil eye. So now the heroes stayed the night on shore, building a shrine for Minoan Athene before setting sail again. The next night caught them far from shore in a terrifying darkness:

> ... that night which they name the Pall of Darkness; the stars pierced not that fatal night nor the beams of the moon, but black chaos descended from heaven, or haply some other darkness came, rising from the nethermost depths. And the heroes [knew not] whether they drifted in Hades or on the waters...

Jason, for once master of his fate, raised his arms to the sky and invoked Apollo, weeping as he prayed. While these tears may represent genuine emotion, as well they might, a wailing invocation is pregnant with meaning for us by now. Apollo responded, swiftly descending from Olympus, to stand atop one of the Melantian rocks. He raised his bow (described here as of gold like the sun, but generally a lunar silver). Dazzling beams of light pierced the darkness, like arrows perhaps, or the simple radiance of the divine weapon. An islet was revealed to their grateful eyes, where they drew anchor. By the dawn light the island was shown them, and they named it Anaphe, meaning Revelation, as the god had revealed it to them in the depths of darkness. Here they built a shrine and celebrated a rite interesting in its details. As the heroes had little to offer the god at the dedication of the shrine, they poured libations of simple water in place of precious oil or wine. The handmaids of Medea, amused at this unusual and plain offering, laughed aloud. The champions, gallantly grasped the humour, and a ribald exchange took place between the men and the maids. This tale is told in explanation of the local rites, when the men make offerings to Apollo and their womenfolk make fun of them Similar ribaldry occurred even at holy Eleusis; there the women told bawdy jokes, in memory of an old lady cheering bereaved Demeter in this way. Such customs are of course far more ancient than the elegant Olympian state cult. They originate at the archaic level of religion, when nobles and tyrants shunned the 'rustic' rites of Demeter and Dionysus.

The next morning being fair, they again set sail towards their homeland. Now Apollonius' story is drawing to its close, he did not intend telling of events after their return. He has but one last great event to share with us while the journey continues. When they were underway, Euphemus, with whom we have recently become acquainted, recalled a dream of the previous night. This was in fact a revelation of his own. We are told that in deference to Hermes, called the god of dreams, the hero took pains to recall each detail of the dream. This is an interesting example of practical piety; such dreams are prophetic, and capable of bringing us good, but to attend to them is also a duty. This is what he recalled:

> ... the god-given clod of earth held in his palm close to his breast was being suckled by white streams of milk, and that from it, little though it was, grew a woman like a virgin; and he, overcome by strong desire, lay with her in love's embrace; and united with her he pitied her, as though she were a maiden whom he was feeding with his own milk; but she comforted him with gentle words: *Daughter of Triton am I, dear friend, and nurse of thy children, no maiden; Triton and Libya are my parents. But restore me to the daughters of Nereus to dwell in the sea near Anaphe; I shall return again to the light of the sun, to prepare a home for thy descendants.*

All this he committed carefully to memory before he told his dream to Jason. Now, Apollonius gives the distinction of dream interpreting to the leader of the quest; but centuries before, Pindar, subtle poet and healer with music, had already called this the prophetic *word of Medea*:

> ... spoken at Thera, which of old the passionate child of Aeetes, queen of Colchians, breathed from immortal lips. For these words spake she to the warrior Jason's god-begotten crew: *Hearken O sons of high-hearted mortals and of gods. Lo, I say unto you that from this sea-lashed land the daughter of Epaphos shall sometime be planted with a root to bring forth*

cities that shall possess the minds of men, where Zeus Ammon's shrine is builded.

So as to be clear, and to reconcile this prophecy with the details as our author gives them, Jason's interpretation, suited to dream and prophecy, was this:

My friend, great and glorious renown has fallen to thy lot. For of this clod when thou hast cast it into the sea, the gods will make an island, where thy children's children shall dwell; for Triton gave this to thee as a stranger's gift from the Libyan mainland. None other of the immortals it was than he that gave thee this when he met thee.

This island, after long travels, would be home to the descendants of Euphemus' son, driven from Lemnos, to Sparta, and thence to the isle of Thera grown from this Libyan earth. From Thera they would in turn become the founders of Cyrene, *to do honour therein to your gods*, all as lofty Triton had intended from his humble gift. With this prophetic word of the goddess of sorcery ringing in our ears, concerning a united worship of African and Greek gods, a short paragraph later Apollonius bids farewell to the Argonauts and to us, with these final words:

Be gracious, race of blessed chieftains! And may these songs year after year be sweeter to sing among men. For now have I come to the glorious end of your toils; for no adventure befell you as ye came home... and gladly did ye step forth upon the beach of Pagasæ.

Orishas and Greek gods of the weekdays

As Santeria is blessed in lacking a central authority, Orisha attributions to the weekdays are highly variable; the following highly useful scheme comes from Philip John Neimark's *The Way of the Orisa*. In Voodoo, Monday is frequently associated with Legba (aka Ellegua, Exu &c.) and begins the week. Compare the weekdays' attribution in the *Grand Grimoire*, commencing with Monday ruled by Lucifer; in Palo a similar figure to Exu bears the name Lucero.

WEEKDAY	ORISHA
Monday	Exu
Tuesday	Ogun
Wednesday	Babalu-Aiye
Thursday	Olodumare
Friday	Ochun, Chango
Saturday	Yemaya
Sunday	Obatala

Babalu-Aiye is identical in origin with Omolu in Quimbanda, and bears quite a resemblance to the chthonic Apollo as plague god and healer. A goetic adaptation of these tables could readily attribute him to Sunday in place of Obatala.

WEEKDAY	ORISHA	GREEK	NOTES
Monday	Yemaya	Thetis	+/− equivalent
Tuesday	Ogun	Hephæstus	+/− equivalent
Wednesday	Oya	Hecate	+/− equivalent
Thursday	Chango	Zeus	+/− equivalent
Friday	Ochun	Aphrodite	+/− equivalent
Saturday	Exu	Kronos	As Lord of Misrule
Sunday	Obatala	Helios	Equivalence doubtful

Comparative 'Goetic Olympic' and ATR syncretism

Sign	Greek deity Neo-goetic	ATR approximate	Orisha, lwa etc
♈	Athene/Medusa	Quimbanda &c	Pomba Gira
♉	Aphrodite	Santeria &c	Ochun
♊	Apollo	Quimbanda &c	Omulu
♋	Hermes	Quimbanda &c	Exu
♌	Zeus	Santeria &c	Shango
♍	Persephone, Hecate	Santeria &c	Oya
♎/♏	Hephæstus/Ares	Santeria and Palo	Ogun and Zarabanda
♐	Artemis, Cyrene	Santeria &c	Oya
♑	Dionysus	Quimbanda &c	Exu (and Ghede lwa)
♒	Hera/Lamia	Quimbanda &c	Pomba Gira
♓	Thetis	Santeria &c	Yemaya

Note archaic Libra was considered the claws of giant Scorpion, and the overlapping Mars/Vulcan forms.

Afterword to the Argonautica

Sir Isaac Newton is said to have enumerated connections between the *Argonautica* of Apollonius and the zodiac. Robert Graves speculated, with reasonable conviction that such a connection was formed in Alexandria. His grounds were that by using Egyptian forms it is simple to make such an equation. This is in fact the case, although he does not give a complete list. As this astrological conceit is of interest, given that the Twelve Labours of Hercules run concurrently with the quest, and are often so associated, I have here listed what seem the likeliest links.

Aries is none other than the Ram of Phrixus; Taurus the Bulls of Aeetes and Gemini the Dioscuri as heavenly twins. Cancer presents a little more difficulty but perhaps is Aristaeus as 'Aetnaean Beetle', while Leo is the Lion of Rhea and Cybele. Virgo is no less than Medea as Virgin, the significance of which need hardly be underlined, but two magical lunar zodiacs in the papyri commence with this sign. Libra is Alcinous' judging the case of Medea and the Colchians, Scorpio the Serpent guarding the fleece at Colchis or the apples of the Hesperides in Libya. For Sagittarius there is Chiron the Centaur or Apollo or Heracles as Archer; for Capricorn the Libyan nymphs in their goatskins and Aquarius the water carriers of Aegina. For Pisces there are the Nereides disguised as dolphins, or mighty Triton whose deeds conclude the tale just as Pisces, opposite the Virgin, is last of the Signs.

Having reached the end of the *Argonautica*, according to the best traditional chronology of Greek myth all but one of the Twelve Labours of Hercules has also been performed. The last and most difficult of these, bringing Cerberus from the Underworld into the light, I will next undertake in his place.

NEBIROS
HERMES CHTHONIOS

Orcus [Hades] is also a god; and the fabled streams of the lower world, Acheron, Cocytus and Pyriphlegethon, and Charon and Cerberus are also to be deemed gods. No, you say, we must draw the line at that; well then, Orcus is not a god either.

Cicero

THE NAME OF THE SPIRIT called Nebiros in *The True Grimoire* is found in different forms in other magical books. He is occasionally referred to as Nelbiroth. In Eliphas Lévi's *Mysteries of the Qabalah* he is called Nibbas. In the well known *Goetia of Solomon the King* he is called Naberius. In the more reliable and authoritative works of Agrippa's pupil Weyer – the ultimate source for most of the spirit catalogue of the *Goetia of Solomon* – the name is rendered as Naberus, with the alternative of Cerberus. Misspellings are frequent in various texts, and have created considerable confusion. The most consistent forms: Nebiros and Naberus, are close enough to be considered as equivalent, and the former will be used throughout this study. A Greek origin for this name may be traced in *nebros*, meaning a fawn skin. This was an attribute of Bacchus, and many terms from this root are associated with the cult of Dionysus (Bacchus). This etymology links the older Thracian deity Dionysus with the god known in Classical times as Hermes Chthonios, the underworld Hermes. In addition it connects Nebiros with the rites of Bacchus, often thought to connect with the origins of the Witches Sabbath. In similar vein, the demon name Frimost translates *Bromios*, a title of Dionysus, from Greek to Latin.

The alternative name of Cerberus also points to the origin of this important spirit in much older lore, for this is the name of the monstrous guard dog of the Underworld in Greek mythology, a figure with a major role in ancient magic. If the other names are not merely corrupted spellings it is possible that the name Naberus or Nebiros derives from a syncretic combination of the names Anubis and Cerberus, such as Anuberos. While such syncretism is entirely valid in the context of Hellenistic magic, it would be unwise to assume Cerberus initially derived from Anubis. A canine guardian of the heavenly afterlife with similar name and attributes to Cerberus appears in very early Indian scriptures such as the *Rig Veda*; Cerberus was initially a distinct Indo-European deity and apparently celestial rather than chthonic. Nevertheless, as Egyptian and Greek underworld deities Cerberus and Anubis were associated in the Magical Papyri, in which context such combinations are neither uncommon nor invalid. In short, whether or not a combined form of the name gave us the reading Nebiros, the alias of Cerberus is an important one for understanding Nebiros in the grimoires.

As long ago as 1905, Maurice Bloomfield brought scholarly attention to the likely identity of Cerberus with two dogs appearing in the *Rig Veda*. This is of course the oldest religious text of ancient India, and has echoes in later Persian lore, and through to the cultures of classical antiquity. A full argument for the identity is beyond the scope of my treatise, but the linkage requires briefly stating. These two hounds were the dogs of Yama, god of death. The afterlife of the period was not a gloomy one, nor was it subterranean. It resembled the afterlife of late antiquity, raised from below to the sky once more. The deceased mounted to heaven, passing as they did so the orbits of Sun and Moon; these luminaries were the watchdogs of Yama whom the spirit of the deceased had to pass. One of them had the name Çabala – tolerably close to variant forms of the Greek name Kerbelus and Cerberus &c. Both dogs of Yama bore the epithet *four-eyed*, which has been variously explained but likely indicated spots over the eyes as well as keen eyesight, but lends itself to interpretations of more than one head. This Vedic precedent does not diminish the connection drawn between Cerberus and Anubis; Anubis, like the Vedic Çabala was one of a pair, Anpu and Apuat. It should also be understood that the description of Cerberus as three headed was only finalised comparatively late, by the Romans; two had been tolerably common among the Greeks. The association, in very early Indo-European lore, of these watchdogs with Sun and Moon is well suited to the later Hellenistic eschatology. The luminaries in this phase were 'Islands', ruled by Hades or Dis Pater, and Persephone.

Cerberus and Anubis

The sages ascribed to their Mercury, personified in Egypt as Hermanubis, a dog's head, and to their Sulphur, represented by the Baphomet of the Temple or Prince of the Sabbath, that goat's head which brought such opprobrium to the occult associations of the Middle Ages.

Eliphas Lévi, Transcendental Magic

The name Cerberus is an ancient name for a guardian of the Underworld, the Hound of Hades. The *hound of hell* is mentioned, though neither named nor described, by Homer. Hesiod is the first to describe and mention him by name. He described Cerberus as a dog with fifty heads; later descriptions credit him with two, a hundred or the more frequent three. In art, serpents often twine around and between his necks and sometimes even these are omitted, perhaps to preserve the elegance of the prevailing sculptural conventions. Literary descriptions convey a far more monstrous form. Around his heads and extending down his back is a great mane of snakes, and he has for a tail the head and body of a serpent. In Dante's *Inferno* Cerberus appears as a *great worm*: a great serpentine dragon, with three canine heads and doglike clawing limbs. Most vividly conveyed is the description of his thunderous barking voice that stuns the mind, and cannot be shut out. In emphasising the size and the sound of Cerberus, Dante echoes the Roman author Virgil, in the *Aeneid*: *these are the realms huge Cerberus makes ring with the barking of his threefold jaws, reposing his enormous bulk in the cave that fronts the ferry.*

The parentage of Cerberus underlines that he is much more than a guard dog, but a true chthonic monster. He was the offspring of Typhon and Echidna. The better known Typhon – who terrified the Olympian gods until Zeus found resolve enough to restrain him beneath a thrown mountain – is associated with the Egyptian god Set. Echidna – herself important in Greek lore – was a beautiful woman from the waist up, a great speckled serpent from the waist down. This appearance matches that of Lamia, who as seen earlier connects with the Sibyls. It is appropriate to this connection that she appears to have originally been an oracular death goddess, before the ascendancy of the Olympian cultus that reduced many older gods to monsters or heroes. This parentage reflects the tradition crediting the birth of Anubis – dog-headed funerary god of Egypt – to Set and Nepthys, whereas other traditions make his father Ra, or Osiris; Anubis however is a much older god than Osiris.

The duty of Cerberus was to guard the entrance to Hades; his den being on the far side of the river Styx, where Charon brought the shades of the dead in his boat. Here he prevented the living from entering the Underworld, and the dead from leaving. This is also strongly reminiscent of Anubis, with his jackal head; the abode of the dead being in the desert on the sunset side of the Nile where howling jackals roamed.

The Classical Greek god of the Underworld, Hades (called Pluto, meaning *riches*, to avert ill-fortune from speaking the name of the God of Death), is frequently depicted accompanied by Cerberus. This partnership has had important repercussions, of which one famous case deserves our attention here. When the first Ptolemy ruled in Egypt he introduced the worship of Sarapis, a form of Osiris who for political reasons united Greek and Egyptian elements. According to Plutarch:

1 Ptolemy Soter saw in a dream a gigantic statue of Pluto – one which he had not previously seen and whose form he knew not – which ordered him to bring it to Alexandria.

2 And when he did not know and had no idea where the statue was to be found even after he had described his vision to his friends, there

was found a great traveller, named Sosibius, who said he had seen at Sinope just such a colossus as the King had seen.

3 He [Ptolemy] accordingly sent [his agents], who after expending much time and effort, and not without the assistance of God's providence, removed it secretly and brought it away.

4 And when it had been brought to Alexandria and publicly erected, [his Greek and Egyptian advisors on the Mysteries] Timotheus and Manetho, immediately came to the conclusion that it was a statue of Pluto – judging by its Cerberus and great Serpent – and persuaded Ptolemy that it was no other God than Sarapis; for it did not come from Sinope with this name, but after coming to Alexandria it received the Egyptian name for Pluto, namely Sarapis.

There can be no doubt that the image of a dog as part of this colossus lent itself to the identification with Osiris, through his association with Anubis; and Hades, through his association with Cerberus. Note too, that while Pluto was identified with Osiris, Persephone – the Queen of the Greek Underworld – was similarly identified with Isis in her Underworld role.

Having mentioned Manetho and syncretism of Egyptian and Greek gods, this Egyptian hierophant is also a major source for the chronology of the Pharoahs. His account included a divine dynasty of gods complete with Greek counterparts of the relevant Egyptian gods. While fragmentary, this equating of gods was evidently highly influential; references to it survive in Byzantine scholiasts and elsewhere. The close relationship of Hephæstus and Helios in the *Argonautica* and elsewhere, while deeply connected to traditions of Asia Minor, likely also refers to this Hellenistic tradition. In Manetho's list they appear as consecutive rulers; father and son.

Manetho's King List

Egyptian	*Syncretic*
Ptah	Hephæstus
Ra	Helios
Shu	Agathodæmon
Seb	Kronos
Osiris	Osiris
Set	Typhon
Horus (1)	···
Thoth	(Hermes?)
Ma	···
Horus (2)	Horus

To resume, Cerberus is an important figure in many well-known myths, particularly those concerning the descent of heroes into the Underworld. Of these heroes Orpheus, a major magical figure, charmed Cerberus to sleep with his lyre, while Hercules dragged him bodily to the surface of the Earth. On this occasion the potent and poisonous herb aconite first grew where drops fell from the slavering jaws of Cerberus.

These myths are retellings of older traditions, and should not be taken at face value. They have connections with old rituals, involving a descent into the Underworld, purificatory and initiatory rituals of descent (*katabasis*). It is significant in this exact respect that in most accounts of Hercules' encounter with Cerberus the hero was prepared for the ordeal by initiation into the Eleusian Mysteries. A central figure in these Mysteries was, of course, Persephone. Plutarch, who was initiated into both these and the Mysteries of Isis and Osiris, considered them to be essentially identical, as at this time – if not before – they largely were.

Anubis was associated with magic in Egypt from early on. A magical papyrus of the third millennium BCE includes a description of its discovery beneath his statue in a temple. In the Magical Papyri of the Greek and Roman period, Cerberus (Kerberos) is frequently invoked along with Hecate, unsurprisingly given their close connection in Greek myth. In other closely related invocations he is called Anubis, the two having become in many respects interchangeable. In one of the papyri, while addressed as Kerberos, the god — evidently in semi-anthropomorphic form — is described as wielding a thunderbolt. Hecate herself was frequently represented with three heads, including one of a dog. One of her ritual titles indeed, was Black Bitch. Her offerings also included the sacrifice of a dog.

Anubis, the familiar jackal or dog headed god of the Egyptians, was for much of their history the god of embalming and the protector of cemeteries; at least officially. Indeed, as his worship is far prior to that of Osiris, he was very likely an earlier Lord of the Dead. As Egyptians knew, real dogs and jackals were all too likely to dig up and eat dead bodies and scatter the remains, and they were associated with all the frightfulness and fear of death. The Egyptians made a regular practice of harnessing as well as propitiating negative forces; much as, in modern times, security agencies seek to turn enemy agents. Anubis, associated with the practice of magic from the early period in Egypt, is a powerful example of this principle. Examples can be found in the magic and religion of the Egyptians throughout their long history. Budge says of him that, in the period when Osiris was the Lord of the Underworld: *as the guide of heaven and the leader of souls to Osiris he was a beneficent god, but as the personification of death and decay he was a being who inspired terror*. So also in papyri of the first millennium BCE and probably earlier he commands huge numbers of messenger demons; while in Magical Papyri dating to Roman times he acts as the main enforcer of curses. As the study of Egyptian culture has progressed, it has become apparent that the more hostile and fearsome aspects of many deities, Anubis not least among them, had formed a large part of folk magic from earliest times. The more respectable or positive forms of the gods were a feature of state religion, rather than of popular belief, which often viewed them rather differently. It is in this form that they appear in the Papyri, which while late in Egyptian history, preserve very substantial elements of both Greek and Egyptian magical cosmology and methodology that are extremely ancient.

The Anubis of the Græco-Roman period is an extremely important figure, both in the Magical Papyri and the widespread Mysteries of Isis. He features strongly in the magical cult of Hecate, wherein he holds the key of the Underworld. He also frequently bears the caduceus associated with Hermes (who was associated with crossroads as Hecate was associated with junctions of three roads; they are occasionally combined in the Papyri as Hermecate). Both the key and the caduceus are important symbols in the iconography of Hecate, and frequently appear in her rites. Clearly Anubis is considered a psychopomp, or guide of the dead, and one of her retinue. In this capacity as well as in his official capacity of guiding shades in the Underworld, he could be appealed to by those who wished to summon the spirits of the dead.

This capacity to bring souls both to and from the Underworld is illustrated in the dual role of Anubis in the legend of Isis and Osiris. The role of Anubis in embalming Osiris and guiding the deceased (who were always entitled Osiris) to the underworld is important to the first part of this role. There is however another aspect to this, for Anubis also assisted Isis and Nepthys in the reconstruction of the body of Osiris, equivalent in many respects to a resurrection.

In *The True Grimoire* Nebiros is under the rule of Astaroth, a demonised form of the goddess Astarte. This relationship is best understood as similar in nature to that between Cerberus and Hecate.

A fuller discussion of the relationship between Astaroth and Hecate, already covered in *The True Grimoire*, is out of place here. For the benefit of clarity here, one or two relevant points require mention. The myths of Hecate and Astaroth portray a goddess active in the three worlds of Heaven, Earth and the Underworld; in addition a major symbol of Hecate is equally prominently connected to Astaroth. This is the pole or pillar, known as the Asherah in the cult of Astaroth, which is also the oldest symbol of Hecate. In her honour a simple pole was raised at places where three roads meet, and embellished with a mask facing each direction. Its original nature was more similar to both the shaman's ladder, and a World Tree or Axis, connecting the worlds.

The dual nature of Anubis, dark and light, is also found in the more respectable philosophical writings of Græco-Roman times. According to Plutarch:

> ...when Nepthys conceives Anubis, Isis adopts him. For Nepthys represents that below the earth and invisible [dark], while Isis represents that which is above the earth and visible [light]. And as the circle called 'Horizon' [horizontal], touches upon the confines of light and darkness alike as common to both, so it has been called Anubis. It is likened to a dog according to its characteristics; for the dog is watchful both by day and by night alike. Anubis possesses this power, as Hecate with the Greeks, being at one and the same time Infernal and Celestial. Others believe that Anubis signifies Time [Kronos], but this is an initiated doctrine.

Plutarch also describes the offerings made to Anubis of two roosters, one white, the other tawny, connecting it with Set, or as Plutarch calls him, Typhon. His double characteristics are also evident in the description by Lucius Apuleius of his image in processions of Isis in Roman Italy:

> ...immediately after these came the Deities...the foremost among them rearing terrifically his dog's head and displaying alternately a face black as night, and as golden as the day; in his left hand the caduceus, in his right the green palm branch.

Note that he appears first among the deities here, as also in the rituals of the Magical Papyri, first Anubis is summoned in vision; as messenger he then brings in with equal facility either the Celestial gods, or demons and the shades of the dead. Many attributes of Anubis connect him strongly with the Greek messenger god, Hermes, the caduceus and palm branch not least of all. That they were associated by the ancients is not in doubt.

Bear in mind however that Hermes too possesses dual forms, with different roles and even different parents. Hermes was not only the herald of Zeus, but, as Hermes Chthonios, also of Hades, god of the Underworld. It is in this capacity, as guide of the spirits of the dead, or psychopomp, that Anubis most resembles him. The *Hymns of Orpheus* include a hymn to both these forms of Hermes, underlining the distinction in roles. We give that of Hermes Chthonios here:

Hymn to Hermes Chthonios

(The Incense: Storax)

Hermes I call, whom Fate decrees to dwell
In the dire path which leads to deepest hell
O Bacchic Hermes, progeny divine
Of Dionysius, parent of the vine,
And of celestial Venus — Paphian queen,
Dark eye-lash'd Goddess of a lovely mien:
Who constant wand'rest thro' the sacred feats
Where hell's dread empress, Proserpine, retreats;
To wretched souls the leader of the way
When Fate decrees, to regions void of day:
Thine is the wand which causes sleep to fly,
Or lulls to slumb'rous rest the weary eye;
For Proserpine thro' Tart'rus dark and wide
Gave thee forever flowing souls to guide.
Come, blessed pow'r the sacrifice attend,
And grant our mystic works a happy end.

Mirroring the relationship of Isis and Anubis, Hecate and Cerberus, Nebiros is a deputy of Astaroth, who is the most approachable of the three great Chiefs. Nebiros is an extremely important spirit, governing more follower spirits in *The True Grimoire* than any spirit of equivalent

rank. He is an excellent spirit for a practical magician to form an agree-
ment with, as his many followers will provide the operator with assistance
in workings for many purposes.

Among those who are his followers he has a particularly close relationship with Huictigaras. Besides the spirits who follow him, Nebiros has an
affinity with Claunech, (who is under Satanachia, a deputy of Lucifer).
These two affinities are interesting, for Claunech is the first among the
spirit followers of the deputies, as Huictigaras is the last. Additionally,
Claunech is said to be beloved of Lucifer, so this affinity also underlines
the importance of Nebiros in the scheme of the grimoire.

His astrological correspondences are similarly universal, his day being
solar, his zodiacal degree lunar, and The Star being a title of his sphere.
These three symbols of course are also components of the standard talisman of the Grimoire. Nebiros can be readily invoked in operations of
Sun, Moon and the Stars, (including geometrical stars formed from conjunction cycles of the planets).

His Nature and Powers

There are few signs of his former glory in the Naberus alias Cerberus in
Weyer, or the Naberius in those grimoires derived from Scot, such as the
Goetia of Solomon. In these books he is described as a crow, a bird with
similar associations to the jackal admittedly, but no Hound of Hell. His
hoarse bestowal of the gifts of oratory and rhetoric is also appropriate
to a Hermes Chthonios, but otherwise he is a shadow of his former self,
though he fares rather better in the truly goetic grimoires. The Nebiros
of the *Grand Grimoire*, a close cousin of *The True Grimoire* and of that of
Honorius shows him clearly, his status and nature undiminished in any
significant respect from the Anubis of the papyri:

> Nebiros can do evil to whomsoever he wishes, make known or cause
> to be found the hand of glory, and the qualities of metals, minerals,
> vegetables and animals pure and impure, and prediction – especially
> by necromancy.

Nebiros can *do evil to whomsoever he wishes*: or, to render the intention more accurately, whomsoever the magician wishes. This is Anubis as the chief enforcer of curses, invoked as a chthonic force, Cerberus to whom offerings or ritual deposits are made at crossroads and in the cemetery. He can bestow the Hand of Glory: the *main de gloire* – which in medieval and later folklore was made from the hand of a hanged criminal still upon the gallows, which were frequently located at crossroads. The French main de gloire was originally the mandragore or mandrake, a magical plant of the very first degree, associated with Hecate and with Astarte. So too, the hand can be formed from the root and stems of a fern gathered on St. John's Eve, along with the seed of the fern, which confers invisibility. That this date approximates the Summer Solstice, when Anubis visits all the cemeteries and a great festival is held by his worshippers, is more than fortuitous.

In its later form, and possibly its original form too, this hand (a term rich with meaning in Hoodoo and Afro-American conjure traditions thriving today) was said to be the tool of criminals, able to send the occupants of a house into a magical sleep. It is an interesting possibility that this instrument of magical robbery was borrowed from treasure hunting rites, which connect with journeys to the underworld. In any case, these associations with the crossroads and corpses, with criminality, especially theft, are certainly appropriate to a Hermes Chthonios; and to a dog headed god, an infernal Hermanubis, and a semi-Egyptian Cerberus. These though are outer meanings of the symbolism; for the initiate of the Mysteries, or to the archaic shaman to whom these themes belong in their primal glory, the significance of the great Underworld talisman is that it confers powers of invisibility, of entering the Underworld unharmed; returning with wisdom, and healing power to defeat the evils of disease, or of ignorance. He can discover the *qualities of metals and minerals*: this too is clearly derived from an underworld role. Hades, as king of the lower world had possession of everything under earth, including metals, minerals and *all the productions of the earth*. The King of the chthonic elementals or Gnomes has the same power, whether or not he be dark Pluto himself.

This partially explains too why this power of Nebiros extends to *vegetables and animals pure and impure*. Indeed, among plants Hades claims the myrtle tree, the narcissus and the maiden-hair. Let us not forget either the poppy or the pomegranate, and their place in the legend of Persephone. Or that Hecate the companion and Demeter the mother of Persephone, dark Hades bride, also represent fertility, besides their long association with death and its mysteries. These goddesses of the Underworld are always associated with crops, and with herds. Potnia Theron – Lady of the Beasts – is among their oldest titles. Nor are such associations exclusive to the feminine Underworld deities, as a beast himself, and a Lord of the Beasts, this power too belongs to our syncretic Hermes Chthonios. Nor should we forget that Nebiros is a deputy of Astaroth in the very grimoire to which this description belongs. The Hecate qualities of the ancient Astaroth include the same rulership of the animal and vegetable kingdoms. A sophisticated application of herbal lore is involved with the Solstice rites associated with Nebiros, as will be seen later.

Lastly Nebiros has the power of *prediction, especially by necromancy*, which he can confer upon the magician. In the Magical Papyri, Anubis is frequently invoked in operations of general divination and of necromancy. Both he and Cerberus are also invoked in other rituals involving spirits of the dead. There are many rituals given in the papyri for divination in a vessel of water, a method known as hydromancy. This method is employed to bring in gods, spirits of various kinds, and the dead through the mediation of Anubis in his role of Chthonic Hermes. Which gods or spirits were to be summoned also decided which kind of water was used: *rainwater if you are calling upon heavenly gods, seawater if gods of the earth, river water if Osiris or Sarapis, springwater if the dead*. There are very strong links between this form of hydromancy and the practice of necromancy, and when spring water is used – as in a related process in *The True Grimoire* for example – it invariably indicates this connection is in force.

While there are variations in the form, many of these rituals involve Anubis, particularly those of the demotic papyri; on occasion, the vessel employed is referred to specifically as the cup of Anubis. The reader is told that this cup is to have the face of Anubis engraved within it. Most often such a cup is used for the obtaining of visions, of spirits of various kinds through the mediation of Anubis. There are related forms of hydromancy which interpret the results of casting three stones into the bowl. Possibly the areas of his face (particularly the ears, eyes, nostrils and mouth) were used to interpret the positions of such stones. (Hydromancy is described in greater detail in the *Book of Elelogap*, the three stones could be round, triangular, and square with appropriate sigils). In the *Papyrus of Unas*, which is much more ancient than the Magical Papyri, the face of Anubis represents the face of the deceased enabling him to go forth without fear while confronting the spirits in the Underworld. The expected veracity both of the messenger god, and by extension of divination involving him, is indicated in the Socratic Oath. Whenever the noble philosopher swore an oath or made a statement in regard to truth, he said *by the dog*, in token of the faithfulness of that animal as a divine symbol. In Plato's *Gorgias* he extends the form of this oath to *by the dog, the god of the Egyptians* (*Gorgias* 482b). This is strikingly appropriate to Anubis the weigher of souls in the Egyptian underworld, where the heart of the deceased was weighed against the feather of righteousness in the Hall of Truth.

This description of the powers associated with Nebiros, examined thus detail by detail, shows him to resemble the Anubis and Cerberus of the older magical tradition exactly. So too, in the grimoires in which this description appears, he is – like Anubis – one of the great commanders of the infernal armies, a Field Marshal no less. Nor is this less than might be expected, known and understood by a medieval European magician. Agrippa (*Three Books of Occult Philosophy* III ch. 18) reminds us:

> Porphry saith, their Prince is Serapis, who is also called Pluto by the Greeks, and also Cerberus is chief amongst them, that three-headed dog: viz. because he is conversant in three elements, [Air/Water/ Earth], a most pernicious devil; whence also Proserpina, who can do very much in these three elements, is their princess.'

While in chapter 16 he informs the reader whose eyes are open to the pagan roots of medieval sorcery:

...four most mischievous kings do rule over the others, according to the four parts of the world; under these many more princes of legions govern, and also many of private offices. Hence the wicked Gorgons, the Furies. Hence Tisiphone, Alecto, Megera, Cerberus.

In the Magical Papyri reference is made to *Anubis threads*; these appear to be knotted threads, the direct implication being the genre known as ligature spells. Surprisingly enough, though the most commonly encountered contexts of such spells are malefic, this is not always the case in the Papyri. There an example occurs of use of knotted cloths to stop haemorrhage after childbirth, (and possibly heavy periods and bleeding after childbirth). Another context of binding, where Anubis is invoked while tying with a cord of 365 knots, arises in PGM IV 296–466. Here the spell is from the class of aggressive love magic. In addition, Anubis often appears in magical inscriptions, and upon amulets such as the Gnostic gems. In short, whether as Nebiros in *The True Grimoire*, or as Anubis or Cerberus in the Papyri, in magic his power is extremely versatile, even comprehensive.

Offerings

According to Plutarch, Anubis was offered two roosters, one white and the other of a saffron colour. Or as we might say, one white, one red, which colour the Egyptians associated with Set. This is in accord with the nature of Anubis; half light, as Son of Osiris, and half dark as Son of Set.

As an Underworld offering it was customary for heroes to offer Cerberus a ritual cake, made from barley mixed with honey, in order to enter the Underworld while in life. Such a cake was also buried with the dead to appease Cerberus, and perhaps elicit his aid in reaching the Underworld, rather than wander as a lost soul. Two such cakes were carried by visitors to Underworld oracular shrines, one for Cerberus and one for the ghostly Python. Not surprisingly, such offerings occasionally figure in the Magical Papyri, but there can be no doubt of their earlier provenance. An ideal place to make such offerings in modern practice would be a cemetery, or a meeting of three ways or four.

Holy Days

In Egypt Anubis was associated with a date which coincides with our Summer Solstice (the entry of the Sun into Cancer), and on that day was said to visit every cemetery in the land. In other parts of the ancient world deities associated with death and fertility, such as Adonis and Attis, had festivals on or around the same date. In a modern attribution of the 28 spirits from the main hierarchy of *The True Grimoire*, he corresponds to the seventh Lunar Mansion, which also represents 0 degrees Cancer.

Verum Spirits and Mansion Cusps or Critical Degrees

Lucifer	Nebiros	Klepoth	Segal
0 ♑	0 ♋	0 ♎	0 ♐
Satanachia	Astaroth	Khil	Frucissiere
12 ♑	12 ♋	12 ♎	12 ♐
Agliarept	Syrach	Mersilde	Guland
26 ♑	26 ♋	26 ♎	26 ♐
Tarchimache	Claunech	Clisthert	Surgat
9 ♉	9 ♌	9 ♌♏	9 ♒
Flerity	Musisin	Sirchade	Morail
21 ♉	21 ♌	21 ♏	21 ♒
Belzebuth	Bechaud	Hiepact	Frutimier
4 ♊	4 ♍	4 ♐	4 ♋
Sargatanas	Frimost	Humots	Huictigaras
17 ♊	17 ♍	17 ♐	17 ♋

(The order of chiefs and deputies employed in this table attributes the chiefs to 1st, 6th and 9th position, corresponding to the Middle Pillar of the Perfected Tree; their deputies flank them on the side pillars).

In this schema the Emperor Lucifer is associated with the Aries Equinox; Klepoth, who corresponds to his female counterpart Pomba Gira in Brazilian Quimbanda, takes the Libra Equinox; the spirit Segal the opposite Solstice to Nebiros.

Summanus

A deity of ancient Rome associated with the 20th of June should be mentioned here. Summanus is thought to have been originally a Sabine or more likely an Etruscan god. He ruled the night sky, and particularly nocturnal thunder, He may have been absorbed by Jupiter prior to the conflict of Rome with Pyrrhus of Epiros in 278. At that time an image of him was struck by lightning, and a new temple on the Capitoline Hill was dedicated to him shortly thereafter on the 20th of June. From then on he received a sacrifice every year on this date. In addition he received propitiation in the form of wheel shaped cakes called *summanalia*, perhaps symbolising the wheel of his chariot. The Latin poet Plautus (died 184 BCE) represented him as the god of thieves, of whom night time is the friend. However he was a mysterious entity to the Romans, Ovid (born 43 BCE), a well informed mythographer was unable to provide any details.

A fine Italian tomb gable depicts him with shaggy locks and paternal beard, bearing a fistful of thunderbolts and with two great serpentine legs. The derivation of his name has two explanations; the most likely and widely accepted is from the Latin *sub-manus* – before the morning. This is likely to be the original sense, but was overshadowed by a later theory which has merit in its own right. The sinister reputation of Summanus led to an alternative derivation which has been extremely influential, deriving his name from Summus Manium, *the greatest of the Manes*, which is to say the chief of the dead. This was accepted by Martianus Capella (4th century AD), who called him Dis Pater (Father Hades, i.e. Pluto). This derivation has been an enduring influence on later writers, constituting a tradition in its own right. Milton's *In Quintum Novembris*, when describing Satan visiting Rome employs the mythic analogy:

Just so Summanus, wrapped in a smoking whirlwind of blue flame, falls upon people and cities.

The difference between Zeus Chthonios, or Zeus Meleichos, and Hades – or other underworld figures such as Trophonios – is in any case never wholly clear. Historiography – the study of interpretations of history, rather than the cataloguing of facts – commends the latter derivation, which has enjoyed wide currency and influence, as an appropriate term for nocturnal or chthonic chiefs. This, and the solsticial date of his feast, recommends a syncretic link of Summanus with Nebiros, a necromancer and Field Marshal of Hades. Bear in mind also the cakes offered to both Summanus and Cerberus.

Considering the thunderbolt wielded by Cerberus in the Papyri, this association may well have influenced their composition. In this context, the use of 365 knots in magical ligatures is very significant. Three hundred and sixty five is the number given to solar-pantheistic forms of deity, such as Abraxas. Such gods, as discussed at length already, were essentially helio-chthonic. This suggests Cerberus attained the power of Zeus IAO or Dis Pater, and the guise of Summanus would be extremely apt.

Solsticial Rites

In European folklore much of the older belief surrounding the Solstice was transferred to the Eve and Day of St. John the Baptist (23rd and 24th of June). The significance of this day continued in magical traditions of the New World, for example, from the early days of Voodoo in New Orleans the greatest rite of the year has been held on Saint John's day. In Europe, Morocco and Algeria the Midsummer rites, with their bonfires, survived from pagan times until the nineteenth century and later. Midsummer also holds pride of place among the festivals of British Neo-paganism, a position which is unlikely to be unique to those Isles. Near identical customs and beliefs could be found from North Africa, to Sicily and Sardinia, and across Eastern and Western Europe. The survival of these Midsummer customs in Islamic countries where a lunar calendar is used, by which no fixed solar date is or can be marked, is particularly striking.

European rites were often celebrated on hilltops, and even mountains, often with a river or spring below, in fields and pastures, at crossroads and in marketplaces; North African rites were held in courtyards and at crossroads, as well as on threshing floors and in the fields.

Many of these festivals are described in Frazer's *Golden Bough*, which while dated in some respects is still a useful reference regarding such customs. There is an enormous amount of magical lore associated with plants connected to this date. Included among these plants are several named after or associated with Saint John, especially the Midsummer fern and St. John's wort. Judging from Frazer, in the North African rites the herbal associations of these rites at first appear more extensive. His account includes giant-fennel, thyme, rue, chervil-seed, chamomile, geranium and pennyroyal, and this is simply a selection from among many aromatic plants. However, the herbal lore associated with the European rites is also extensive, and in some respects more revealing.

The bonfires are frequently composed of specially chosen woods. Some traditions speak of three types of wood, others of nine; still others add a toadstool to the nine woods. Besides the woods a number of plants are also gathered. These are also intended to be burned in many cases. Some commentators have assumed this is a simple weeding of potentially dangerous plants from pastureland. Certainly some of the plants are potentially dangerous, but an examination of what these rites are intended to achieve reveals more complex motives. The intention is to protect from witchcraft, thunder, hail and disease, and specific pests. The fires are often deliberately to windward of pasture land, or of crops and orchards. A major part of the rite is the production of smoke, and several of the plants involved are powerful against various parasites, internal and external. While it is likely enough that ridding pastures of these toxic plants is a consideration, closer examination shows there was also clear recognition of their virtues. Some of these plants and their uses are known to have been employed in the Roman world, and the plain implication is that these rites involve survivals from much earlier times.

It is believed, probably quite rightly, that the smoke kills fleas. Cattle are driven through or between fires, or over the place where the fire burned the previous night. People expose children, the sick and themselves to the smoke which heals and removes ill fortune from men, animals, crops, and fruit-trees. Many ailments are said to be prevented by these rites, and these also correspond to the virtues of the plants. It is significant too that not all plants gathered are burnt; some – often in the form of wreaths – are kept for later use. So too is a residue of ash and some charred brands from the fire. These are put to various magical uses, detailed below. That some herbal preparations – such as tinctures and decoctions – involving these same plants were in widespread use is a likely enough assumption.

Fire and smoke from the fires drove off evil spirits, witches, dragons, trolls believed to be abroad that night. This is a common feature of fire festivals, although the identification of disease and demons shows a very practical aspect to the ritual.

The main features of such fire festivals were and are primarily: fires lit on high places, torchlit processions, rolling of a fire wheel or wheels down the hill. Launching fire disks from flexible rods was another activity commonly associated with these celebrations, in anticipation of modern fireworks. Secondary features included visits to healing springs, washing in three wells to see those who will die in the coming year and drowning rather than burning an effigy.

Fire rites were productive of magical elements retained for protection during the coming year. Keeping stumps of torches, or charred brands, to protect house and fields from lightning, foul weather and from pests. Keeping ashes as protection from fire; these were often put on the roof of the house, or inside the house, but could be scattered on fields to protect crops from corn cockles or darnel.

In similar vein, keeping wood from the fire to relight the next years was a common practice. In some instances three charred sticks were planted in flax fields that same night, and remained there until after the harvest. Similar harnessing of the same protective power involved placing such a stick in thatch as protection from fire.

By dancing around, or simply seeing nine bonfires, a girl ensured being married that year. Leaping over the fire prevented back ache when reaping the harvest, and protects from fever or ague, and promoted fertility. Repetition seven times added power, as with incantations in *The True Grimoire*. Burning a male effigy and fire jumping by boys frequently went together, suggesting sacrifice of a male personification of vegetative growth. High flax was assured by sympathetic magic, either by the height of the flames or of the jumping over the fire. This was general regardless of crop, assuring high hemp, corn and so on. Fire jumping by young couples was not necessarily a fertility rite; the highest jump favoured the yield of their parents' harvest.

Herbal Associations

Herb lore was a major aspect of these rites wherever practiced. Looking at the fire through larkspur preserved the eyes. Mugwort and vervain particularly, which are both highly regarded in magic, were used to make chaplets worn at the rite and subsequently kept for their protective power. The burning of such chaplets rid the former wearer of ill luck; it was customary to keep singed wreaths for good luck, and employ parts of them over the year. Uses included burning a little in thunderstorms with a prayer, giving some to sick or calving cattle, and fumigating livestock stalls and the home for health and protection. A wreath of mugwort protected from ghosts, witches, from sickness, from sore eyes and so on.

Burs and mugwort were also placed on pasture gates; walnut gathered at the time of the fire protected against toothache and hair loss, as well as controlling many disease causing organisms. Mullein, another common magical herb, protected cattle from sickness and sorcery.

The same plants assured abundant crops or vintage (vines), protection of people, crops and cattle from pests and disease, dizziness, convulsions, plague, witchcraft and harm of every kind, sickness, fire and lightning. While many of these plants are replete with magical associations, a powerful connecting factor with all those mentioned was the association with the fire on this day.

There is in short a wealth of lore and tradition surrounding these dates, much of it directly employable in magic and modern folklore. It is a comparatively simple matter to re-appropriate St. John's Eve to Nebiros and invoke him as patron in the use of herbs and remnants from the fire associated with the day. Frazer gives details of a Brotherhood of the Green Wolf in Normandy which annually elects a Green Wolf as their leader and token sacrifice. While assimilated to St. John's Eve and Day and involving Church and clergy at various points, their rite bears the marks of great antiquity. In addition, the solemnities of the daytime give way to great noise and indulgence by night. This is certainly a survival of bacchanalian debauches through until dawn after such rituals, which belonged to the peasantry in the archaic period.

Both the brotherhood and the individual Green Wolf, who wears a long green mantle and conical hat, should remind us of the fire festivals celebrated by Sabine wolf-men in honour of Soranus. In him we have an Eastern style sun-god, complete with lupine hypostases symbolising his chthonic connections. The associations with our jackal-headed Anuberos, perhaps after rising to solar-pantheistic status in the Græco-Roman period, are clearly appropriate.

The Spirits under Nebiros

As befits Anubis the leader of spirit hosts in the Egyptian underworld, and as the Field Marshal of Infernus in the grimoires, Nebiros commands innumerable spirits. While the vast majority are nameless followers, *The True Grimoire* mentions several of the most powerful by name and enumerates their abilities. Three of these are distinct from the others; they are named among the eighteen spirits who collectively, due to their nature and type, are also said to be under Duke Syrach; as well as in groups of three under one or other of the six deputies of the chiefs. All of these appear to be Salamanders or of the nature of fire, and those under Nebiros are as follows:

Morail, known also as Menail: can make you or anything invisible. Frutimiere, known also as Glitia, prepares all kinds of feasts and sumptuous banquets for you. Huictigaras: causes sleep in the case of some and insomnia in others.

Also under Nebiros are two sub-chiefs named Hael and Sergulath; Hael is one of the most important spirits in the whole Grimoire, as he can assist in the composition of pacts, and the magical discovery or correct drawing of sigils for any spirit.

Hael: Enables one to speak in any language he will, and also teaches the means whereby any type of letter or characters may be written truly. He is also able to teach those things which are most secret and hidden.

Sergulath: Gives every means of speculation. In addition, he instructs as to the methods of breaking the ranks and strategy of opponents.

Subject to Hael and Sergulath are the eight most powerful subordinates: *Proculo* causes a person to sleep for 24 (otherwise 48) hours, with the knowledge of the Spheres of Sleep; *Haristum* can cause anyone to pass through fire without being touched by it; *Brulefer* causes a person to be loved by women; *Pentagnony* gives invisibility and love of great lords; *Aglasis* can carry anyone or anything anywhere in the world; *Sidragosam* causes any girl to dance in the nude; *Minoson* is able to make anyone win at any game; *Bucon* can cause hate and spiteful jealousy between members of the opposite sexes.

Their Conjuration:

Serguthy, Heramael, Trimasael, Sustugriel; Agalieraps, Tarithimal, Elgoapa, Nebiros, Hael, and Sergulath; and you also Proculo, Haristum, Brulefer, Pentagnegni, Aglasis, Sidragosam, Minosums and Bucons, come together by the Great, Powerful and Holy Adonay, thou shalt appear, come, by the will and command of N... N... and bring all your power, place yourselves in the power of he who calls, heeding all that he desires.

Sanctus, Sanctus Regnum Verba praeterague nihil! Omnis spiritus rexurgat! Pax voluntas, fiat voluntate mea.

[Holy, Holy Royal Word, surpassed by none! All ye spirits arise, come peacefully and do my will.]

✦✦✦

Various things stand out in this catalogue of spirits under Nebiros. Firstly, Morail and Pentagnony (aka Pentagnegni) share the power of invisibility. Similarly Huictigaras and Proculo are both concerned with sleep and dreaming. These are appropriate powers for spirits under Nebiros, who possesses the secret of the Hand of Glory. Invisibility is one of the pre-eminent shamanic powers, signifying the ability to travel in the underworld; the helmet of invisibility associated with Hermes is borrowed from the god Hades (who some mythographers take to be originally an elder Hermes). The power of the Underworld guide over the world of dream is very well represented by several spells in the Magical Papyri. An invocation of Anubis or Cerberus over a wax image of a dog forms the principal part of several spells to send dreams, and visitations of spirits in dream (Cerberus in PGM IV. 1872–1927; Anubis in PDM suppl. 101–116, 117–130). These could be readily adapted to involve an invocation of Nebiros and a conjuration of his spirits Huictigaras and Proculo. Similarly a spell for obtaining a divinatory vision in sleep is found in *The True Grimoire*. As has been explained before, the spells in *The True Grimoire* operate by means of the spirits of the Grimoire. Accordingly this simple spell can also be adapted for work with Nebiros and his spirits. This spell consists of writing the operators name in the central circle of the standard *Verum* talisman, and appropriate spirit names within the circumference. Then, when going to bed, saying a prayer that these spirits will reveal what you wish during the night, placing the talisman so it will lie under your right ear as you sleep.

The *Grand Grimoire* and the *Red Dragon* names further spirits under Nebiros. These are Ipos, who knows all things past, present and to come, and can also make men witty and bold; Naberus, a form of Nebiros himself, who can confer knowledge of all arts and sciences, particularly rhetoric; Glasya-bolas, who appears as a winged dog, he can also make known all arts and sciences, cause bloodshed and manslaughter, teach all things past, present and to come, and confer invisibility. Together these spirits represent divination, knowledge, courage, invisibility and power over enemies. Like those spirits listed above, this is a compendium of the powers associated with Nebiros.

Last, but by no means least, the two spirits Pentagnony and Bucon are connected etymologically with the ancient household gods of Roman religion. In this way the spirits under Nebiros are familiar spirits attendant upon the goetic magician, and the collective conjuration given above forms a suitable part of rituals accompanying regular offerings to them.

THE MAGICAL PAPYRI

IT IS EVIDENT ENOUGH BUT SHOULD NOT BE FORGOTTEN that the grimoires are not an oral folk tradition; nor, despite outside influences, are
they merely an adaptation of an imported Eastern system. They were
from their very beginning a Western literary genre. While superficially
similar, the ritual materials inscribed for Assyrian kings and the magical
papyri of Egyptian pharaohs bear a relation to this long lived genre which
is distinct socially, culturally and geographically.

As remarked by Joseph Peterson, and noted by Skinner and Rankine
in their *Veritable Key of Solomon*, the earliest texts of the Solomonic genre
are Greek: both Hellenistic (*The Testament of Solomon*) and Byzantine
(*The Hygromanteia*). As indicated earlier, the grimoires have their earliest
ancestors in the Orphic books. Between the Byzantine Solomonic books
and those of Orpheus lay the Græco-Egyptian magical papyri and the
lost magical books of Ephesus &c. The Orphic books, the Magical Papyri,
the Byzantine and subsequent Solomonic texts constitute the phases of a
continuous literary tradition; in all these phases the texts existed on their
own merits without the warrant of a ruling minority, whether aristocratic
or theocratic.

The collection of ancient magical texts, published as *The Greek Magical
Papyri in Translation*, is difficult to over-value. As a collection, it collates
virtually the entire surviving examples of this genre. The principal exception is what can be extrapolated from surviving ritual deposits such as the
defixiones, and engraved gnostic gems. Its importance to this study, and
to a critical re-evaluation of goetic magic, is inestimable. Various things

become apparent to the student of magic when comparing the papyri with the grimoires. Details emerge which explode assumptions concerning goetia from hostile perspectives. Firstly, it is necessary to underline certain salient facts. Betz observes in his masterly introduction that the Underworld in the papyri has assumed massive importance. It appears to me that this may not be such a recent development, when the transferral of the Underworld to the sky is properly considered. According again to Betz, the Underworld has also expanded to encompass deities who formerly had no Underworld role; this too requires appraisal in a wider context. Betz also notes what he takes to be cases of reversion to pre-Classical forms, of gods reassuming their earlier daimonian nature. It is more likely though that a prior sublimation of these daimonian forms was not in fact general; that in the appropriate contexts these forms had remained intact.

If Betz is right, then cultural reasons may have existed for the apparent expansion of the Underworld; the pessimism of civilisations conquered by Rome foremost among them. Perhaps too it is here, rather than in Christianity, that we find the original demonisation of the pagan gods. However, when he gives Helios as an example of this tendency to chthonicisation, certain major difficulties arise which require examination a little later.

However, in terms of magical cosmology and practice, the comprehensive importance of the Underworld has significance separate from these considerations. It plainly marks the major part of the magic portrayed therein as goetic, in that it emphasises spirits of the dead, Underworld experiences and other chthonic considerations. In this respect it either reprises or simply continues the magic of a much earlier period. Indeed, it is a fact that the old Mystery cults became a major concern of Hellenistic intellectual life in the period in which these documents were composed. That the Magical Papyri are the ancestors of the later grimoires is a given, the relations between them are plain. There is, firstly, the presence of Solomon and Moses as magical heroes and the use of Jewish god-names (by no means exclusive, but sufficiently prefiguring later use). Alongside these are other elements, from other cultural roots, such as the use of magical symbols and letters known as characters. These are often identical with symbols found in the grimoires, or of a plainly similar type. There is also, as shown earlier in the chapter concerning Nebiros and in the chapter of *The True Grimoire* concerning Astaroth, a considerable foreshadowing of the principal dramatis personæ of the grimoires.

Alongside this is another important issue, the identity of the processes of the papyri with those described in the *Theurgy* of Iamblichus. This equivalence shows quite plainly that the distinction understood to exist between ancient theurgy and goetia is largely false. While goetia had become a derogatory term its identity remains clear; a species of magic concerned with the Underworld that perpetuated older perspectives, albeit in reformed guise. The only real distinction is that what was called goetia was often practiced by persons outside the intellectual and philosophical elites. Iamblichus, a major leader of the Neoplatonist school, gave the old magic respectability through supplying it with a philosophical interpretation. Thereafter the term theurgy was the designation preferred by magicians who saw themselves, or wished to be seen, as religious conformists or as morally and intellectually superior to more marginalised magicians. However, in practical terms – sometimes conceptual terms as well – there was little difference. Lack of philosophical acumen on the part of practitioners did not prevent them claiming to be theurgists to avoid the opprobrium associated with the devalued term, nor were philosophers immune to charges of goetia.

That after the Orphic books the Papyri are the next ancestral source of the grimoires is, as said above, a given. The arrival of this ancestral stream in the world of Christian Europe is not problematic either. One route was the survival of Hellenistic civilisation under the Christian Byzantines, who influenced the successors of the Western empire, and was the most direct route of Solomonic forms. The other however was the Islamic world that enthusiastically absorbed and added to hellenistic learning, including its magical lore. In modern occult circles, the most accessible evidence of this inherited lore transmitted in turn to the West, is in the compendium of magic known as the *Picatrix*.

This tome, compiled by an Islamic scholar, was first translated for Europeans in medieval Spain. In it the names of Greek sages are constantly mentioned: aphorisms are attributed to Empedocles and clear statements made of Neoplatonist theory: the great chain of being, sympathia and so forth. Magical books attributed to Aristotle, Hermes, Hippocrates and others are quoted briefly or at length, as will be seen in a later chapter. An unknown work attributed to one Kriton, a common Greek name, is cited alongside Apollonius and others. That these attributions are no mere literary device is plain enough from the descriptions of talismans and other details, which plainly have pagan origins. Most of the designs of magical images in the *Picatrix* found their way into Agrippa and elsewhere. Several are recognisable as similar in design to earlier gnostic gems and talismans manufactured by, or according to the instructions of, hellenistic magicians.

As mentioned in Book One, there has been debate concerning the relation of the hermetic corpus and the Magical Papyri. Some see the first as high or learned Hermetica, and the other as low or popular Hermetica. Such a distinction is utterly irrelevant in the *Picatrix*, where sophisticated Hermetic philosophy forms the basis of magical practices directly related to the papyri. The two form a continuum, and this is more likely than not to reflect Hellenistic forms. This is not to say there were no individuals who specialised; simply that one did not exempt its exponents from the other.

Abraxas

Much ink has been expended on the mysterious Gnostic deity known as Abraxas, with ideas ranging from the erudite to the farcical. The importance of the figure to this study is in the self-evident but scarcely remarked relation of Abraxas to Helios, god of the Sun. This close identity is apparent in several prominent features: firstly, as is well known, the name Abraxas sums to 365 in Greek gematria, the number of days in a solar year. Secondly, it is by no means unusual to see Abraxas represented in a chariot, a standard emblem of Helios. Indeed, even when the chariot is absent a charioteer's whip is usually present. Abraxas, in Greek letters as in English, has seven letters, signifying his dominion over the planetary spheres, as well as every day of the year. The pantheistic nature of Abraxas is fully in accord with Neoplatonist ideas concerning Helios in late antiquity, wherein he is the most important of the old gods, the heart of the cosmos. This status simply reflected his exalted status in Orphism, which was of long standing.

Jewish iconography too was influenced by late Helios theology, and mosaic floors have been excavated in synagogues representing God in his chariot, surrounded by symbols of the seasons. The mysteries of the Chariot, central to Merkavah mysticism lends itself to such associations. There has been considerable speculation concerning the attributes of the Abraxas figure, with its rooster's head, upraised flail and shield. None, so far as I am aware, have pointed to the resemblance of the serpent legs to images of chthonic giants, or of Typhon. By far the likeliest interpretation of this element of the image is dominion over the earth and Underworld, as major components of his universality.

Betz' comments notwithstanding, what could be perceived as a chthonic role for Helios developed at least as early as the sixth century; when his night journey in a cup entered Greek myth. Apollo, whose chthonic qualities derive from gods such as Nergal and Reshef as well as his close association with Dionysus, was first perceived as a Sun god in the fifth century; this development originated in Orphic and allied sources. Similarly Plato, in his *Laws*, clearly identified Helios and Apollo, giving them the same official to preside over their cults. In this, he simply followed Orphic precedent; Orpheus refused honours to Dionysus, giving them instead to Helios, who he called Apollo.

Although the state cult of the Roman period elevated the Sun to the main deity, the roots of this idea can be perceived much earlier, in philosophical, magical and popular traditions. Also derived from Plato, and prior Ionian sources, was the idea of the Underworld in the night sky. In this schema, Sun and Moon were identified with Hades and Persephone, and the zodiac and Milky Way with paths or rivers of the Underworld etc. Persephone's identification with the Moon explains the title Children of the Moon, given to Orphic initiates, who had expiated the original sin implicit in the Titans murder of Dionysus, her son.

Weekday	Planet	Greek gods from papyri
Sunday	☉	Helios
Monday	☾	Selene
Tuesday	♂	Ares
Wednesday	☿	Hermes
Thursday	♃	Zeus
Friday	♀	Aphrodite
Saturday	♄	Kronos

(Helios & Selene = Hades & Persephone)

Franz Cumont in his *Oriental Religions in Roman Paganism* speaks of Solar pantheism developed in Syria in the Hellenistic period under the influence of Chaldean astrological religion. From there this view of the Sun-god as a pantheistic deity or demiurge became official in the Roman Empire. In this respect, as in others, Hellenistic Syria was as important to the development of Western magic as developments in Egypt in the same time frame. From his Eurocentric stance, with inbuilt Judæo-Christian bias, Cumont emphasises the importance of this deity in the development of religion: *The last formula reached by the religion of the pagan Semites and in consequence by that of the Romans, was a divinity unique, almighty, eternal, universal and ineffable, that revealed itself throughout nature, but whose most splendid and most energetic manifestation was the sun. To arrive at the Christian monotheism only one tie had to be broken, that is to say, this supreme being residing in a distant heaven had to be removed beyond the world. So we see once more in this instance, how the propagation of the Oriental cults levelled the roads for Christianity and heralded its triumph.* Today we might legitimately wonder whether this separation from the world was such an advance. For the time being however it is merely important to bear in mind that the separation was not a feature of the pantheistic sun god, quite the contrary. Though later theology might obscure this element of his nature, part of the purpose of what follows is to underline the implications of his chthonic connections.

Jupiter Heliopolitanus was indeed originally a solar god of Syria, whose stupendous temple survives at Baalbek, reflecting his importance in Roman religion before Christianity. Prior to the Roman adoption of the god, the Greeks had associated him with both Zeus and Helios. As a pantheistic deity he subsumed the seven planets, busts of the gods of which are found decorating the front of some statues of the god below a winged solar disk. On some such statues, very recognisable Greek forms are found: it is Helios & Selene, Mars & Mercury, Jupiter & Venus that appear in pairs with Saturn alone beneath them. The order of appearance from right to left and top to bottom is the order of the days of the week associated with these planets. On occasion seven Eastern deities appear instead, and on other occasions the signs of the zodiac. All of which underlines the identification in the papyri of Helios with Abraxas. There, though he appears elsewhere in other guises, he is plainly equivalent to Aion, all encompassing god of eternity.

Zeus or Jupiter Heliopolitanus are obviously Greek and Roman names for a native god. In Syria he was called Baal, and he was associated with the Egyptian Set, as well as Reshef. Baal as a Sun god is easy to find in the *Picatrix* and elsewhere, and he rules over fire as well as the Sun. This is the source of the name as one of the Four Kings of the Elements in demonology. An alternative for this name, Oriens, is a title of the Sun in the Roman cult of the god. Like Helios and Abraxas the god holds a whip. His Roman title, Iovi Optimo Maximo Heliopolitano (most high and great Jupiter of Heliopolis), provided a mystic formula: I O M H. Associating this pantheistic solar god with Abraxas involves no leaps, since Syrian and Chaldean cosmology were part and parcel of the Hellenistic synthesis, and the conceptions involved scarcely differ.

Whether disconnection from the world equates with a superior concept of deity is a moot point. In any case there are conflicting accounts of the cosmology of Basilides, in whose school Abraxas appears to originate. Depending which is correct, Abraxas may be either: the greatest of the Gnostic Archons (supported incidentally by the fact that the name Sabaoth is written on the Abraxas gems), or the First Principle from which all originates. The latter is a conception of deity which connects with the Unknowable God of Neoplatonism, of Kabbalah, and of the very theology which Cumont considered so exceptional. My point stands without diminishing the perceived connections of this same figure with the Hekalot of the Jewish tradition, and the zodiacal Sun god represented on ancient synagogue mosaics. In the appropriate cultural context the typhonian and chthonic associations of the solar pantheistic deity nevertheless argue for a manifested and personal god, though on a supreme scale.

An interesting feature of Hellenistic syncretism is the association of IAO-Sabaoth with the Bacchic cry of *Io Sabazios*. This essentially identifies Dionysus as the supreme god, as appropriate to the prophecy that he would ultimately supplant Zeus as ruler of the gods and the universe.

Regarding the Abraxas gems referred to already, there are two descriptions of related stones in the Magical Papyri. PGM XII. 201–69, and PGM XII 270–350 both describe the making of magical rings bearing engraved stones, on the first is a snake with its tail in its mouth, inside this Selene (a crescent moon) tipped by two stars and above these Helios (a sun). Beside Helios the name Abraxas is to be engraved, the same name is to be written on the other side of the stone, while around the border is engraved IAO-Sabaoth. The consecration of this ring involves what is unmistakably a chthonic offering. Prior to a sacrifice and libation a pit is dug, at a place *open to the sky*, or if this is not possible a clean, sanctified tomb; a fire is then built over it for a burned offering.

The second involves engraving on a heliotrope stone, green with red flecks, as commented in *The True Grimoire*. In this text Helios is to be drawn in the form of the circular snake emblem, inside which is a scarab surrounded by rays, on the back of the stone the name in hieroglyphics. All kinds of aromatics may be used in the offering to the god, except frankincense which is specifically excluded. The identical prohibition occurs in the Orphic *Hymn to Dionysus Chthonios* (*The Orphic Hymns* no. 52). This is reminiscent of the assumed connection between Sabaoth and Sabazius in Hellenistic syncretism.

Although neither the translator nor the editor have noted it, the consecration ritual of the first of these rings appears to be the *spell for all occasions* cited in other rituals of the papyri. Both are Helios rites, containing comparable and connected themes.

The Spell for All Occasions or Consecration of all Purposes (PGM IV 1596–715) invokes Helios as the greatest god, it specifies that his power extends *over the world and under the world.* He is entitled the Agathos Daimon, an important honorific, and the celestial heaven is termed his processional way. He is also specifically called the great Serpent, again identifying him with the snake with its tail in its mouth, representing the whole of creation and of time. The ritual is an all purpose consecration rite; accordingly instructions are given to rewrite the petitions involved as required, to give power to whatever is being consecrated, citing its purpose. A fusillade of barbarous names then follows, among which the Abraxas title, Sabaoth, is conspicuous. This introduces a twelve stage incantation, where the god is greeted in terms of twelve times, images and names, and the petition *give power to this image, talisman etc, made for N* spoken after each. This series relates to an ancient division of both day and night by twelve rather than twenty four. Each 'hour' is further associated with one of twelve traditional animal images collectively known as the *dodekauros:* giving us Hellenistic hours of the cat, serpent &c. In this particular ritual these symbols were further associated with a divine name, as follows:

HOUR	FORM OF THE GOD	DIVINE NAME
1st hour	Cat	Pharakouneth
2nd hour	Dog	Souphi
3rd hour	Serpent	Amekranebecheo Thouth
4th hour	Scarab	Senthenips
5th hour	Ass	Enphanchouph
6th hour	Lion	Bai Solbai
7th hour	Goat	Oumesthoth

8th hour	Bull	Diatiphe
9th hour	Falcon	Pheous Phoouth
10th hour	Baboon	Besbyki
11th hour	Ibis	Mou Roph
12th hour	Crocodile	Aerthoe

After each *in the N hour you have the form of N and your name is N* the specifics of the consecration in hand are recited.

Finally, *earth & heaven, light & darkness* are conjured by the god who created all, the Agathos Daimon, to accomplish all that is intended by the ring, stone, image or other item being consecrated. The climactic words are themselves a final formula: *The One Zeus is Sarapis*; this reaffirms Helios as a universal deity, since it identifies Zeus (a conception similar or identical to Zeus Heliopolitanus is surely implied) with Sarapis, whose chthonic nature is explicit.

To summarise: the essential feature of the rite after the opening prayer is a rehearsal of the 12 forms and names of the solar pantheistic god, with a final petition at the end of each. As usual in Egyptian magic the intention has to be added by the operator (*add the usual*, or *do the NN matter*). The important thing is that this consecration ritual is designed for adaptation as required, constantly redrafted as appropriate to specific operations. In fact several rituals in the Papyri specify its use, and their diversity certainly confirms the universality of its intended application. To illustrate that its purpose extended beyond talismans and amulets, one of these (PGM IV 1872–1927) involves the making, not of a talisman but a magical statue of Cerberus for use in amatory rituals.

The *consecration for all purposes* bears comparison with later grimoire consecrations, in particular one in *Verum* entitled *The Orison of the Instrument*. Not only is the *Verum* ritual itself a general purpose consecration, it also uses similar terms and invokes a pantheistic deity who besides commanding the elements is *the Creator of the Sun and Angels*. By comparison and extrapolation it is very plain that the *Verum* rite could be applied as well to talismans and spells as to instruments; similarly the *Consecration for everything* could be applied equally well to the magical instruments typical of the grimoires.

The Byzantine Legacy

The following table represents 12th century Byzantine planetary correspondences; expertly and conscientiously culled from pagan sources:

Planetary god	Mineral	Plant	Animal
Kronos	Lead	Hyacinth	Ass
Zeus	Silver	Lily	Eagle
Ares	Iron	Violet	Wolf
Helios	Gold	Rose	Lion
Aphrodite	Tin	Pimpernel	Dove
Hermes	Bronze	Madder or Anenome	Snake
Selene	Crystal	Narcissus	Cow

Contemporary with early grimoires this Byzantine knowledge of Hellenistic material was both extensive and well informed. Indeed the survival of Platonic Paganism in some Byzantine philosophical circles endured until the medieval period and beyond. The existence of out and out pagan magicians in adjacent Bulgaria, where those out of favour with the authorities were wont to flee, is not simply possible but extremely likely. So, in Arthur Bernard Cook's estimation, *these Byzantine attributions represent a systematised selection from the customs and cults of the Roman Empire.* For example, the Sun emerging from a rose appears on the coins of Helios' island of Rhodes (from *rhodos*, a rose).

The association of Ares with violets is less obvious, but the nature of Mars underwent such enormous changes historically that this is not to be wondered at. Violets were associated with the rites of Dionysus – who had martial roles – and Ovid's portrayal of Roman offerings to the Manes includes them. Whatever the original meaning of this attribute, we can at least see here a convergence equal to the sharing of household ritual space by the ancestors and Mars. So too we see the wolf attributed to him, the same animal anciently associated with Apollo, reflecting his chthonic origins. Most interesting of all, the Typhonian and Dionysian ass is here attributed to Kronos. This god was, like Typhon, punished with imprisonment in Tartarus. This was prior to assuming a more dignified and privileged role in the Underworld of the initiated, perhaps reminiscent of the revival of fortunes Typhon experienced in the Hellenistic era.

Cook emphasises also that silver and the lily represent in particular a Syrian solar Baal of the town of Doliche, known to the Romans as Jupiter Dolichenus. This god was among other things a god of precious metals. In several dedications the title *where iron is born* is added to his name. He was popular with Syrian soldiers serving Rome. One inscription speaks of him as *born where iron arises*. These expressions do not indicate ironmines in the neighbourhood of Doliche, for *there is not a particle of evidence to show that such mines were ever to be found in that locality*. It is no accident that the same description is associated with our Chalybes, described by Greek lexicographers as *a Scythian tribe, [dwelling] where iron is born*. Strabo informs us that in his time they were known as Chaldeans and had once worked silver as well as iron. The association of the Chalybes with the Chaldeans does not impress modern scholars; but Babylon too had been Persian, and its astrological theurgists sometimes confused with Zoroastrian magi. In any case his statement that they had once worked silver remains interesting. Homer after all describes the Halizones as coming: *from far-off Alybe, where silver is born*. So too the poet Timotheos sang of *earth-born silver*.

So it appears certain that in Asia Minor, with its great mountain-ranges full of mines, iron and silver were considered to be gifts or even children of Mother Earth. While the roots of this idea may be prehistoric the Syrian conception is likely derived directly from the Hittites, who worshipped a great mountain-mother. She is identical for our purposes with the Cretan mother of Zeus, her son and lover who was born, slain and risen. Jupiter Dolichenus is readily connected with her through his attributes, the bull and double-axe. These motifs are associated with in the first place the Hittite father god and in the second the son, and are strongly linked also with Cretan cults. Thus it is a safe assumption that the title *where iron is born* indicates that he was the successor of earlier sons and lovers of the goddess.

This Jupiter Dolichenus was also frequently identified with Jupiter Heliopolitanus, so that we can view him as both a pantheistic deity among the highest conceptions of late paganism, and more primitively a god of fertilising sunshine and storm. The interplay of roles associated with the Sun and the planet Jupiter is of course a frequent theme with both Zeus and Baal in various forms, as has been seen at various points in this study. The association of this god with precious metals points also to the primitive origins of the god Hephæstus, with all his connections with Helios. That the metals were born of fire, associated also with the brightness of the sky and the sun, underpins all these connections.

Incidentally, while tin is often more commonly associated with Jupiter in the grimoires, the correspondence of silver is by no means lost in the transition from Byzantine to later Western magic. Agrippa lists silver as associated with Jupiter, and he (and thus Barrett) also says of Jupiter's talismanic figures that being engraved on silver they grant all the benefits associated with the planet; silver is also the only metal mentioned in the description of the Pentacles of Jupiter in the *Key of Solomon* (see in particular the fourth Pentacle of Jupiter).

This discussion of the solar-pantheistic deity who rules over fire and metals concludes with an invocation linking the subject with the next to follow. Its highly syncretic approach to the ancient gods is not surprising in a text of similar date to the Papyri. The cryptic gematria in the closing line represents the value of the Greek letters IHΣ, a mystic formula representing Dionysus:

Ode to the Sun

Latium invokes thee, Sol, because thou alone art in honour after the Father the centre of light, and they affirm that thy sacred head bears a golden brightness in twelve rays, because thou formest the numbers of the months and that number of hours. They say that thou guidest four winged steeds, because thou alone rulest the chariot of the elements. For dispelling darkness thou revealest the shining heavens. Hence they esteem thee Phoebus (Apollo), the discoverer of the secrets of the future, or because thou preventest nocturnal crimes. Egypt worships thee as Isoean Serapis, and Memphis as Osiris. Thou art worshipped by different rites as Mithra, Dis, and the cruel Typhon. Thou art also the beautiful Atys and the fostering son of the bent plough. Thou art the Ammon of barren Libya, and the Adonis of Byblos. Thus under varied appellations the whole world worships thee.

Hail, thou true image of the gods and of thy father's face, thou whose sacred name, surname, and omen, three letters make to agree with the number 608.

Martianus Capella, 4th century AD

TYPHON-SET

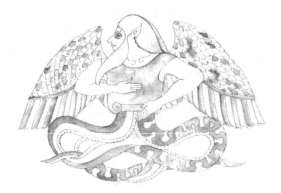

THE MAGICIANS WHO COMPOSED and used the Magical Papyri had two principal patrons, Hecate and Typhon-Set. Both of these deities are extremely important in this context, with an influential presence far beyond their initial cultural environs. Hecate had brought that status with her to Egypt and the Roman Empire from her existing position in the Mystery religions of Asia Minor and Greece. Typhon merged with Egyptian Set and proceeded to become the premier deity of magicians throughout the Roman world. Hecate evolved from one original character, through various phases, to become the premier female witch deity. Typhon-Set's evolution has a different character, in which well-known Egyptian elements are as prominent as Greek. Nevertheless, as a composite deity, his status in Greek tradition also preserves important themes. While there have been many recent studies of Hecate, the role of Typhon in late pagan magic is also of uttermost importance. Indeed, his importance persists in various forms throughout modern occultism, but many historical and mythic elements are under emphasised. An examination here, highlighting the neglected Greek elements, is the least the god demands.

The correspondences of Typhon-Set are very clear from ancient sources: his colour is red; his metal is iron; the kind of water appropriate to him is seawater; his pre-eminent animal symbol is the wild ass. The Greek Typhon is the mythological embodiment of the power resident in storm, volcano and earthquake alike. He is represented as either a ravening wind storm or an immense fire-breathing giant. His form was most remarkable: in appearance his body was human down to his thighs; from them extended a colossal mass of vipers, long enough to reach up to his head, and constantly hissing. His whole body bore many wings, while springing from his head and cheeks were masses of filthy hair which floated in the wind. He had a hundred serpentine heads springing from his arms – in place of fingers according to some – and devouring flame gouted from his mouth and eyes.

This is perhaps why, while represented with three human heads or a single one of an ass, a hundred heads are his frequent attribute, occurring sometimes without mention of any others. The sound of him was as abominable as the sight; each of his heads spoke in a frightening voice. Some spoke in the speech of the gods, a different sound and language to that of men. Others bellowed like a bull, or whistled, or barked like a dog, others uttered horrific cries as of the shrieks of wild beasts.

Typhon was the largest and most formidable creature ever born, his height was above the mountains and his head frequently scraped the stars. When he stretched out his arms to either side he touched the two horizons of East and West. There are several accounts of his parentage, and all are of interest.

The first, and in some respects the most interesting version of all, credits Hera with creating Typhon without male intervention, a duplicate of the myth of Hephæstus, whose myth connects with that of Typhon at various points. According to this version she gave responsibility for raising her creation to the monster Python at Delphi. However the *Homeric Hymn to Apollo* and the *Scholiast* to Apollonius of Rhodes actually identify Python with Typhon, which may be simply the Cilician pronunciation of Python. This thesis is supported by the appearance of a Corycian cave at both locations and in both myths.

Second: some, such as Hesiod and Apollodorus, reckon him the young-est son of Gaia and Tartarus. Angry at the defeat of the Giants, her sons, she brought Typhon to birth in Cilicia to avenge them. The Cilician loca-tion is an important part of the myth in all its forms; the 'Roman' cult of Mithras, with its cave, originated here in later times.

Third, according to others: Gaia, in revenge for the defeat of her sons the Giants, slandered Zeus to Hera. Hera sought assistance from Kronos in avenging the slight and received two eggs coated with his semen which when buried would produce a demon capable of depriving Zeus of his throne.

Typhon attacked Olympus, belching fire, hissing and screaming with his many mouths, while hurtling blazing rocks like comets. This so terri-fied the gods that they fled to Egypt in horror and disguised themselves as animals: Zeus a ram; Hermes an ibis, Apollo a crow, Hera a cow, Dionysus a goat, Artemis a cat, Aphrodite a fish and so on.

While Zeus is included in this mythological aside, both he and Athena are exempted of this shameful behaviour in the main account. Zeus is said to have responded with a barrage of thunderbolts as Typhon advanced. When Zeus and Typhon came to close quarter fighting, Zeus produced the adamantine sickle of Kronos (which as we have seen is also the sickle of Demeter, made by the Telchines). Typhon then fled and Zeus pursued him, until Typhon made a stand at Mount Kasion in Syria. Here Zeus closed again with Typhon, perceiving him to be badly wounded; Typhon however caught Zeus in the coils of his many serpents, deprived him of the sickle and cut out the tendons of his hands and feet. Wading through the ocean to Cilicia carrying Zeus a helpless prisoner, he next rested at the Corycian cave. Here he secreted the severed tendons in a bearskin, and set Delphine – half maid, half serpent – to guard it.

According to one version, Hermes and Pan recovered the tendons and restored Zeus unobserved. Another has it that Cadmus – himself a mon-ster slayer – regained the sinews for Zeus by a stratagem.

When Zeus had recovered his strength he pursued Typhon to Mount Nysa where the Fates falsely informed Typhon that he would gain strength from eating the food of men. Following their advice he lost more of his strength. Mount Nysa of course is strongly associated with the myth of Dionysus, whose myth also includes a dethronement of Zeus.

Battle was rejoined in Thrace at Mount Haimos, this mountain was also associated with Boreas, the god of the North wind. Although Typhon (from whence our word typhoon) is strongly connected with winds, being the parent of the Furies who were – among other things – wind demons, Boreas is not reckoned his son. It is curious then that this important element of the Typhonian myth should happen here, as if an ancient mythographer were identifying Typhon with the wind god in defiance of alternative traditions. In the ensuing combat Typhon threw huge mountains, but Zeus hurled them back upon him with thunderbolts. The blood from the wounds these inflicted upon Typhon is given as the reason for the name of the place. When he set out to flee across the Sicilian sea Zeus cast Mount Etna upon him, trapping him under its immense bulk. To this day flames arise from it.

Etna was not the original prison of Typhon, earlier accounts give the region known as Tartarus that honour. However, according to Hesiod the embodied and personified Tartarus was the father of Typhon in the first place. Moreover, Homer knows nothing of this version, but places Typhon's resting place in Cilicia, in the Arimian mountains which Zeus lashes with thunder:

> ... offended Jove
> In Arime, Typhon with rattling thunder drove
> Beneath the earth in Arime; men say the grave is still
> Where thunder tombed Typhon, beneath a monstrous hill.

Typhon still occurs as a man's name in Turkey, and the Chalybes (mistaken for Chaldeans) worshipped the god of fire on mountains in this region. So once more the Typhonian mythos reminds us of Hephæstus. So too the flames of Etna simultaneously represent the forge of Hephæstus and the breath of Typhon. However, Ovid in his *Metamorphoses* piles not merely Etna but the whole island of Sicily atop Typhon: his right hand beneath the cape named Pelorus, his left beneath the promontory of Pachynus and his legs beneath that of Lilybaeum. Etna in this account lay only upon his head, from which he spat smoke and flame. Ovid further reckoned the tremblings of the earth, occasioned by the struggles of Typhon to free himself, caused Hades to visit the island. This he did to assure himself that there was no danger of a breach that would permit daylight to penetrate his dark realm. It was on the occasion of this visit that Hades saw and abducted Persephone to be his queen.

There are thus strong linkages with Demeter and Persephone, with Dionysus and with Hephæstus, embedded in the key accounts of the Typhonian mythos. These chthonian links are also echoed in the legend of Aristæus (see Book Four) being hidden beneath Etna to preserve him from the slaying of the Titans by Zeus. This legend, as mentioned previously, also connects Aristæus with Hephæstus, since the beetle – the local equivalent of the scarab, is the Hellenistic Egyptian equivalent of the Cancerian crab with its tongs. So too these amphibian tongs signified the Telchines, magical workmen of Rhodes.

Typhon was the father of many notable monsters; besides being the self evident father of the Harpies in the guise of winds. He was the sire of Cerberus, Geryon and Orthos. Also, by Echidna: the Chimera, Ladon, the Theban Sphinx, the Hydra, the Sow of Crommyon, the Nemean Lion and the eagle which so tortured Prometheus. This catalogue is very reminiscent of the offspring of the goddess Tiamat. She was the mother of monsters who were the Zodiacal constellations in primitive form. The animal forms of the Greek gods in the Typhon myth may imply another version of this motif; the Olympians themselves were after all associated with the Signs. In any case many of the monsters sired by Typhon were encountered by Heracles in his twelve labours, often associated with the zodiac.

According to Homer, Typhon lived beneath the earth in the country of the Arimi, which Suidas took to mean the mountains and peoples of Mysia and Lydia. As interesting as this is Strabo, likely more accurately, places it in Syria; presumably near the Turkish border. This would suit the associations with Cilicia and Mount Kasios. Virgil mistook the allusion and located him beneath the island of Inarime off the Campanian coast of Italy. While Virgil may have been practicing the legitimate art

of elastic mythic geography, many details of the myth originate with the
Hittites; so there is no mistaking Homer's intention.

In keeping with that elasticity there were two mountains known to the
Greeks as Mount Casius or Kasion. In fact, locations linked with Typhon
were particularly prone to this duplication; there was a Corycian Cave
in Cilicia, and another near Delphi. The primary Mount Casius is on
the border of Syria with Turkey, and has a very long sacred history. Zeus
Kasios is the Greek name for a succession of older Baals whose connection with the place goes back millennia. The contest with Typhon undoubtedly connects with epic battles this god had with gods of the sea
and of death. Another Mount Kasios was located near Pelusium in Egypt,
near a huge and very deep lake heavily impregnated with bitumen, called
the Serbonian bog, which once swallowed most of a Persian army. In the
Argonautica Typhon is located in this lake, rather than in Sicily. The prefix
Cassio that appears before some classical names indicates a dedication to
the sacred mountain and its god. Cassiopeia, the name of a constellation
named after the mother of Andromeda is such a name. Perseus rescued
Andromeda from a sea-monster in Greek myth, but as I have mentioned
elsewhere the rescuer in an Egyptian form of the myth was no less than
Set himself.

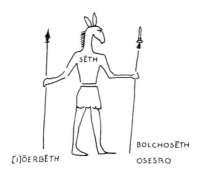

Set from the Græco-Egyptian Papyri

175

As is widely known the Egyptian counterpart of Typhon, the god Set, exemplified the ferocity of the warlike Pharaohs Rameses and Seti; until the rise of Osiris theology put his chaotic ferocity and cunning beyond the pale. The language with which Seti and Rameses recorded their deeds has a parallel in Aeschylus' *Seven Against Thebes* when the ferocity of Typhon is associated with a warrior chief, whose shield bears his likeness:

> *No vulgar cunning did his hand possess*
> *Who carved the dread device upon its face,*
> *Typhon, forth-belching, from fire-breathing mouth,*
> *Black smoke, the volumed sister of the flame;*
> *And round its hollow belly was embossed*
> *A ring of knotted snakes. Himself did rage,*
> *Shouting for battle, by the god of war*
> *Indwelt, and like a Mænad, his dark eyes*
> *Look fear. Against this man be doubly armed,*
> *For, where he is, grim Fear is with him.*

Of course, the Egyptian and Greek contexts involved in this comparison have their dissimilarities as well as resemblances. Can we truly compare a Pharaonic monumental inscription with a Greek tragedy? As remarked elsewhere in this study, the occasion of most daimonic intensity in the *Iliad* begins with the storm-like onset of Achilles. Despite their cultural differences, Rameses and Homer spoke the primal language of epic; celebrating the superhuman deeds of earthly demigods.

While of another order of poetry, Aeschylus' verses contain luminous phrases pregnant with meaning: *by the god of war indwelt*, this clearly means possessed by Ares, the Greek Mars; *like a Mænad* – an ecstatic devotee of Dionysus – this again implies an ecstatic state, an ecstasy of war rather than wine. The warrior is not only possessed by a god himself, he inspires the presence of another in opponents. The perception here is of fear as a spiritual presence; the image is so powerful we at once appreciate that modern talk of the personification of abstractions does not diminish one iota its role as an active force.

Typhon as Demiurge

Finally, we come to a vexed matter implicit in Typhon's role as patron of magicians. This and associated concerns has inspired considerable debate among scholars, and many confused and nigh unsupported statements by otherwise competent academics. Firstly, it appears quite unjustified to suggest a historical equating of the biblical Seth with the god of the Papyri. Nor does Typhon-Set equate with Gnostic or occult forms of Jesus Christ, despite the linking of the name Aberamenthou with both of them on separate occasions. This aside, there is no doubt whatever that Typhon-Set was commonly identified with the sun in the Græco-Roman period, and not infrequently with Abraxas. Similarly, there are many occasions when Jewish god-names occur in invocations of Typhon-Set. Identification of both Typhon and Dionysus with the Jewish god is also a common theme in late antiquity. Despite assertions by respected reference works, I am not inclined to epitomise every instance of this as anti-Semitism, even though such traits certainly existed. Set had a newly acquired demiurgic and solar-pantheistic status that was evidently sincere, this was neither necessarily or still less inevitably connected to ethnic politics. Similarly, Dionysus was a hugely popular god; identification of him with Eastern deities is perfectly in character, even if controversial due to the status of one in particular.

What is certain is that in late pagan magic Typhon-Set was frequently associated with Jewish names and titles. This is apparent from many relevant passages in the Papyri, as also from defixiones found in Rome. The magician in these cases is plainly more interested in conjuring his own god than in insulting that of another nation. In modern interpretations of the later grimoires, these names are termed Kabbalistic; in reality, this means they represent a Christianised Neoplatonist view of the universe, expressed in Jewish rather than pagan Greek terms. Even so, Renaissance Neoplatonists frequently employed the names and images of the Greek gods, along with appropriate Orphic hymns.

Imputations of anti-Semitic tendencies to modern usage of these names strike me as erroneous; the fact is that the very notion is quite alien to many practitioners. Similarly, magical use of Jewish god-names occasionally incurs accusations of cultural appropriation. Again, the fact is that these names have become traditional; it is however extremely significant that late pagan use of them predates similar Christian usage. While apparently counter-intuitive to modern sensibilities, for an ancient pagan it was perfectly feasible to accommodate figures from henotheist or monotheist cultures. In some cases, particularly in Asia Minor, such accommodation reflected a deep respect for and involvement with Jewish culture, which however stopped short of conversion. On the other hand, there is no necessity to retain wholesale usage of these names; the conceptions of deity involved are not the sole province of any particular theology, and slavish reliance on past forms is no indication of magical competence.

Having disposed of this issue in short order, the more immediately relevant fact here is that Typhon-Set bore the status mentioned. In doing so, he demonstrates the mutability of views of the gods from one epoch to the next. It is a simple fact that perceptions of the nature and attributes of any ancient deity was subject to change. Consequently, the favouritism of one modern pagan grouping or individual for one or other past expression does not render those of another wrong per se. That Typhon-Set preceded Jehovah as premier deity of ceremonial magicians, often invoked under exactly the same names, is both historically true and potentially significant to various modern practitioners, and that is what matters here.

... an art of depraved curiosity which they either call magic or by the more detestable name goetia or by the honourable title theurgia. For they try to distinguish between these arts and condemn some men, whom the populace calls malefici, as devoted to illicit arts, for these, they say, are concerned with goetia; but others they want to make out praiseworthy as being engaged in theurgy. But they are both entangled in the deceptive rites of demons who masquerade under the names of angels.

The City of God, Saint Augustine 354–430 CE

G IVE OR TAKE A LITTLE THEOLOGICAL PREJUDICE, the linkage by Augustine of goetia and theurgy, of angels and demons is essentially correct. While goetia possesses many centuries of historical precedence, in practical details goetia and theurgy are intimately related. In large part, Theurgy (as a formal school rather than an appropriated term) is a reformation of the older goetic tradition by Neoplatonist philosophers. To a large degree the writings of Iamblichus on Theurgy are a philosophical appraisal of magic as it already existed rather than a new system of magic. Such an interpretation follows from viewing goetia as representing, or originating within, the magical aspects of popular religion in the Hellenistic world; for it is exactly these which his work reprises and reinterprets.

While the origins of the term goetia are in oral prehistory, eventually emerging in literature in the 5th century BCE, those of theurgy are in the 2nd century CE. This is not to say that no mystery attaches to the origin of the term, or any of the concepts surrounding it. That would be very far from the truth. However, the origins of theurgy as a term are relatively easy to trace, and the names of its earliest exponents are known.

The first occurrence of the terms theurgy and theurgist is in reference to Julianos the Theurgist, who flourished in the reign of the Emperor Marcus Aurelius 161–180 CE. This magician – for such he was – is said to have been of Chaldean origin, and appears to have written in Greek. He is thought to have played a major part in the composition of the *Chaldean Oracles of Zoroaster*; whether as author, collector or redactor is uncertain. The term theurgia is derived from two Greek words, *theos* meaning god, and *orgia* meaning work. The meaning therefore is along the lines of *the divine work*, or more precisely: *working with (or upon) the gods*. The obvious comparison, which was probably intended, is to *theologoi*; from which comes our term theologians – from *theo* god and *logoi* word – those who talk about the gods. A theurgist by contrast is one who works with or upon the gods. While not necessarily devoid of or irreconcilable with a theoretical philosophy, theurgy is a practical art.

The philosophy with which it is primarily associated is Neoplatonism. However, while Theurgy originated earlier, it was not originally part of Neoplatonism as taught by Ammonius Saccas, Plotinus or Porphyry. Theurgical principles were enthusiastically integrated into Neoplatonism by Iamblichus; the successor of these teachers and chief of the Syrian school. Despite this acceptance Theurgy also retained a distinct existence as a Mystery school; Proclus, the successor of Iamblichus, was separately initiated into Theurgy.

Dodds, in his essay on Theurgy, makes the observation that the kind of magic represented by the Greek Magical Papyri used fragments of ancient religious rites for mundane ends, while Theurgy used magical procedures resembling those of the Papyri for religious ends. Disregarding the fact that what he takes for such fragments appear to be the original compositions of magicians, drawing an impartial distinction between religion and magic has never been easy. It is not present in the origins of the 'goen', who officiated at oracles, lit sacrificial fires and guided the dead. Equally the combination of religious and magical roles personified by the 'goen' is visible in the Magical Papyri. Nor is a distinction between religion and magic drawn in the writings of the theurgists. What Iamblichus provides is an elucidation of magical and religious rites. They are handled without distinction, within one and the same framework. Nevertheless, Dodds' observation accurately indicates the close, even intimate, correspondence between goetia as represented by the Papyri and the methods of the theurgists.

As a theoretical explanation and justification of religious and magical rites as a single genre, the treatise of Iamblichus is an extended commentary and justification of the authentic goetes, within a philosophical framework. This is not to say there was no difference between Theurgy and what Dodds calls *vulgar magic*, and which the literati of the day would have called goetia.

Theurgy was chiefly concerned with bringing the practitioner into communication or union with the gods. This is the interpretation put upon it by Iamblichus; and the *Chaldean Oracles* show it to have been equally true of Julian, or those he was interpreting. Goetia was frequently turned to a variety of short term purposes, just as the ancient Oracles answered a variety of questions, both personal and political, many of them as mundane as anything magic endeavoured to resolve. The philosophical framework provided by Iamblichus explains how divination works, regardless of the nature of the question. In the same way the theoretical basis he provided is applicable to any magical operation, whether or not it is concerned with divine union. However, between priest and magician, whether their arts are termed goetia or theurgy, no necessary and often no actual division exists. The concern of the operator with the divine work is central to both. Goetia – the art of the Goen, a founder and celebrant of Mysteries – is the earlier form of Theurgy; working with the gods. The short term purposes of specific magical operations should not obscure the perceived religious role and identity of the operator. It is this role and identity which distinguishes the magician, both in magical lore and popular belief.

Stephen Flowers, an occult author with a firm academic background, draws a distinction between goetia and theurgy. With him however the distinction is one of degree: goetia is a practical art, involving external materials and practices; theurgy is a further step upon the road, when self deification has been achieved and magical processes have been internalised. While his *Hermetic Magic* is both useful as a corrective regarding Classical goetia, and valuable for those exploring the Magical Papyri, this distinction is not entirely satisfactory. The classic handbook of Theurgy, *The Mysteries* of Iamblichus, describes a great many operative procedures. Most typical of these is the making and empowerment of magical statues of the gods, a procedure well represented in the goetic papyri. This certainly involves physical materials (particularly herbs, stones and animals according to the laws of sympathia), and in the papyri it frequently involves material or mundane objectives. This was so central to theurgic practice as to lead Psellus to interpret theurgy as the making of gods. This making of gods connects them with the goeten as founders of the Mysteries, such as Abaris who made the Palladium from the bones of Pelops. Indeed, the powers Julian the Theurgist and his father are credited with place them in direct descent from the goeten. There are accounts of feats of weather magic, and purifying cities from plague. They possessed the ability to cause men's souls to leave their bodies, and it is fair to assume they could do so in their own right. Theurgy is essentially a reformation of magical religion, a restoration of archaic goetia.

The idea of a magical assistant, so frequent in the papyri, undoubtedly precedes the Holy Guardian Angel of *Abramelin* and modern occultism. The magical assistant or parhedros is often an invoked emanation of a solar pantheistic deity, again matching modern Qabalistic conceptions. Theurgical practice is also anticipated in the manufacture of magical images to embody such an assistant, incorporating appropriate materials according to the laws of sympathia. In modern usage a key example of such an image is the magical head, its seven holes reflecting the seven letters of the name Abraxas.

Although Julian the Theurgist is the reputed founder of Theurgy, the distinction of having penned the definitive treatise on the subject belongs to Iamblichus. His work, known as *The Mysteries*, is a response to a letter of Porphyry questioning the nature of magic and the rites of religion. Porphyry inquires how the various genera of higher beings are distinguished from each other; in what they differ, and from what these differences arise. Why do ceremonies take the forms they do, what in the nature of the gods and other entities requires such rites? He asks also what divination consists of, and what explanation there is for the active and passive forms such arts take. How is it that divination can be performed in conscious or unconscious states, ecstatic or somnambulant? He enquires into the nature of image making in the invocation of gods. In this connection arise the magical laws of Sympathia whereby plants, stones, animals and other material objects or qualities equate with different qualities of the gods.

The Cosmology of Theurgy

The cosmological hierarchy of spiritual entities described by Iamblichus consists of gods, the higher demons, heroes and purified souls. Subdivisions of these classes also appear in his writings: the archangels, angels, cosmocrators, archons and so forth; these are terms that represent subdivisions among the gods and higher demons. This places angels – wherever they may originate – in a philosophically pagan worldview, subject both to their various planetary gods and to major pantheistic figures. Essentially all types involved in theurgical workings relate to one or other of the four essential categories. All these, gods, the higher demons, heroes and unpolluted souls were of a higher nature than unredeemed souls, which includes the major portion of humanity. It is worth comparing this cosmology with the row of Agrippa's *Scale of the Number Ten*, labelled: *Ten Orders of the Blessed according to the traditions of men*. The apparently Cabalistic orders represented there quite obviously reflect older Theurgic and Neoplatonist classifications.

Hierarchical Table of the Superior Genera

Genera	Subdivisions	'Cabalistic' equivalents
Gods	Gods	Elohim (Gods)
	{Archangels}	
Demons	{Angels}	Beni-Elohim (Sons of the gods, or Demi-gods)
	{Higher Demons}	
Heroes	Heroes	Cherubim (Cabirs)
Pure Souls	Pure Souls	Ishim (Flames)

Gods and Angels (concise)

Planetary & related pantheistic gods	example Angels (Byzantine KoS plus * = PGM refs)	Notes & alternatives
Kronos	Sakatael, Uriel*	Cassiel in the grimoires
Zeus, Baal	Raphael* Boel*	Sachiel in the grimoires
Ares	Samael, Shamuil*	Samael, Zamael in the grimoires
Helios, Baal Typhon/Abraxas &c	Mikael* Boel*	As grimoires, cf. Reshef & Nergal Solar pantheistic: Mikael or Uriel
Aphrodite/Astarte &c Baalit	Agathoel Anael*	compare Hagith, agathadaimon. as grimoires, variant Haniel
Hermes Aristaeus, Mēn &c	Uriel*	In Testament of Solomon & Enoch I. many other attributes. Raphael in the grimoires.
Selene/Hecate &c Baalit, also Mēn &c	Gabriel*	As grimoires (Gabir/Cabir)

Note that Mikael, as either Solar or Mercurial angel, certainly adopted attributes and roles of Anubis of the PGM (including the balances), and that both Mikael and Uriel have solar pantheistic, helio-chthonic roles.

Proclus accorded each of the gods a retinue of these genera; Iamblichus has the various genera of the particular retinue attend a sacrifice to the appropriate god. The most traditional astrological attribution schema on Greek lines, predating planetary and other schemas, would first reflect the zodiac via the months. Such an approach is the direct equivalent to modern magic's Hebrew names of God ruling archangels, angels and spirits of various Spheres, Signs etc. As superior genera to that of ordinary mortals, it was considered right and just, as well as intellectually respectable, that any of them might be honoured with rites and sacrifices. By the same reasoning, consultation through divinations and oracles could be sought of them. In short, all were encountered by means as religious as they were magical.

There is however – disregarding the Ishim or Souls as people often do – a major difference between generic Hebrew and Greek classifications. That is, in corroboration of the essential equivalence of goetia and theurgy, two categories of superior being invoked in this way include the illustrious dead. While Theurgy is thought of as a dignified philosophical movement, with its origins in the thought of Plato and Pythagoras, invocations of the dead constitute a form of necromancy; a term with which goetia is and always has been associated. An authentic invocation of an oracular hero at his cenotaph is part and parcel of the heritage from which goetia as we know it has its origins. Just such respectable necromancy as originally distinguished the older tradition was equally at home in the magico-religious worldview of the Theurgist. This concern with the mighty and illustrious dead provides the clearest possible demonstration that Theurgy and Goetia were in many respects equivalent in conception and application.

Theurgic Methods

The methods of the theurgists were several. The highest form of theurgy was divine union through pure contemplation, which was the most difficult and strictly for the few. More accessible, and in some ways more definitive, was the making of magically charged images of gods, incorporating the methods of sympathia. Closely related to this were methods of self-deification, often employing similar means to the making of divine images. In addition to these modes, the theurgists practiced ritually induced trance – the term mediumship is best avoided in favour of prophecy – for the reception of divine oracles.

The Theurgy of Iamblichus and the Neoplatonists explicitly involves: incantation, talismans and seals, ecstatic states and trance, the doctrine of correspondences, as well as hierarchies of spirits that were deeply influential on the development of the grimoires. Despite this it is a peculiar fact that a sizeable number of modern ceremonial magicians see Iamblichus as anti-magic! This is perhaps more connected with modern controversies – and simplifications – than a true appreciation of his work.

There are two possible explanations for this misidentification, which are not mutually exclusive. One is a misunderstanding of the ability of an advanced Theurgist to dispense with ritual. This is not at all incompatible with far older traditions, where an advanced magician attains 'deification' and can dispense with the external apparatus previously essential. This attainment was seen as rare, and existed alongside an entirely positive view of ritual in the writings of Iamblichus. Theurgy as developed by him provided a highly influential theoretical basis for a wide variety of ritual and divinatory methods. That this influence reached the grimoires, of the 15th century and later, through such direct influences as Ficino, Mirandola and particularly Agrippa is an evident fact. Secondly there is the controversy surrounding the use of blood; here too Iamblichus is being misunderstood. He explicitly states not that blood is forbidden or inessential, but that it is more appropriate to some beings than to others. Any blanket demonisation of such beings is of far later date than Iamblichus, who includes them among *the superior genera*. Controversies over the use of blood, of vegetarianism and so forth, have been present in mystical and magical traditions for millennia, and to stigmatise a key thinker in this way is a false form of purism. It is false because it overlooks the eclectic and syncretic tendencies at work in magical traditions. While these tendencies inevitably produce some internal contradictions, they also contribute decisively to the richness of these traditions. In any case, such contradictions will not be overcome by the simplistic expedient of rejecting Iamblichus!

Theurgy in the Grimoires

As seen, St. Augustine refused to recognise a distinction between Theurgy and Goetia as practiced in the Roman Empire. That it was a false distinction when the historical contexts in which the terms arose are understood is clear enough. Nevertheless some space must be given to the fluctuations such terms have undergone in the later history of magic. In the period of the grimoires, and by imitation in modern magic, the erroneous distinction is still frequently encountered and often arises from its misuse in influential texts. Mirandola and others asserted that Goetia operated exclusively by evil spirits, and that the higher magic they preferred was to be distinguished from it. Often as not this lawful magic was clearly based on principles of sympathia, which has been termed natural magic. However others, who practiced magic based on invocation, either alongside or in place of natural sympathies, claimed to be practicing theurgy. Naturally in a Christian context this omitted the heroes and daemons of the old pagan theurgy; focussing mainly on angels. Agrippa referred to this later type of theurgy as follows in the 46th chapter of his *De incertitude et vanitate scientiarum*: *Now many think that Theurgia is not unlawfull, as if this be governed by good Angels, and a divine deity.* So it is that in the *Lemegeton* we find the book of evil spirits referred to as the *Goetia*, and that of supposedly higher forces called *The Theurgia of Solomon*.

The distinction is, of course, false; unsupportable either from the derivation of the words or from the texts exemplifying their use. For example we find one of the goetic spirits, Vassago, described as good in nature, while those of the Theurgia are described as partly good and partly evil. This makes nonsense of the simplistic distinction underlying the classification, even as redefined. In any case, going beyond this particular grimoire, the classification is fundamentally unsound. As has been seen, the angel Cassiel frequently takes on demonic form in practice, so that using theurgy to refer to angelic magic swiftly exceeds the supposed bounds of the term. Moreover, as should be abundantly clear from the outline of early goetia, it was not concerned with evil spirits exclusively, and even when it was frequently took the form of exorcism.

The Christianised magic represented by the grimoire literature is derived from ancient sources, in which moralistic distinctions latterly employed in the grimoires did not apply. They are similarly absent from the Arab material which formed one of the major routes by which learned antique magic reached the West. As will be seen in the *Picatrix* material which follows shortly, the natures of the seven planetary spirits are determined by their planetary associations, rather than any moralistic division into good and evil. The spirit of Saturn (subsequently called Cassiel by Christian magicians), is a thinly disguised planetary god, capable of any action consistent with his planetary nature. What makes him seem prone to contradictions in the grimoires is the theological recasting of the material, which is foreign to the sources; without this veneer, the things required of him are completely consistent.

In closing this brief appraisal of Theurgy, an original document of unknown date is worth presenting. The *Nuctemeron* is attributed to Apollonius, and certainly originally written in Greek. Although cryptic, it bears the imprint of Neoplatonism of the theurgic type in its references to fire, which echo the tone and language of the *Chaldean Oracles* and the *Prayer of the Salamanders*. It is sufficiently brief for quotation in its entirety.

The Nuctemeron of Apollonius of Tyana

The First Hour:
In unity, the daimons sing the praise of God: they lose their malignity and fury.

The Second Hour:
By the duad, the Zodiacal fish chant the praises of God, the fiery serpents entwine about the caduceus and the thunder becomes harmonious.

The Third Hour:
The snakes of the Hermetic caduceus entwine thrice, Cerberus opens his triple jaw and fire chants the praises of God with the three tongues of the lightning.

The Fourth Hour:
At the fourth hour the soul revisits the sepulchre; the magical lamps are lighted at the four corners of the circles. It is the time of incantations and illusions.

The Fifth Hour:
The voice of the great waters celebrates the God of the heavenly spheres.

The Sixth Hour:
The spirit abides immoveable; it beholds the infernal monsters swarm down upon it and does not fear.

The Seventh Hour:
A fire, which imparts life to all animated beings, is directed by the will of pure men. The initiate stretches forth his hand, and pains are assuaged.

The Eighth Hour:

The stars make utterance one to another, the soul of the suns corresponds with the exhalation of the flowers; chains of harmony create unison between all natural things.

The Ninth Hour:

The number that is not to be unveiled.

The Tenth Hour:

The key of the astronomical cycle and the circular movement of human life.

The Eleventh Hour:

The wings of the genii move with a mysterious and deep murmur; they fly from sphere to sphere and bear the messages of God from world to world.

The Twelfth Hour:

The works of the light eternal are fulfilled by fire.

GOETIC GALLERY:
METAMORPHICA

Pythagoras

PYTHAGORAS IS IMPORTANT to this study in various ways, although in other ways quite separate from its main purpose. He is important, in the same way as his mentor Pherecydes, as a link between two phases of culture and religio-magical thought. Important too as a link in the chain by which Dionysian associations predating the rise of goetia were transformed in Orphic and other movements; and as adapting these and eastern forms of Demeter worship. This may have extended further than adaptation, to the extent of propagating them. Such matters as his contributions to numerical mysticism, flowering later in the Qabalah, as also his role as moralist are, on the other hand, utterly separate. My sketch of him tries to steer a middle way between these sides of his legacy, while emphasising the former more than has previously been the case.

Pythagoras was born on the island of Samos, and flourished in the period 540 to 510 BCE. His ancestry may well have been part Syrian, and was certainly affluent. He was trained from youth in music, poetry, eloquence and astronomy, as well as being a distinguished athlete, winning the prize for wrestling in the Olympics when 18 years old. According to tradition he then sought the wisdom of the East, travelling to Egypt and Chaldea; reports that he also studied the wisdom of the Magi all appear rather to refer to the Chaldeans. In these nations, he is said to have gained the respect of the priests and learned from them *the theocratic art*, by which the aristocracy and the people are governed by the wise. This principle resembles that sought by Plato to reform the Greeks when the old traditions began to lose their force. He spent many years acquiring their traditions relating to the nature of the gods and the soul. He returned for a while to Samos, but although welcomed was disgusted by the form of government that prevailed there. He appeared again at the Olympic games, on being recognised and hailed as a Sophist or wise man he disclaimed the title, calling himself instead a lover of wisdom, that is, a philosopher. He was the first to call himself by this name. He then visited the republics of Sparta and Elis before making his home in Crotona, a Greek colony in Italy. A local tradition claimed that Dardanos, associated with the Samothracian and Phrygian Mysteries was born there.

At Crotona Pythagoras founded his school, admitting both males and females. This was strikingly distinct from contemporary Greek custom, the closest contemporary analogy being the form of sexual equality practiced by the barbarian Scythians. While conventional enough in considering marriage a holy role for women, he evidently esteemed female intelligence highly. Diogenes Laertius held that much of his system originated with Themistoclea, the priestess at Delphi; famous examples of female Pythagoreans are also present in the literary record.

He taught by example as well as eloquence, practicing an austere style of life while discoursing upon music, healing, mathematics and natural philosophy. He taught a frugal and benevolent philanthropy in place of hedonism and materialism. He paid due reverence to the rites of the gods, whose temples he regularly visited. At an early hour of the day, he made his devotions and apparently attired himself in the manner of the Egyptian priests, making continual purifications and offerings. Herodotus, who wrote in Southern Italy near the site of known Orphic interments, tells us that the deceased Orphic initiate is wrapped not in wool but linen. He notes this as consistent with both Egyptian and Pythagorean practice; purification rites are also typical of Orphic practice. Pythagoras is also widely thought to have written poetic works under the name of Orpheus.

Pythagoras famously taught a doctrine of transmigration of the soul, recalling his former lives. Two of these previous lives are noteworthy here: Aethalides – a son of Hermes numbered among the Argonauts – who had the power of dwelling in Hades as well as upon Earth, and was thus acquainted with all things; Hermotimus who had the power of leaving his body. An unnamed wise man mentioned by Empedocles was credited by him with the wisdom acquired in twenty or thirty prior existences; this man is likely to have been Pythagoras. Empedocles was not being merely vague or coy; it was Pythagorean practice not to refer to *that man* by name.

His instruction was adapted in accord with the temperament of the individual: those among his pupils who were inclined to talk overmuch were obliged to remain silent in his presence for five years, while the naturally quiet and thoughtful were encouraged to speak after two. It is supposed that he learned the use of hieroglyphic signs in Egypt, and through similar principles he and his followers were able to correspond, and to recognise each other in distant regions. He taught also that numbers underlie all things, which together with emphasis on the number ten as perfect is a doctrine that arises later in the Qabalah.

His mentor was Pherecydes, a Syrian, who was well versed in Chaldean star-lore. The astronomical knowledge of Pythagoras is acknowledged in the tradition that it was he who realised the identity of the Morning and Evening stars, appearing in the heavens at different times, in one planet, Venus. This tradition also represents the astronomical achievements of Greek astrology, building on Chaldean foundations. Other Pythagoreans were to make other significant astronomical advances.

Accounts of his initiations into Mystery cults vary; Porphyry the Neoplatonist records a tradition that the Idaean Dactyls initiated him on the island of Crete. There he was *purified with a thunderbolt* and laid on the seashore covered with black lamb's wool for a night. Thereafter he spent *thrice nine hallowed days and nights* – a lunar month – in the cave of Zeus before emerging for his initiation. His transformations into various forms – closely resembling those of Empedocles – relate to Cretan cult forms. There are other accounts of his retirement to a cave, from which he emerged after some months both pale and ghastly in appearance, announcing that he was returned from Hades. This compares with the practice of fasting in sacred caves at various Oracles, as well as the legend of Epimenides.

The visits to Sparta and Elis were most likely to have been in search of wisdom, rather than – as elsewhere suggested – marking approval of their form of government. Abaris – the supposed disciple of Pythagoras who in reality predated him – had founded the temple of Persephone at Sparta. The Dactyls were worshipped at Elis, which had been the seat of Pelops, which name recurs in association with many figures examined here. This hero, said to be originally from Phrygia, received honours as high above all other heroes as Zeus above the other gods. A significant aspect of the legend of Pelops involved him being slain, dismembered and served up to the gods. Only Demeter, distraught due to the abduction of Persephone, did not recognise the meat as human and ate his shoulder. The gods then restored him to life, replacing his shoulder with one of ivory. Pythagoras is reputed to have had a golden thigh, which was a sign of his own more than human status. The resemblance of legends such as these to shamanic initiatory ordeals, involving dismemberment by spirits and replacement of parts of the body, is extremely striking. That the legend of Pelops includes clear reference to the Mysteries, those involving Demeter and her daughter's Underworld experience, shows the close relation of the theme to the Mystery cults.

While long well received and influential at Crotona, in time the Pythagoreans fell foul of political rivals. Violent persecution followed with many slain, Pythagoras fled, by the best accounts, to the city of Metapontum. Here an earlier Greek shaman, Aristeas, had founded a cult of Hyperborean Apollo. Pythagoras, who also honoured Apollo and the Muses, took refuge here briefly and appears to have fasted unto death. Although said to have sought sanctuary in the temple of the Muses, there is a recurrent tradition that the 'house' where he ended his days was afterwards known as the Temple of Demeter.

Other accounts of Pythagoras accorded him the power of bilocation, appearing in two distant places at one time. He was similarly credited with power over animals, such as taming a bear and arresting the flight of an eagle. He made in addition many discoveries and proofs in mathematics and particularly geometry. His fame was great throughout the ancient world, and he was accorded divine honours upon death, his home being treated as a temple, and statues erected in his honour. Iamblichus counts Abaris among the disciples of Pythagoras, while Suidas reverses this association. Aristotle mentions a mysterious identity between Pythagoras and the Hyperborean Apollo.

Modern scholars, eschewing the excessive rationalism of the nineteenth century, believe that a great many of these traditions are not late romantic accretions, but rather part of Pythagoras' own self-deifying legend. Certainly all the early sources, such as Xenophanes, Heraclitus, Empedocles, Ion and Herodotus portray Pythagoras as a magician in accordance with the popular tradition. Timon of Phlius, a philosophically inclined Greek poet who lived in the time of Ptolemy II, wrote of Pythagoras that he *sought the reputation of a wizard*. The term Timon used was goen. Modern scholarship, as with Empedocles, is learning not to distinguish the 'mythologised' mystic and magician from the mathematician and natural philosopher; seeing them instead as two aspects of the same role.

Among magical authors Cornelius Agrippa makes very frequent mention of Pythagoras. He is cited as practicing hydromancy; as healing others by magical power; in relation to arithmancy and gematria; to transmigration into other bodies and of becoming a god; of absenting oneself from the body; of laying in seclusion to obtain prophetic power and of secrecy in sacred things. In all these and other matters, Pythagoras, his followers and his precepts were ever in Agrippa's mind.

One particular element of Pythagorean thought in Agrippa involves the Muses and Apollo. As seen when considering the *Vision of Er*, Plato attributed the spheres of his universe to the Sirens. Pythagoras, from whom the Music of the Spheres originates, attributed them rather to the Muses. As shown in Book Three, Agrippa delivered such an attribution from an otherwise lost Orphic source.

There are also many significant references to Pythagoras and Pythagorean teachings in the writings of Giordano Bruno, and as many – with as much approval but without the same degree of interest for us as in Bruno – in the writings of Pico della Mirandola. He and his teachings are also referred to by Doctor John Dee in his *Hieroglyphic Monad*.

He was mentioned in Trithemius' *De Septum Secundeis*, while the same author's *Steganographia* may well have been partly inspired by the ability of Pythagoreans to communicate with one another at a distance. Additionally seven precepts attributed to him are cited in the famous and influential *Picatrix*.

It is extraordinarily interesting that Johann Reuchlin, in his epoch making *De Arte Cabalistica*, which is in the form of a three way dialogue between a Moslem, a Pythagorean and a Kabbalist, portrays the Pythagorean as belonging to the tribe known as the Alans; a steppe people identical with the shamanic Sarmatians encountered by the Greeks.

Take the status of Pythagoras in the grimoire tradition, along with his links to ancient chthonic cults and to Chaldean astrology. Put aside his importance to mathematically inclined Renaissance magicians – perhaps excepting the Hermetic extremist Giordano Bruno – and all avowed enemies of Goetia of later date. It is not that these are without interest, or beyond incorporation in the magical perspectives of some among us. It is simply that these are – so to speak – lofty pinnacles, or ivory towers, obscuring a more fundamental issue. While these are certainly Pythagorean, at the same time he is a link to an earthier theme of Greek shamans and the legacy of Dionysian cults. While Pythagorean principles may be of interest to few, his generally unacknowledged status as a link in this chain requires recognition. It points us to a more primal mystery, from which philosophy and numerous other gifts to our culture had their beginnings. It is that fountainhead, which is also the unacknowledged pagan source of goetic magic, which concerns us here.

REFORMERS
& BACKSLIDERS

THE CLOSELY WOVEN INTEGRATION of traditions from Crete, mainland Greece, Thrace and Asia Minor, arises constantly in classical accounts of the Mysteries. Such syncretism of traditions may well have been the work of major religious reforms undertaken by teachers such as Pythagoras and the semi mythical Orpheus; both of whom, somewhat unexpectedly from some perspectives, were major revivalists of chthonic religion. Their reputation and image among 'transcendentalists', freemasons &c. has somewhat obscured what this means for those rediscovering the significance of goetia as the spiritist or even animist origin of Western magic. Ironic as it may be, these ascetic moralists are our link with older orgiastic traditions, and to necromantic magic.

It is of course from the Magi that the term magic derives in Western languages. Who were they? The answer involves some surprises, given some of the vague ideas that have circulated about them. Occult literature and old classical dictionaries alike concur in crediting Zoroaster the Persian with founding the religion of the Magi. However, firstly the Magi were not Persians, but Medes, who had existed as a specialist religious caste long before the coming of Zoroaster. Rather than a founder, he was a reformer, and the religion he wished to reform was that of the Magi. The Greek experience of Persian magic in the Persian Wars, as recorded by Herodotus, is clearly not Zoroastrian at all; it included sacrifice of human beings by burying alive, as well as the more usual animal sacrifices, namely horses, both of which it is fair to assume Zoroaster would have opposed. In other words, the adoption of the term occurred at a point in time when the magic of the Persians as known to the Greeks was pre-Zoroastrian. Nor was this, so to speak, an isolated case of mistaken identity. In Classical sources *Zoroaster*, *Persia* and *the Magi* are often very misleading terms. They have tenuous links at best with the traditions concerned, traditions more appropriately attributed to Chaldea and Phrygia.

Zoroaster, like Pythagoras and Orpheus, was a reformer of an ecstatic or wild religion, in his case the 'primitive' worship of the Devas. Persian influence in Asia Minor appears not to have reduced the cults of the old gods; even those traditions reminiscent of Persian cults frequently have more archaic elements.

The contrast between the reputation and the reality creates problems of understanding. A tradition generally has to exist already in order to be reformed. Additionally, elements of the older tradition often persist, if indeed it does not make a partial or complete resurgence. Such resurgences of the older tradition are then frequently associated with the teachings of the very reformer who may have tried to suppress them. The case of Zoroaster is one example; he apparently reformed the traditions on which the practices of the Magian caste were centred. However, many of the older practices appear to have persisted, and the Magi remained an influential priestly caste. A further complication is the frequent confusion of Chaldeans and Magi, with the former having much more to do with the planetary magic of the grimoire tradition. The whole spectrum of older tradition, reforms and later manifestations of one or both are associated willy-nilly with Zoroaster and the Magi, regardless of where the various dividing lines may have been. Thus, the pre and post Zoroastrian Magian traditions, as well as those of the quite separate Chaldeans and others, become extremely difficult to distinguish from one another. In such circumstances, false assumptions readily arise, and later views are mistaken for the teachings of the reformer or of his predecessors.

The same situation exists in relation to Pythagoras. He is associated with the doctrine of reincarnation, and also with vegetarianism. It is often supposed that his reforms involved rejection of animal sacrifice, since animals could be reincarnated humans. There is then a temptation to associate Pythagorean teachings with the Indian doctrine of reincarnation and their attendant vegetarianism; contrasting this with older Greek rites of sacrifice. Against this interpretation there are traditions that he sacrificed a hundred bulls in thanks for one of his mathematical discoveries; also that he was initiated at a Cretan sanctuary, a process involving sleeping wrapped in the fleece of a sacrificed ram. There were also specifically

Pythagorean teachings relating to the sacrifice of piglets, a practice closely resembling ancient chthonic rites associated with Demeter. Similarly the Pythagorean magician, Apollonius, is credited with conjuring the hero Achilles without blood sacrifice. However he also visited the sanctuary of Trophonius, where the pre-ritual diet consisted entirely of meat of sacrificed animals. Despite this he traditionally credited the teachings he obtained at the sanctuary as being totally compatible with Pythagorean principles.

The likeliest and readily supported resolutions of this dilemma are in keeping with the Thracian connections in the Pythagorean tradition, rather than supposed connections with India. Following this reading there was originally no Pythagorean doctrine of reincarnation for all, this interpretation was a subsequent development, superimposed later. Originally being empowered to live on after death was the result of religious or magical practices in life. From this followed the opportunity to increase that power in successive lives, which again was the preserve of the magicians, not of all humanity.

Dietary restrictions such as vegetarianism are more problematic; they are unlikely to originate in the Dionysian cult that preceded Orphism, given the regular performance of bloody rites in which women regularly took part. They make most sense as an element of the reforms introduced by Orphic teachings. There remain the contradictions regarding Pythagoras and Apollonius of Tyana, here again the Eastern 'Demeter' cult that underlay the teachings of Pythagoras is unlikely to have involved strict vegetarianism. While in relation to Orphism the relevant sources point to lifelong vegetarianism after initiation, it is not unknown even in modern religions for particular foods to be allowed or disallowed at different points in the ritual calendar. It is also important to bear in mind that Orphism was not a unified movement with one doctrine, set ritual and prescribed practices. On the contrary, Orphism is a generalised term for a variety of analogous sects and teachings. Similarly the cults of Dionysus, like the god himself, were constantly transforming and breaking established forms, as well as combining with local cults and other traditions.

More important than the dichotomy of asceticism and orgiastic elements in these traditions is the nature of the goal. This was identity with a divine figure: collectively while in life in the case of primitive Dionysian rites, individually in the after-life in the case of the Apollonian mystics. From this background emerged the concept of a divine man, personified by Pythagoras, Empedocles and others who aspired to and attained that goal. The helio-chthonic Hero of ancient Thrace underlines the inter-connectivity of many forms of the theme, which transcends even apparently major dichotomies in expression. The solar-pantheistic god complete with chthonic powers, which features so largely in the magical papyri, is the highest form of the concept of parhedros or magical assistant; today's Holy Guardian Angel. It was with such a god also that the magician ultimately sought identity.

FAMILIAR & UNFAMILIAR SPIRITS

I T IS FITTING TO RETURN TO THE SUBJECT OF FAMILIARS and household spirits that arose in Book Six. This has an important bearing on the development of magical traditions, justifying a review of the prototypes of these figures in Greek and Roman lore. For the non-academic reader today the usual impression of Greek and Roman myth is of stately deities in cleanly laundered robes, with satyrs providing little more than light relief and contrast. Prominent snake cults are probably the last thing this impression would lead us to expect. Yet a temple of the 13th century BCE at Mycenæ, excavated in the 1960s, contained ceramic images of twelve deities and seventeen snakes; a ratio of approximately two deities to three snakes. In fact, snakes played an extremely important role in the entire history of Greek religion, and similar features were not lacking in ancient Italy.

The manifestations of snake worship in general comprised two main strands, the domestic and the chthonic. Household gods or spirits manifested in the form of snakes; snakes were also very commonly associated with the dead, particularly but not exclusively with the heroes. As will be seen in the course of this chapter, while initially the two where quite separate they became largely synonymous in the course of time. Even modern academics occasionally insist that the household spirits had always been connected with an ancestor cult. For our purposes the distinction, while real, is less important, since the later developments are a potent influence on magical traditions regardless of earlier distinctions.

Household Snakes

The snake as an important element of the Greek household cult makes its first appearance in Minoan Crete. In Cretan religion temples played a very minor role, the focus instead was sanctuaries in caves and upon and under mountains, and in the house or palace. The snake never appears in the cave and mountain sanctuaries, it is purely a part of the household cult. Here the role of the snake is strongly emphasised, clay images of them adorn modelled clay honeycombs, and upright tubes. Although similar objects appear later in association with the dead and the hero cults, in the Minoan context there is no trace of such associations. The snake is a guardian of the house, and is treated in a similar way to the familiar spirits of folklore. Bowls, as if for offerings of milk, were found alongside the snake tubes at Knossos. While these offerings may have been purely symbolic they are strongly reminiscent of the actual feeding of house snakes in Balkan villages and elsewhere.

The Manes

The Manes (the good beings) were spirits of the dead in ancient Italy. Counted among the infernal gods from early times they were known as the Dii Manes. The Romans in particular honoured the Manes with great solemnity. They presided over burying places and monuments to the dead and dwelled beneath the earth under the rule of Larunda, who bore the additional name or title of Mania. Towns throughout ancient Italy possessed a pit called the *Mundus*, conceived of as an inverted sky, representing the abode of the underworld deities, particularly the Manes. These were dug before the town was built, then vaulted over and provision for a removable stone put in place. An offering of corn was then cast in and an altar erected. One such was located on the Palatine hill in Rome, one of the oldest parts of the city. The gap in the vault was overlaid with a stone called the *lapis manalis* which was seen as a door to the underworld, for ingress and egress.

The augurs, as the diviners or Rome were known, invoked the Manes when commencing their religious duties; such invocations were repeated three times, as this number was reckoned sacred unto the Manes. At the festivals of the chthonic gods – Dis Pater corresponding to the Greek Hades, Ceres corresponding to Demeter, and Proserpina corresponding to Persephone – the lapis manalis was taken up at a ceremony called the Mundus patet, which occurred three times a year: August 24th, October 5th and November 8th. As the dead were at large on these dates they were considered unfortunate for marriage or business and propitiatory offerings to the dead called *inferiæ* were made. A greater festival, with similar overtones was celebrated at the Parentalia from the 13th to the 21st of February; friends and relations of the departed gathered and sacrifices and feasts were offered to the Manes. In the Imperial period this rite was said to have been founded by Aeneas. Virgil, probably under Homeric influence, portrayed Aeneas as sacrificing to the infernal gods including the Manes; the blood of the victim was received in a trench, resembling a similar rite performed by Odysseus. Although he too attributed them to Aeneas, Ovid portrays rites of greater Italian antiquity, performed at the graves and at home: small gifts were brought to the tomb on a tile wreathed in garlands, a scattering of meal with a few grains of salt, bread soaked in wine, and some loose violets.

The last day of this period was called the Feralia, and again Ovid comes to our aid, describing a curious domestic ritual. An old woman would visit the home, and sit with the girls of the household. With three fingers she set three small lumps of incense under the sill, fastened threads together with lead and turned seven black beans over and over in her mouth. She cooked the head of a sprat with its mouth sewn up with a bronze needle and sealed with pitch, and dropped wine upon it. Presumably at this point she spat out the beans. According to Ovid the custom was that she drank the rest of the wine before rising, she then declared that hostile speech had been silenced and departed the house slightly drunk. This ritual was under the auspices of a goddess of the dead known as Larunda; this important figure is delineated in a later part of this section.

Larvae

The Larvæ or Lemures were restless and malevolent spirits of the dead. The name Larvæ is thought to originate in the word *larva*, meaning a mask. They were seen as the spirits of wicked men, who wandered at night particularly, tormenting the living, haunting houses and bringing bad omens and misfortune. The word *larvatus* means bewitched, suggesting the employment of these spirits in malefic magic which was essentially an induced haunting. To propitiate them the festival known as the Lemuria was celebrated on the nights of the 9th, 11th and 13th of May, at which time the temples of the gods were closed and marriages prohibited.

The roots of the Lemuria were exceedingly ancient and it was celebrated with primitive rites. Not much is known of the public rituals but there is more information concerning the domestic ritual:

Ovid tells us in his *Fasti* that at midnight the head of the family rose and made a sign with the thumb inside closed fingers (the Sign of the Fig) to be free of fear of meeting a ghost and after washing his hands in spring water he took nine black beans and either threw them over his shoulder or more likely held them in his mouth and spat them out, being careful not to look behind him, as is usual with many chthonic rituals. After this he spoke the incantation nine times: *hæc ego emitto; his redimo meque meosque fabis* (*with these beans I redeem me and mine*). Washing his hands again he and probably others of the household beat metal pots together like cymbals, walking through the house saying nine times: *Manes exite paterni!* (*family ghosts, depart!*)

The same type of beans were also cast onto the graves of the deceased, or burned as an incense of exorcism, the smell being disagreeable to the spirits; incantations were muttered and drums and metal pots beaten.

Penates

The Penates, more properly the Dii Penates were supposedly inferior deities of the Romans; accounts of them are contradictory. In historic times they were household gods and ruled over private houses and the affairs of the household. Their name derives from the Latin for the innermost part of the house, where their shrine was located, identical with the family store room or larder, which they protected and blessed with powers of increase. However, the hearth was also associated with them, possibly by conflation with other similar household gods such as Vesta. Like many such deities they are in reality older than the gods of the city or the state. However as the state was conceived of as a greater family there were also state Dii Penates, and the two should be distinguished although they are evidently related.

The conception of the Dii Penates of the state and home was influenced by Greek cities in Southern Italy on Roman tradition. Accordingly they were seen as two young men and associated with the Cabiri (the theoi megaloi or great gods of Samothrace), and thought to have been brought from Troy by Aeneas. Hence Virgil's expression: *the home gods and great gods*. They were sometimes portrayed as seated, sometimes dancing and occasionally holding spears. As household gods of the state they were often associated with Vesta, goddess of the hearth. Both their connection with the Cabiri and with Vesta concern fire; the Greeks had similar domestic gods of the hearth, who appear to be more primitive forms of Hephæstus and Athena. There too the fiery connection persists, Hephæstus is a fire god and already associated with the Cabiri, and Athena was occasionally portrayed as assisting him at the forge.

The Latin tradition was that the head of the household nominated the particular god worshipped by the house, which in practice meant the household cult was a hereditary cult. For these reasons while the Penates are reckoned inferior deities they often bore the names of such important deities as Jupiter. Similar practices are found among the Greeks, where household cults of major deities were passed on from generation to generation. Some divide the Penates into four classes, celestial, marine, infernal and such persons as had received divine honours upon Earth. The last category resembles the old domestic cults of heroes among the Greeks, which preceded the adoption of a particular hero by the city. Others suppose the Penates to be spirits of the dead, identical to the Manes, but subsequently identified with greater deities. Images of the Penates could be of wax or earth, superior versions being of silver or ivory. They received offerings of wine, incense and fruits, and occasionally a sacrifice of lambs or sheep, and also goats. When these offerings were made they were garlanded and adorned with garlic or poppies, the last particularly suggesting chthonic connections. Their rites occurred during the festival of Saturnalia. It is not uncommon to find them identified with the Lares, but while confusion existed among the Romans themselves the two are distinct, as the location of their shrines and other details makes clear.

Lares Familiaris

Scarce had he finished, when, with speckled pride,
A serpent from the tomb began to glide;
His hugy bulk on seven high volumes rolled,
Blue was his breadth of back, but streaked with scaly gold.
Thus, riding on his curls, he seemed to pass
A rolling fire along, and singe the grass.

The Lares were Roman spirits attached to any and every household. They were also associated with the Lares Compitales or Lares Viales, who are more strictly the spirits of crossroads and of roads respectively. They were early on confused with the Manes, and later Latin authors also drew little distinction between them and the Penates; thus, it is hard to distinguish them from one another in the old texts. This is less important in tracing their relationship with later magic, when the confusion or interconnection is part of the picture, than in the history of Roman religion in its various stages. However prior to the time of Caesar they were far more distinct, and were referred to in the singular as Lar Familiaris. Lar may well connect with the Etruscan terms Lars meaning conductor or leader, or Lar meaning lord, king or most importantly, hero. In the later phase the domestic spirits were seen as a pair rather than a single spirit as before.

It was once commonly assumed that the Lares were ancestral spirits, associated with the ancient practice of burying ancestors beneath the house. This assumption likely derives in part from the ancient connection of the Lars with the Manes. However, it now appears more likely that the Lar Familiaris was identical with the Genius Domus (see my *True Grimoire* for what appears to be an important Solomonic use of this term). These were a form of domestic Genius Loci, similar in nature to the brownie of later folklore (see discussion of Luridan the familiar in Book Six: *Volcanic Conjurations*). As they were associated with a dwelling place the name of the spirit was also applied to the house itself. Some images resembled monkeys and were covered with dogskin, at their feet was placed the image of a barking dog in token of their care for and vigilance over the safety of the house; once the idea of a pair of Lares had arisen they were often represented as a pair of dancing youths similar to the Curetes. Ovid refers to them as the night watchmen in his *Fasti*, which term translates the name of the *Verum* spirit Bucon, just as Penates connects with the name of the spirit Pentagnony (*The True Grimoire*).

In the private cult of the household images of the Lares were placed in a shrine known as a sacrarium or lararium, these niches were situated behind the door of the house or at the hearth. These were frequently decorated with paintings of snakes, similar to the household spirits of ancient Greece; a well preserved example may be seen at Pompeii. They received offerings at mealtimes when a small statue was placed on the table, and incense was frequently burned at their altar. Greater offerings, involving the sacrifice of a sow, fruit and garlands were made in May, they received offerings too at the Kalends, Ides and Nones and on the birthday of the householder. At these times their images were crowned and polished with wax causing them to shine, and – since the Latin for shining and smiling are very closely related – this rendered the spirits of the house happy, as in the *smiling household gods* of the second *Epode* of Horace.

Incidentally, the Roman dates given here are in the old Julian calendar and may be converted by adding eleven days to obtain the date in the current Gregorian calendar. Each Roman month had three days known as Kalends, Nones, and Ides which possessed importance in dating festivals and other matters. The Kalends was the first day of the month; the Nones nine days before the Ides reckoning inclusively while the Ides was approximately mid month. The Ides of March, May, July and October fell on the 15th, and thus the Nones were the 7th day of those months; in the other months the Ides fell on the 13th and the Nones on the 5th.

Lares Compitales

The Lares Compitales on the other hand were spirits of the general neighbourhood centred on a crossroads or highway, whose worship was later united with the domestic cult. These deities were two in number and honoured by the entire local community. It appears that they were two in number due to the meeting of two roads. In myth, they were the children of Mercury and Lara, also known as Larunda. Larunda was an underworld goddess of the old Roman religion and was also called Muta or Tacita in token of the silence of the dead. Her name of Mania is bestowed upon her as mother of the Manes, while Larunda may well connect her with the Lares. The ritual of the Feralia described earlier involved her, and the connections of that rite with silence are evidently appropriate to her. Originally seen as the mother of the spirits of the dead, the later Roman mythographers connected Lala with the Greek *lalein* connected with speech, even gossip. In an attempt to explain the former meaning of silent they invented a story whereby the god Jupiter was enamoured of Juturna and since she spurned him he requested the complicity of the nymphs, but Lala refused her help and informed Juno of his intentions. Enraged by her actions Jupiter cut out her tongue and instructed Mercury to conduct her to the underworld to remain a water nymph but of the world below. Mercury, evidently in his own chthonic role, became enamoured of Lala in turn and from their union arose the twin spirits known as the Lares. Their nature was similar in nature to Mercury himself; as in the myth in question he conducted souls to the Underworld, thus the Etruscan term conductor underlines their chthonic nature.

The influence of these spirits extended not only to the crossroads but also to the general neighbourhood. Their association with the crossroads connects them to traditions of magic from ancient times through the Middle Ages to the traditions of the New World and on to contemporary magic.

The connection of the household Lares with Mercury and the Lares Compitales has some important undertones that require underlining. The original Roman Mercury is often said to differ markedly from the Classical Hermes; however, the Lares in Italy may well connect with the primitive Hermes via either Etruscan influence, which has links to Asia Minor and the Mystery cults, or the early migration of Greeks to Southern Italy. The supposed Greek equivalent of the Roman Mercury, Hermes, was anciently represented by a phallus. A Roman legend makes King Servius Tullius the son of a Lares Familiaris and a slave of Tarquin, named Tanaquil. The Lares is said to have arisen from the hearth in the form of a phallus made of ash.

Vesta

The Goddess of the hearth, and particularly of its flame, Vesta closely resembles the Greek Hestia in name and function. However her cult was ancient in Italy long prior to the period of Greek colonisation, this suggests a common origin in Indo-European traditions. The later mythologists connect her with the most ancient goddesses, such as Rhea or Cybele as well as Demeter, Persephone and Hecate. Although these connections are late these goddesses share genuinely archaic features. Thus despite her famous virginity Vesta is associated with the Great Mother of the Gods, and is a goddess of fire.

The original custom of honouring her with an ever burning fire in the household was later extended to the city and to the state. Nevertheless her role as household goddess was both primitive and enduring. So important was the custom that colonies transplanted fire from the fire of their place of origin. Vesta was closely associated with the Penates. The custom of transplanting fire gave rise to the Roman notion that their cult – and the sacred fire – had originated in more ancient Latin settlements. This idea was subsequently extended as the idea of a Trojan origin arose.

The sacred fire of Rome and other Latin cities was tended by a college of virgin priestesses, who dwelled in the Atrium Vestae. The word *atrium* indicates the open central room of a Roman dwelling, the forecourt of a temple and the hall of any other building. The Atrium of the Vestals was not inside the city but at its forecourt. Excavations of the site point to a continuation of primitive customs. The shape of the building was round, like the earliest Latin huts. It commemorated the outline of a chieftain's hut, whose daughters the Vestals would originally have been, with the duty of tending the fire on behalf of the community. While the public cult was the responsibility of these Vestal Virgins, the private cult of Vesta was continued in every home.

At the Vestalia in mid-June (June 9th old calendar) the ladies of the city walked barefoot in these processions to the temple of Vesta. Banquets were prepared in front of every house, and millstones were garlanded. The young donkeys which turned these stones on other days were garlanded with flowers and did no work, but were paraded around the city. A Greek inspired explanation of this was that the goddess was saved from the amorous advances of the phallic god Priapus by the braying of an ass. It is necessary to note however that the ass was the beast most closely associated with Priapus. Significant here perhaps is Burkert's comment regarding Hestia, that although the hearth fire is subject to sexual taboos, it is also experienced as a phallic force.

Gods and Goddesses of Fire

An archaic element of the duties of the Vestals involved their making offerings to another goddess, with the unprepossessing name of Caca. She
has a relationship, perhaps to the point of identity, with another goddess
named Cloacina, originally associated with purification by a Roman river,
who became goddess of the Roman sewers, without, strangely, suffering
devalued status in the process. Due to this relationship perhaps, as well
as her name, Caca became associated with excrement. Leaving Cloacina
aside, the fact is that Caca was initially quite different, a goddess of the
hearth fire who may well be more ancient than Vesta herself. Few traces of
her ancient cult remain, having been assimilated by Vesta. However there
are significant elements in her myth, more particularly those involving her
brother Cacus. The details of his myth converge with topics arising elsewhere in this study, and contain interesting pointers to archaic rites and
the nature of more important gods.

According to the best known Roman myth her brother was a son of
Vulcan named Cacus. He was a three headed fire breathing giant, and
a dangerous robber in ancient Italy; his mother according to some was
the snake-haired Medusa. He dwelled in a cavern stronghold which John
Dryden's translation of Virgil describes thus:

> The monster Cacus, more than half a beast,
> This hold, impervious to the sun, possess'd.
> The pavement ever foul with human gore;
> Heads, and their mangled members, hung the door.
> Vulcan this plague begot; and, like his sire,
> Black clouds he belch'd, and flakes of livid fire.

Legend has it that he stole some of the cattle which Hercules was driving
through Italy (having himself stolen them from another three headed giant named Geryon). Cacus showed cunning in concealing his crime, drag-
ging the cattle backwards into his cave so the hoof prints seemed to lead
away from it. The ruse was betrayed either by the lowing of the cattle or

by the treachery of Cacus sister, the hearth goddess Caca who had fallen in love with Hercules. Hercules then either defeated Cacus with his club, or according to another version, when Cacus closed the entrance to his cave with stones Hercules tore off the top of the mountain and killed him. King Evander then purified Hercules of the murder and made him welcome. The keeping of a perpetual flame in honour of Caca is supposed to derive from this incident, but a perpetual flame would already have been her attribute. Hercules supposedly founded rites at Rome in honour of this feat, which Carmenta refused to attend. Thereafter women were excluded from the rites.

By this account Cacus was an unpleasant fellow, but there are strong traces of other quite different traditions about him. An Etruscan mirror depicts Cacus as a long-haired young prophet with a lyre singing what must be a rhyming prophecy which his pupil records in writing in an enigmatic script. Behind the pair are two armed warriors approaching intent on capturing them. This theme is not uncommon in classical lore; it resembles the capture of Proteus and other figures to force an unwilling oracle. Another tradition, probably late, links Cacus with Marsyas, who has escaped the cruelty of Apollo and invaded Italy; significantly, given the depiction of Cacus as a prophet above, this tradition credits Marsyas with the invention of augury. The same traditions link him with free speech and the rights of the lower classes. The freedom implicit in the popular Dionysian cults are here clearly contrasted with aristocratic tyranny represented by Apollo. Statues of Marsyas were the gathering place for popular demonstrations, and the Phrygian cap is still known as a liberty cap to this day. Another tradition concerns a man of great strength, named Cacius, who lived on the Palatine Hill and entertained Hercules. Taken together these traditions suggest Cacus may not be as black as he is painted; on the contrary he and his sister appear to be Italian fire deities with oracular functions and Etruscan connections. It is perhaps not impossible that Cacus has some relation to the prophet Calchas, whose cult certainly reached Italy; while purely speculative the alteration in his name could be due to Etruscan usage.

Another figure who is plainly related to Cacus, at the very least as half brother and possibly identical with him is Cæculus. The myths surrounding Cæculus are contradictory, and may reflect the changing relationship of Rome with the city he is said to have founded, Præneste. This was one of the most ancient towns of Latium, 21 miles South East of Rome. From around 499 BCE it was allied to Rome, but after the coming of the Gauls became one of its enemies until assimilation after the Social War. An important and famous feature of the city was the oracle of Fortuna. The oracle was consulted by drawing lots known as Prænestinae sortes. The lots were written in ancient characters upon small pieces of wood kept in an olivewood chest and consultation consisted of randomly extracting one of these, which provided the answer. The foundation myth of the city comes in two forms: the Greek form is interesting enough, attributing its foundation to Telegonus, son of Odysseus and the sorceress Circe, or his supposed grandson Prænestus. The other version is the older and attributes its foundation to Cæculus, son of Vulcan.

The legend of Cæculus is that two shepherds named the Depidii lived near the site of Præneste. A spark from their fire flew into the lap of their sister who conceived Cæculus. In some versions the girl is said to have abandoned the child near the temple of Jupiter, but he was found beside a fire by local women who brought him to the brothers, who raised him. These brothers were *dii indigetes*, ancient indigenous Italian deities, and appear to be a form of Lares or Penates. Cæculus' name is said to mean blind (*caeco*) for the smoke from the fire had made his eyes water. This seems to be a rationalisation, and since his name appears also as Cœculus there can be no certainty about the derivation. His name may equally derive from the related term *caecus* which has the additional meaning of invisible or secret.

'Vulcanian Cæculus' grew up as a famous robber and gathered some companions to him with whom he built Præneste. A multitude gathered for the spectacle but he was unable to convince them to become citizens. He then implored Vulcan to show whether he was truly his father. Thereupon a fire suddenly shone forth around the crowd, which parted when Cæculus approached. Many then gladly came to be under the protection of the fire god and his son. According to the legend as given by Virgil, Cæculus was born in a fire, and subsequently fought against Aeneas. As Aeneas is the legendary founder of the state this probably represents the conflict between Præneste and Rome. More importantly the role of Vulcan in the legend of Cæculus reflects his role as the god of the city hearth.

That the heroes Cæculus and Cacus are strongly linked is evident. Not only are their names similar, but both are sons of Vulcan, both are 'robbers', both are connected with oracles and Evander appears in both their legends. Conflict with Præneste may have devalued some forms of the god, and may also account for Carmenta's refusal to attend the rites of Hercules if she was the oracular goddess of the rival city. However another factor that should be considered is the role of Vulcan himself. A fire god, he differed from Vesta in representing destructive fire, rather than the kindly and sacred hearth. It appears likely that his sanctuary the Volcanol, common in Italian towns including Rome, was for propitiatory offerings against fire. However, he was also clearly regarded in some places as a hearth god, and this role is visible in the legend of Cæculus. The benign and malefic roles of the god may then be equally native to his son.

IMPLICATIONS FOR MODERN PRACTICE

Mia Labores: Goetic Devotions

MY MAGICAL WORK concerns goetic processes, and involves a strong devotional aspect while dealing with spirits of the earth and the Underworld. This does not imply that I am a Satanist, but that my approach to the spirits differs from medieval demonology and the later derivatives. The ancient Greek word *goetia* is understood in different ways in modern times. Some reflect its devalued status in classical and medieval culture, others the exaggerated importance of the *Goetia of Solomon*, both creating a stereotyped impression of actual goetia. In essence however goetia is the archaic root of a great deal of spirit work in Western magic, and a principal and venerable ancestor of modern ritual magic.

In classical antiquity the term goetia generally referred to rituals of an earlier phase of culture, or practices reflecting them. It dealt particularly with the spirits of the underworld or of the earth, as opposed to heavenly or Ouranian deities and entities. These ranged from ghosts and demons to deities such as Demeter, Hades and Persephone. My understanding of such work shares with many African Traditional Religions the idea that God is a remote and unapproachable figure largely unconcerned with the material universe. To varying degrees much the same applies to other celestial beings. The chthonic spirits on the other hand are approachable, and practical magical relationships may readily be formed with them. Where these relationships are long term a definite rapport is formed. Maintaining this relationship involves cultic activities on the part of the magician, such as the making of offerings on a regular basis.

Is this worship? To answer this involves a simple exercise in semantics. It is significant that in Christian marriage vows the phrase *with my body I thee worship* is used partner to partner. If we examine the word we find that worship derives from the same root as worth, worthiness &c. So if we wish to use the word worship it must be understood that it represents the recognition of the spirits partnership with the magician, and does not diminish the magician in relation to them. In fact, in several convergent traditions relevant to this approach the posture of kneeling while communicating with spirits is strictly forbidden. In accordance with this, when not standing or moving a squatting or seated posture is appropriate.

Images

Traditionally, and practically, one of the best ways to communicate with spirits involves images of them placed in a suitable shrine. A cabinet with cupboard space below and shelves above is a very suitable basis for such a shrine. Images typically take two forms, one is a clay head, and the other is a statuette. Preferably these will be handmade and consecrated, although an Ellegua head may be obtained from a Botanica or suitable mail order supplier. Instructions for consecrating clay may be found in the *Key of Solomon*. In many cases whether a statuette or a head is chosen the image will contain various items, be they appropriate herbs, seven coins or other things. In some cases the image may be bought or adapted, so long as it is appropriate to the entity concerned. An installation ceremony should also be performed, and the position on the shrine carefully chosen, for example selecting the height of shelf for each image according to the rank of each individual spirit.

Another form of communication by image involves the votive image. The subject of votives is powerfully connected to various types of magic including magical images, talismans and defixiones (a form of aggressive magic, including forceful love spells as well as curses). Sympathetic votives, often in the form of a model of an afflicted part of the body deposited at a temple, are another example of their connection with magic. A reprise of this topic appears in Book Eight, in connection with the *Picatrix*. There are good academic studies of defixiones in print, rather less about votives, but the serious student can readily extrapolate practical applications from the sketch given here.

Ritual

Aside from routine prayers and conjurations, the essential aspect of ritual with a household shrine consists of offerings. These will generally consist of fire and water, as well as food if appropriate. By fire is meant candles and incense, and by water fresh water. Some spirits require these daily, others weekly, and this can be ascertained by divination, or performed according to traditional procedure. Candles are generally offered in thanks for a favour, while water and incense are offered more regularly to maintain the link and feed the spirits. A good idea when performing such offerings to goetic spirits is to consecrate the water and fire in the name of the ruler of these elements in the hierarchy concerned. Suitable songs or incantations are an appropriate adjunct to all such offerings. Be aware that some spirit's likes and dislikes differ from others, some for instance do not like water, and others may prefer other drink. Some may also prefer tobacco to incense.

Sacrifice

Beyond some general comments the process of blood sacrifice is outside the remit of this article. This is for various reasons, not least of all being the controversial nature of such rites in modern Western society. This aside, even such traditions relevant to the practice of goetia where such rites are accepted differentiate sacrifice of chickens from four-footed animals, the latter requiring initiation or at very least experience. Such a distinction makes sense, as chickens are relatively simple and lowly offerings, while goats or other animals require a skilled hand to avoid suffering. Nevertheless this rule pertains mainly to more agrarian societies, and no general rules can be offered herein. The reader must make their own informed decisions regarding this aspect of sacrificial ritual.

Only generalised statements may be made about offerings of food. Western examples may be found in such works as the *Key of Solomon* (Book II, ch. xxii of the Mathers edition), or the *Picatrix*. Food offerings relevant to other traditions, such as Santeria, may be researched in many

217

modern works. Very often particular entities have particular preferences, such as popcorn and seven types of beans for Omolu; other food offerings may be deduced from systems of correspondences, such as hot foods for Martial and square saffron cakes for Jovial entities.

These aspects aside, there are other aspects of sacrifice that can be usefully discussed. Goetic rites in classical Greece drew upon more archaic traditions, and in various ways these are still implicit or explicit in the tradition as it survives today. In the Christian period the term goetia often indicated suspect magical practices connected again to older traditions, those surviving from paganism. Consequently, goetic offerings and rites were – and still are – often deeply conservative in nature. For example, offerings of wine, a comparatively recent innovation in classical times, were not made to older chthonic deities. Barley beer or some older form was preferred, the feeling being that the older rites should be retained for certain kinds of entity, many of whom have precise parallels in modern goetic work. Although the specific example given above may not hold true for the entities with which the modern conjurer works, similar cases and attitudes very well may.

As a part of my own work, for instance I make a point of buying up old coins to serve as offerings. Although most of these are pre-metric English pennies, I also keep some exotic coins, whether foreign or unusual in some way. These come into use in various ways: as permanent offerings on a ritual shrine, or as sacrifice fees, paid by burying in the earth when collecting items from outdoors at various appropriate locations. These 'obsolete' sacrifices reflect the fact that some of the spirits are old, whether spirits of the dead from an earlier time, or gods and nature spirits of earlier phases of culture, whether our own or other's. These coins of course involve a sacrifice in several respects: not only has modern money been earned and spent to obtain them, but very often specific journeys have been made, and time and energy expended, in order to exchange modern currency for older coins.

On the other hand, modern coins such as two pence coins may serve perfectly well on occasion. They may be pressed into the earth when a chance find is made, or offered to a more recent ghost. Similarly, they may be offered even to older entities, so long as these recognise coins in general as viable currency.

Offerings of coins on a shrine, or on other special occasions to a particular spirit, may well involve larger payments. For example a number associated with the spirit may determine the number of coins.

Intermediary Entities in Goetic Ritual

Another consideration of great importance is the presence in many spirit hierarchies of an intermediary spirit who must be dealt with first in order to contact the others. This may well influence the structure of offerings as well as conjuration. Generally the intermediary spirit must be worked with first, in order for offerings to reach other spirits on the shrine.

In my ritual work I am in constant contact with the intermediary spirit of the *Grimorium Verum*, whose name is Scirlin. He is the focus of a good deal of ritual, and the recipient of frequent offerings. In many respects Scirlin acts in the same way as the Holy Guardian Angel in other supposedly transcendental systems. His role is also very similar to important intermediary spirits in African Traditional Religions, as well as Ganesha in Hinduism, and so forth.

There are several devotional aspects to this frequent contact. Some of these are true of other spirits as well, but are naturally emphasised in this particular relationship. One example is that Scirlin possesses property, in the form of gifts and offerings of a permanent nature. He also has a special incense offering, which has to be prepared separately and kept in stock in order for my goetic work as a whole to proceed. The position of his image is at the centre of the spirit shrine, and is seated on a large marble pentacle, surrounded by various items belonging to the spirit. Among these are dedicated divination tools, which may only be used with this particular spirit, and which are strongly in tune with him.

Work

There is a useful expression in Mexican witchcraft or Brujeria that has no direct counterpart in modern Western occultism. The expression is *mia labores*, which literally means my chores, but refers to routine magical work such as cleaning the sanctuary and the performance of routine prayers and spells. There are equivalent duties in goetic practice, and their performance has a strongly devotional aspect. Regular cleaning of ritual tools and the workspace or shrine is prominent among them, and the use of a special wash is a feature goetia also shares with New World religions and magical systems such as Brujeria and Hoodoo. In work with the *Grimorium Verum* the Holy Water is sprinkled with an aspergillus made from three herbs, but a large infusion of these same herbs in boiling water forms a useful wash for mia labores. Naturally the items to be cleaned should be dusted or wiped before sprinkling or being doused in this infusion. Similarly the polishing of ritual metalware and so forth, should precede reconsecration rituals.

The performance of routine prayers and spells is another aspect of mia labores. Although rarely mentioned in manuals, it is an important staple of the pursuit of goetia as an everyday vocation. In *Verum* work (and also in several versions of the *Key of Solomon*) there is a routine prayer that should be recited in the lead up to all magical operations. Assuming the grimoire is the background or inspiration for your magical work as a whole, this prayer will be said every day. In addition the regular offerings and conjurations that accompany them are an aspect of mia labores. The same is true of rituals of consecration, which are not only to be performed when a given ritual item is first made, but repeated on a regular basis.

Similarly, the holy water sprinkler should be regularly replenished on a Wednesday under a waxing moon. Then the instruments should be gathered on the altar and collectively blessed, sprinkled and perfumed with the appropriate incense. In general all such work can usefully be preceded by a ritual bath, also using procedures from the grimoire, or appropriate substitutes. Additionally, as goetic work has a vocational aspect, or is an integrated part of a magical lifestyle, routine prayers and spells can include ritual baths on a regular basis. This is but one aspect of making magical ritual part of daily activities.

Other aspects of mia labores and the pursuit of a goetic vocation involve the physical environment. To illustrate, whenever I move home, which in recent years has been fairly frequent, one of my first actions is to explore the area thoroughly. In particular I am on the lookout on such excursions for the location of nearby crossroads, as many as possible; for cemeteries; particular trees and plants; for watercourses, both streams and rivers.

Watercourses are important for provision of differing types of water as defined in ritual, and also potentially for clay, useful in making images and vessels. Crossroads are important for the disposal of ritual ephemera, be they residues of operations, or the spells themselves. When disposing of something at a crossroads it is important to consider whether you wish the effect of the spell to remain with you, or to be distant from you, as this determines which side of the crossroads it is put. Crossroads are also important locations for various offerings and even some conjurations.

Cemeteries are useful for a variety of reasons, and are places I visit fairly frequently. Once again, my activities should not be confused with Satanism, particularly the variety that embraces any form of vandalism. Cemeteries are the abodes of spirits the magician wishes to be on good terms with, and mistreating their home is unlikely to have such an effect. On the contrary, I often pay a ritual fee on entering a cemetery, and also pay the spirits if I take anything away with me, or if I bring something with me and leave it behind. As mentioned earlier, I keep a good supply of old coins for ritual purposes, and a visit to the cemetery is likely to be preceded by going to the cabinet in which these coins are kept. My access to the place is also accompanied by a little cleaning up, and a good deal of discretion, including both my behaviour and my appearance.

You may one day see someone slowly walking around a cemetery, dressed conventionally and behaving respectfully. Perhaps they are looking keenly at various graves and trees, even at the ground in front of them. Occasionally they may glance around before picking things up, some but not all of which end up in the bin. The chances are you are looking at a goetic magician.

The cycle of rituals and the routine of magical chores is an important aspect of the pursuit of goetia as a vocation. This cycle is the basis of empowerment of the magician, the instruments, and particularly, of the spirit agencies that underpin the more spectacular magical work that is more commonly spoken of, but whose reliance on the adoption of a magical life based on devotion and actual work is too often left unsaid.

Household Gods

Some time back a reference in a Santeria book I was reading set off a chain of thought. The subject was a magical ritual performed in the bathroom, a location of considerable importance in the religion. Many Santeros have a shrine in their bathrooms to the Eguns, spirits of the dead including ancestors. It is also an important location in initiation rituals. By contrast, a well-known modern Kabbalistic writer used to include a request not to take his books into the bathroom, as they contain names of God, and to do so is disrespectful. *Here*, I thought, *is a separation of the ways; which is most important to me? Is the cultural context of one more appropriate than the other?* While Kabbalah has immense prestige in modern magic, the practicalities of magic in the home environment – where most ritual baths will take place – make this taboo problematic; additionally, comparing New World traditions with the Western strand as I am doing here is a far more productive approach.

My chain of thought moved swiftly onwards; Kabbalah and the more obvious systems of correspondences in Western magic include no attribution of bathroom or other parts of the house. Where else might I find one? As the reader may have gathered, the roots of astrology are intrinsically more pagan than is Kabbalah; partially explaining why Albertus Magnus considered many aspects of astrology to be necromantic. Although many parts of its pagan heritage are massively overlaid or obscured, they are far from lost. Accordingly, I resorted to a handbook of horary astrology concerned with finding lost objects; including clear guidelines for locating said item, in whatever part of the house it may have been mislaid. An attribution of parts of the house to the planetary gods swiftly emerged, as follows:

	Parts of a house sacred to the gods	Astrological house corresponding
♄	Doors, stairs, basement Hallway	4th, 10th
♃	Loft, attic	9th
♂	Bathroom, toilet	8th
☉	Dining and/or sitting room, fireplace, child's room	5th
⚥	Bedroom	5th
☿	Study/office	6th
☾	Kitchen, garden, nursery	4th

As well as illustrating the possibility of reclaiming pagan magical principles from astrology, this table has a variety of interesting subtexts. The Moon for example is here connected with the kitchen, where much hoodoo practice takes place, and with the garden, where herbs may be grown. Obvious connections with water, growth and magic are clearly implicit. Additionally a lunar goddess protective of children and the family is recognisable as a basis of the attribution. Saturn's connection with liminal places is striking; the connection of Mars with the bathroom and toilet reconnects us with the origins of this chain of thought. In this context, he presides over purification and elimination of dross. The connection of the location in Santeria with the dead, and thus with eschatology generally, suggests he is here in an Underworld role. So indeed does the association of the Eighth House with sex and death, in a word, Scorpio.

These associations are not rigid; other locations for shrines are possible, even likely, for convenience or other reasons. On the other hand, these places have intrinsic power and meaning that can be utilised in a variety of ways regardless of shrine location. The performance of spells, the placing of talismans or other devices, and the incubation of magical objects for a set period in the appropriate place in the house, all naturally follow from these associations. Of course, this is a more localised approach to mythic geography as discussed in Book One. Very similar principles apply, most particularly the reconnection of the magical with the so-called mundane or physical world.

Types of Water

PGM IV. 154–285 *ll* 220–230

Having commented briefly on the following passage in *The True Grimoire*, this is a suitable place to extend upon those remarks.

> Inquiry of bowl divination and necromancy: Whenever you want to inquire about matters, take a bronze vessel, either a bowl or a saucer, whatever kind you wish. Pour water: rainwater if you are calling upon heavenly gods, seawater if gods of the earth, river water if Osiris or Sarapis, springwater if the dead...

Other references from Egypt support this classification, Seawater being ascribed to Set and river water to Osiris. The role of Osiris in Egyptian magic and popular belief seems to have differed from orthodox religious belief. In magical beliefs he was pre-eminently Lord of the Underworld, and the chief of many demons (or fighter and guardian spirits), potentially dangerous to humans and of course potentially useful to magicians. (Sarapis is a Hellenistic Egyptian Lord of the Underworld with many attributes of Osiris).

The classification appears to hold good in later grimoires, several examples appearing in *Verum* and in its relative *Liber Troisième*.

Rainwater has no examples in *Verum*, but then it isn't calling on heavenly gods! Seawater however is used in *Liber Troisième's* spell *for making it rain*, and instructions for making artificial brine are included for land-locked magicians. Eliogaphatel is evidently one of the *gods of the earth*. Stones from a river are used to weigh down the skin during the parchment making process in *Verum*, and the Underworld associations of the location is likely significant. Springwater is used in the conjuration of Uriel – a rite with strong resemblances to Egyptian bowl divination. The 'angel' Uriel is certainly a dark and ambiguous figure both in the grimoires and in angelology; he frequently represents saturnine and chthonian energies, and his name is likely to be a cover for darker entities, particularly Lucifer (Uriel means *Light of God*, Lucifer *Light bearer*. He has various aliases in angelology too, such as Phanael the Angel Guardian who was conjured into a crystal in Book Three.

Thus, this particular rite suits re-crafting in a variety of ways, choosing different waters and spirits for other purposes, just as in the Egyptian example. Similarly when crafting new spells, for example with the standard *Verum* talisman form and spirits whose nature suited the task in hand, use of water of an appropriate type could be among the considerations.

Given the instructions for manufacturing artificial seawater in *Liber Troisième* some of my readers will perhaps be seeking spring-water at their local supermarket, and there is no prohibition against such initiative. On the other hand, exploring local geography as a magical resource is a source of power and insight. Local crossroads, springs, cemeteries, sources of plants etc. are significant in the life of goetic magicians.

Finally, how Western or traditional is this? Well, firstly the papyri, and Egypt, form a genuine basis for much of the magic of the West. Secondly, though traditional Western magic went into decline for centuries and much has been lost, there are many traces still extant which can be revitalised, of which this is undoubtedly one. When such associations and correspondences are second nature – at our fingertips – they add great richness to magical culture, so that the term tradition gains meaning. Traces of 'our' magic are to be found in unsuspected places. For example, those familiar with Palo practices will have encountered the collecting of dirt or soil from different locations: *dirt from seven banks, seven police-stations, seven prisons* etc. Very similar lists of magical soil have been found in accounts of Spanish magicians of the seventeenth century, one of whom had *dirt swept from the three prisons of Madrid,* along with graveyard dirt and so on. So while these items are thought of as belonging to New World magic, they may equally be survivals of Western magic preserved by another culture with considerable contact with the older one.

Papyrus parallels, which underlie and reconnect the magic of both the grimoires and Hoodoo, are very numerous, and invaluable. I cannot recommend highly enough *The Greek Magical Papyri in Translation* edited by Hans Dieter Betz. It is an invaluable resource for both the history and the practice of goetic magic.

THE MAGIC OF THE PICATRIX

MONG THE ARABS AND PERSIANS, in the centuries called the Dark Ages in Europe, much of the magical lore of the Hellenistic world was not merely preserved but actively thrived. Hermetic, Gnostic and Neoplatonist traditions continued unabated in the East prior to the coming of Mohammed. This included the technical Hermetica of the Magical Papyri. The Nabatean Arabs, who had been in close contact with the Roman world, were but one Arab culture for which astrological magic was a major part of their religion. The Sabians of Harran were among the most influential of these Hermetic Arab communities, and their learning was to make huge contributions to the development of the Moslem world. They were adept astrologers and their cultus was closely akin to the later astrological magic of the grimoires, but as the expression of a star based religion. Mecca itself was saturated in such lore prior to Islam; according to tradition, 365 astrological statues embellished the city.

While I have given due credit to Chaldea, Syria and Asia Minor, the earlier Middle Eastern cultures have been largely examined via the Greek filter by which their contributions reached the West. To a degree, I intend to compensate for that emphasis here. After the fall of the Western Roman Empire the Arab world was the principal heir of much of the learning and magic of the Græco-Roman world. Certainly the Eastern Roman Empire, called Byzantine by Western writers, preserved a great many Classical manuscripts. The fall of this power, and the access gained to its learning were undoubtedly a major cause of the Renaissance in Italy. Nevertheless, the attitude of the Byzantine authorities to magical lore was ambivalent at best, and viciously intolerant at its worst. The Arab world by contrast was a more conducive environment not only for the survival but also for the further development, of the Classical inheritance.

The period of Islamic expansion, particularly in Spain, was the route by which much of this lore was first regained by the West. This process was further accelerated by their defeat and the abandonment of their libraries; containing Greek and Arab works. Ptolemy's *Almagest* was just one such book important to occultism. This was translated by Gerard of Cremona; he to whom is attributed a treatise on Geomancy in the *Fourth Book*. This infusion of pagan learning, including the sophisticated Hermetic theory of magic, was the primary medieval source for the material in the grimoires, prior to the sack of Byzantium. While Christian in appearance the grimoires as magical manuals were very largely dependent on pagan lore. As such it was dependent on learning transmitted first by the Arab world, and subsequently the Byzantine.

Of particular importance in the process of transmission, alongside many other Greek, Latin and Arabic texts, was the colossal compendium of magical lore known as the *Picatrix*. Among the many key elements that it transmitted was a wealth of Sabian lore, the prayers attributed to them in the *Picatrix* have been shown to be genuine rites of their astrological cultus. Such lore is also the major source for conjurations of planetary spirits in the Western grimoires; regardless of how and whether these were crudely reinterpreted as angels, demons &c.

The astrological images, which the *Picatrix* transmitted to Western occultism, reach back to Indian, Babylonian and Græco-Roman originals. The *Picatrix*, in short, is a major example of the transmission of Hellenistic magic to the Western world, from the 10th century AD onwards. Its influence on the grimoires, and on major occult thinkers such as Ficino and Agrippa has been demonstrated beyond any doubt by modern historical techniques.

The materials included in this survey are a small fraction of the Classical inheritance transmitted by the *Picatrix*. The *Picatrix* is, after all, a book far larger than any European grimoire. It is more comparable in size and scope to Agrippa's *Three Books of Occult Philosophy*, which draws substan-

tially upon it. The materials I have included here are principally technical Hermetica, that is, practical magic on the ancient model. The *Picatrix*
contains far more than this, including major theoretical and philosophical
elements; detailed astrological lore and a wealth of Hermetic knowledge.
Were this not the case it would hardly have exerted such a powerful influence on some of the greatest thinkers and artists of the Renaissance. My
selection represents examples of the dependence of Western magic on the
ancient world, from the Greeks to the grimoires. The translation work began many years ago, with the help of my then wife. Notwithstanding the
period elapsed and two major excerpts appearing from other sources, this
material has been largely unexplored. I suspect this is partly due to the
pagan nature of some of the materials, compared with the later Christian
revisions that produced the grimoires. Nevertheless, this material truly
represents the ritualistic and magical side of the *Picatrix*, and explains the
title selected.

The Sabeans

The following material includes several chapters and excerpts from the
Picatrix relating to magical practices attributed to the Sabeans. This term
denotes an important Arab sect (more probably separate communities
with related practices) of the pre-Islamic period, possessing very evident
links to Hellenism and even so-called low Platonism. This is important
in a variety of ways; if, for example, I am guilty of underplaying Eastern
influences on Hellenism, the following material forms a counter note of
caution against underestimating the importance of Hellenism as an influence on Near Eastern magic.

The Sabeans have long been a subject of interest to Western historians:
thus we find E. Cobham Brewer (1810–1897) in his *Dictionary of Phrase
and Fable* (1898) defining them as follows: *An ancient religious sect; so called
from Sabi, son of Seth, who, with his father and brother Enoch, lies buried in
the Pyramids. The Sabeans worshipped one God, but approached Him indi-
rectly through some created representative, such as the sun, moon, stars, etc.
Their system is called Sabeanism or the Sabean faith. The Arabs were chiefly*

Sabeans before their conversion. The description of the Sabeans given by Cobham Brewer indicates a particular form of religious practice. As will be seen, such rites were the evident forerunners of the astrological magic familiar to Western magicians from the grimoires (i.e. the *Heptameron*, the *Key of Solomon* &c.); where operations attributed to the seven planets have colour, gem, metal and animal correspondences as an integral practical base). The *Picatrix* faithfully records many aspects of Sabean ritual; just such colour correspondences &c. were present in the astrological rituals they performed. This is to say the least of it, as among them were prodigiously learned astrologers and mathematicians integral to the advancement of Islamic learning and its influence. The *Picatrix* is a direct forerunner and a powerful influence on grimoire magic, both directly and through the lens of writers such as Agrippa.

In some specific respects, Sabean ritual differs from those most commonly described in the Solomonic texts although parallels are traceable elsewhere, especially in French grimoires. Examples of these are prostrations and widespread animal sacrifice. The latter is mentioned constantly, and there are examples besides of human sacrifice. In *The Golden Bough*, Frazer, whose account matches similar descriptions elsewhere in the *Picatrix*, describes bloody rituals of the Sabeans:

> The heathen of Harran offered to the sun, moon, and planets human victims who were chosen on the ground of their supposed resemblance to the heavenly bodies to which they were sacrificed; for example, the priests, clothed in red and smeared with blood, offered a red-haired, red-cheeked man to 'the red planet Mars' in a temple which was painted red and draped with red hangings. These and the like cases of assimilation to the god … are based ultimately on the principle of homeopathic or imitative magic, the notion being that the object aimed at will be most readily attained by means of a sacrifice which resembles the effect that it is designed to bring about.

Prostration obviously signals the divine status of the planetary gods. So in essence does blood sacrifice, although the diabolical reputation of the practice, especially in a magical context, does much to obscure this fact. In the material following, every planet has an appropriate animal victim. In the case of Jupiter, the victim is a black sheep which may well indicate a ram as in the cults examined throughout this study. In the case of Mercury, the victim is multi-coloured in keeping with the colour correspondences retained in the grimoires. In every case, the liver of the victim is consumed as a sacrament. This may involve similar ideas to methods of divination from examination of the liver; the Romans inherited this from the Etruscans, who are thought to have originated in Asia Minor.

Astrology and the Gods

Albertus Magnus in his *Speculum Astronomiae* spoke of necromantic elements in astrology, and cited the Solomonic books among his examples (see *The True Grimoire* p. 137). The removal of pagan magic from astrology was a major concern of the medieval Church. Via the *Picatrix* the magic of Solomon and Agrippa's astrological magic derive directly from Chaldean and Hellenistic magic, as evident in the magical papyri. Just as modern astrology results from Greek systemisation of Syrian and Babylonian starlore, so the source of these elements in Western magic is Græco-Roman.

The above analogy is precise, in the *Picatrix* we see together elements directly comparable to what we see separately in Solomonic grimoires and modern astrological manuals. The recombination of these elements, to fully regenerate the traditions latent in western magic, is most readily done from a classical pagan perspective. Of course Jewish, Christian or Islamic traditions are all adaptable as masks, through angelology; that is how they obtained the form in which we posses them. The nineteenth century occult revival performed a similar masking with Egyptian god forms, a precedent for which existed in Græco-Egyptian magic. Behind all these masks however lurks a synthesis of Greek and Babylonian thought, of which astrology rather than Cabala is the primary model. In any case, the aspects of Cabala utilised in Western occultism generally represent an abridged and simplified form of astrological symbolism, for which however it is a less effective substitute. Astrology permeated the origins and determined many subsequent developments of Western magic. The public relations office of the Chaldean magi should congratulate themselves on first rate infiltration and subversion of the Græco-Roman mind, and thus of the Western magical tradition as a whole.

As indicated before, the colossal pantheon of Greek myth is not a true representation of local cults with their far smaller dramatis personae. This is equally true of the cultures with which Greece was in contact, and should be carefully borne in mind when considering astrology as the primary syncretic model on which the Western magical tradition was formulated from various cultural models. In the interwoven cultural contexts of the ancient Mediterranean and Middle East, the celestial gods and the planets do not stand in fixed relation to one another. Nor have they always the same claim to local affections; the god Baal may be most popular in one place as Jupiter or the Sun, a father or a young man. Similarly the goddess Baalit may manifest as Moon or Venus, and be popular in one place as a mother and another as a virgin. A goddess, young or mature, might be associated with the Sun; equally, the Moon could be associated with a god, Apollo or Men a young Moon god, or Sin a father. Nergal could be Mars or the Sun, and very possibly lunar besides.

So, the planets and gods are not in fixed relation, but they are two very closely related sets of categories. The very adaptability of their interconnected relations permits flexibility, but also demands it of us. While distinct, these inter-related categories live parallel lives: father, son, mother and daughter inter-relate constantly with solar, lunar, planetary and chthonic symbols. Properly understood, astrology is a pre-integrated and highly sophisticated instrument for the syncretic synthesis or analysis of their inter-relations.

SABEAN PRACTICES

The astronomer Al-Tabari has said of the Sabean practices that the drawing near of the powers of the planets and their servitors is performed by them. The Sabeans, both their chiefs and the servants of the temple of the planets, have all agreed on these descriptions following.

When you pray to a planetary power and desire something of him you must have trust in God, cleansing your heart of ill intentions and thoughts as your clothes likewise of dirt, and clarify and purify thy mind. Further, it is necessary to consider the nature of your wish and under which planet it belongs. Fumigate your garment upon robing and call the planet with thine invocation. The planet concerned is reached in its sphere, which I will denote to thee. When you do this your entreaty will be realised, and you will attain what you aimed at with your demand.

Thus you ask of **Saturn** by entreaties concerning distinguished old men, chiefs, kings, providers, the pious, landowners, tenants, those managing estates, those selling houses, lawyers, farmers, peasant-masters, slaves, robbers, parents, grand-parents and the aged.

When you are sad or have a melancholy illness and any matter that belongs to the nature of Saturn, against his action you must call upon **Jupiter.** He works for the resolving of disadvantages and mental disturbances caused by other planets, but in this case the other planet must first be called.

Persons under Jupiter are those dignified by high positions, the respected, the learned, judges, clerks of law, officials, notaries, doctors of religion, those who interpret dreams, the cultured, the wise, kigs, caliphs, parents, the powerful in all spheres of life, brothers and sisters and all the young. Further call upon him to ask concerning peace treaties and trade relations.

Ask of *Mars* regarding things concerning persons of his nature, as riders, military leaders, rebellions and riotous persons, officers, guards, heroes, soldiers, opposition, all whose actions devastate land and exposes men, of those working with blood or fire or working in iron or handling it. Warriors, stable masters, shepherds, servants, robbers, enemies, those who oppose your cause in any matter, or endanger kin and old folk and disturb peace. Whatsoever is of his nature such as matters of disease of the lower body, or of bleeding the sick. Against him thou callest Venus then she unties what he ties, and makes good what he damaged.

Ask of the *Sun* what you wish concerning kings, caliphs, princes, crowned heads, the mighty, lords, parents, emirs, the brave, heroes. Ask so that he distributes to the good that which they deserve, and to the bad bringeth ruin; also that the praiseworthy shall be loved by great men. Also concerning judges, the right-learned, the wise, philosophers, great lords, prominent scholars, sedate, worthy and respectable persons, those in positions of importance, parents and older brothers and sisters. Regarding these you shall ask the Sun what you desire for them, gold, leadership and all that is under the Sun.

Venus ask concerning affairs of women, singers, servants and boys, and in affairs of offspring and the love of children, love, falling in love, lewdness, sensuality, lesbianism and sodomy, and all such. Also of musical matters as flute playing and singing. Of womanish persons, effeminates, hermaphrodites, castratos, slaves, eunuch servants, pages, flatterers and yes-men, all artists, lewd entertainers, spouses, mothers, aunts, younger brothers and sisters. Call Venus for restraining the influence of Mars, then she loves him and is inclined towards him.

Mercury ask in affairs of secretaries, employees who make calculations, for geometry, astronomy, preachers, orators, philosophers, the wise speaker [leader of prayer, religious doctor], learned persons, theologians, writers, poets, princes, wazirs, superintendents, tax collectors, merchants, leaders in theoretical and practical arts, young male and female servants, young brothers and sisters, artisans, designers, draughtsmen, painters, gold smiths, all that accords with the nature of Mercury. Ask of the Moon in affairs of Kings, Governors and Viceroys, princely heirs, grand tax collectors, postmasters, couriers, ambassadors, travellers, wanderers, builders, landowners, surveyor-geometricians, measurers of fields, lawyers, village tutors, seamen, water managers, the common people, magicians, chosen women, pregnant women, king's slaves, aunts, elder sisters and brothers.

So herein you learn to ask of a planet only what concerns its nature.

Comment

A perusal of the persons connected with operations of Venus shows that the range of love spells was not restricted to heterosexual relationships. Seeking her intervention and favour in cases of lesbian and homosexual attraction is equally as apt to her nature. Pointing this out involves more than simple political correctness; the nature of magic and the forces invoked is considerably clarified by such instances. Neither Venus nor any of the other forces invoked are enforcers of later religious law; they are true to themselves and the principles they personify. An image of the goddess accompanied by magical characters and sigils is equally appropriate for love between men, because love and attraction rather than gender and reproduction are the principles involved. A beautiful naked woman depicted in such an image is not a case of sympathetic magic, but of evocation. It hardly requires a genius to point out that male homosexuals appreciate iconic women; the association of these icons with goddesses is frequently drawn.

SABEAN RITES
OF THE PLANETS

Saturn: first fast seven days from the day of the Sun till the day of Saturn, on the seventh day sacrifice a black raven (and a black dog as some say) saying over it:

In the Names of Asbil who is set over Saturn, and of the Lords of the Highest Houses, attend to my commands and fulfil all I desire of thee.

Then employ the character of Saturn to obtain what you will.

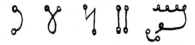

Jupiter: again fast, seven days from Friday to the day of Jupiter. On the seventh day sacrifice a black sheep and consume the liver, saying:

O Rufijail, thou angel that is set over Jupiter, the happy, the good, the perfect beauty! By the Lords of the Highest Houses, hear and attend to my invocation and fulfil all I desire of thee.

Then use the character of Jupiter to obtain thy desires.

Mars: fasting seven days from the day of Mercury to the day of Mars, one sacrifices a wild, black cat, or as some say a spotted cat, consuming its liver and saying over it:

O (Ru) Bijail, thou Angel who is set over Mars, the vehement, the ardent, the inflammatory horseman! By the Lords of the Highest Houses, attend to my demands!

Then one may employ the character to obtain one's will.

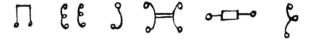

Sun: fast seven days from Monday to the day of the Sun, one sacrifices a calf, eating its liver, saying: O Ba'il, thou Angel that is set over the Sun, the bright, the world keeper, full light and perfect brilliance, the bringer of good and ill fortune, the helpful and harmful! By the Lords of the Highest Houses, attend and do my will!

One may then use the character for ones purpose.

Venus: this operation requires a fast from Saturday unto the day of the planet. One sacrifices a white dove, consuming its liver, and sayeth:

O Bitail, thou Angel that art set over Venus, the Fortunate, Beautiful Star! By the Lords of the Highest Houses, attend and do my will!

Then use the character for one's purpose.

Mercury: for the operation of this planet one fasts from the day of Jupiter to that of Mercury, and on this day one must sacrifice a black and white cock, or as some say a black, green and white cock, eating its liver and saying:

O Harqil, thou Angel who art set over Mercury, the fortunate, noble, beautifully formed one, by the Lords of the Highest Houses, attend and do my will.

Then use his character for your purpose.

Moon: fast seven days from Tuesday until her day. On the seventh day slaughter a sheep and eat its liver saying:

Saljail thou Angel who art set over the Moon, the key and the chief of stars, the light, the quick! By the Lords of the Highest Houses, attend and do my will!

Then use the character to obtain what you will.

These and other rites are found among the Nabateans, including many magical rites, miraculous suffumigations and curious talismans, and some of them are to be found in the work *Nabatean Agriculture.*

Influence and origin of Sabean Magic

The planetary angels of the preceding section are evident equivalents of those in the grimoires. It also employs the 'Chaldean order' of the planets reproduced in the various *Keys of Solomon* &c.

Planet	Picatrix Angels	Grimoire Angels
♄	Asbil	Cassiel
♃	Rufijail	Tzadkiel
♂	(Ru) Bijail	Samael
☉	Ba'il	Mikael
⚥	Bitail	Aniel
☿	Harqil	Raphael
☽	Saljail	Gabriel

Note that in this system, the Sun and Venus are associated with Ba'il, i.e. Baal, and Bitail, i.e. Baalit, (the feminine form, thus Lord and Lady). The association of Bael, the chief god, with the Sun has its equivalent in Orphic solar theology. In the alternative system tabulated below Bel or Marduk is associated with Jupiter, showing its roots in a schema more compatible with the Olympian or Jovist theology. Thus, the variant identifications of the Sun or Jupiter as major deity, encountered in various Greek systems, both have analogues in the Middle East.

Planet	Day	Sabean Name	Babylonian Name	Greek Name
☉	Sunday	Samas	Shamash	Helios
☽	Monday	Sin	Sin	Selene
♂	Tuesday	Nergal	Nergal	Ares
☿	Wednesday	Nabu	Nabu	Hermes
♃	Thursday	Bel	Marduk	Zeus
♀	Friday	Beltis	Ishtar	Aphrodite
♄	Saturday	Kronos	Ninib	Kronos

That these pagan gods are essentially equivalent to the angels named in the Sabean rites we see from further incantations of theirs in the *Picatrix*. These, with other details omitted in the condensed form given here, give their names in various tongues, chiefly Arab, Persian, Roman (Eastern Empire, thus Greek in most cases), Greek and Indian. Despite some little confusion, these names are eminently recognisable in most cases. Still other Sabean incantations given in the same book omit the angel names altogether and simply use the Greek names; while the author says that when sacrificing a bull to Saturn they repeat a prayer of the Greeks. Intriguingly, this series of incantations while using male names for the Sun, addresses her as the queen of heaven and the Moon as Lord.

Saturn

In the name of God, in the name of the Angel Isbil, who is set over Saturn in all coldness and ice, the Lord of the Seventh Sphere, I invoke you by all your names: in Arabic, O Zuhal, in Persian, O Kewan, In Roman O Kronos, in Greek O Kronos, in Hindi, O Sanasara! By the Lord of the Highest House, may you grant my request, listen to my call, and obey me in obedience to God and his rulership, grant me NN

Jupiter

O Rufijail, you angel who are set over Jupiter, joyful and serene, complete, consummate, pious, Lord off beautiful vestments, of dignity and wisdom, far from that which is unclean and from vulgar speech! I invoke you by all your names: In Arabic, O Mustari, in Persian, O Birgis, In Iranian, O Hormuz [Ormazd], in Greek, O Zeus, in Hindi, O Wihasfati! By the Lord of the Highest House, of good deeds and of mercy, may you grant me NN

Mars

O Rubijail, you angel who are set over Mars, you violent, hard-headed, fiery, flaming, brave hearted, blood spiller, rouser of civil war and of the mob, powerful and virile, you who forceth, who overcometh, inconstant, violent, lord of ill deeds, punishment, blows, captivity, deceit, falsely accusing, speaker of uncouth words, pitiless, thou slayer, dwelling alone and apart, bearer of arms and prolific fornicator. I invoke you by all your names: In Arabic, O Mirrih, in Persian, O Bahram, In Roman, O Ares [Mars], in Greek, O Ares, in Hindi, O Angara! By the Lord of the Highest House, attend my word and grant my petition, for see I desire that you do NN by Rubijail, the angel set over your realm

At Dawn to the Sun

O Cause of Causes, you are sanctified and made sacred and ruleth unceasingly and forever, I petition you (insert here a petition for favour and recognition from a specified lord) or from all the kings of the earth. Welcome, thou who bringest forth the light and the life of the world, deign to listen to me and grant me recognition and kind reception. I invoke you by all your names: In Arabic, O Sams, in Persian, O Mihr (Mitra?), In Roman, O Helios, In Hindi, O Aras, O Bara! O light and radiance of the world, who art the centre of all, who giveth life to the world of coming forth and passing away, attending to its growth, o you who standeth in the exalted places, you who holds the supreme place (insert petition for favour), for you are mistress and queen [!] of the planets, they who receive and emit their light and radiance from you. I beseech thee, who guidest everything, take pity on me, my prayer and my petition.

Venus

Hail unto thee, O Venus Anahid (Anahita), joyous mistress, the cool, the moist, constant, clean, beauteous, sweet-smelling, open handed, happy, mistress of ornament, of gold, of gaiety, of dance, of joyous arousal, of finery, of singing and of hearing songs, of flute playing, of beautiful music from plucking of strings, of recreation and jest of company and leisure, thou friendly and receptive, arouser of love, the just, thou who lovest wines, luxury, all joys and union. Thus art thou; I invoke you by all your names: In Arabic, O Zuhara, in Persian, O Anahid, in Roman, O Diana [of Ephesus], in Greek, O Aphrodite, in Hindi, O Surfa, O Astarte! By the Lord of the Highest House, may you hear me and fill us all with your love and the joy of your roving dance. By Bitail, the angel who is set over your realm, come fill us forever and ever again with the sweet breath of your life!

When Mercury is conjunct the Moon

Hail unto thee, O Mercury, O Lord, excellent, trustworthy, replete with wisdom, speaker, comprehensible, who disputeth knowingly, aware of every science, thou that calculateth, scribe, of beautiful manners, who knoweth that happening in heaven and earth, thou lord, noble one, caring little for pleasure, that art useful to goods and in trading, lord of cunning, of deceit and cleverness, thou that aideth, patient, clever, deft handed, lord of revelation and of prophets, of the proof of the divine, of faith, of understanding, of speech, messages, sound teaching, of diverse arts, of perception, insight, sound knowledge, of philosophy, of foreknowledge, of the measuring of heaven and earth, of surveying, of astrology, of augury, of casting lots, of rhetoric, of skill in verse, of accounting, of eloquence, of sweet, swift flowing and elegant speech, of inscrutability, of rapidity in trade, of much travel, of deception, of elegance, of sureness, of assistance, of flexibility, of patience, of wishing good, of fairness, of mercy, of peace, of dignity, of self-control, of the right reverence of the divine, of recognition of rights and sweet spoken. Thou art concealed, so that no nature knoweth thee, and subtle, so that thou art not defined by any description; thus thou art a bringer of fortune with the fortunate stars, male with the male, female with the female, daily with diurnal stars, nightly with nocturnal stars, thou maketh thyself like unto them in nature and in all their actions. Thus art thou, I call you by all your names: In Arabic, O Utarid, in Persian, O Tir, In Iranian, O Haruz, in Greek, O Hermes, in Hindi, O Buddha! By the Lord of the Highest House and the supreme ruler, may you hear me and obey me in all I ask of thee... grant me NN by Harqil, the angel who is set over your realm, may you hear my prayer and attend my petition...'

Moon

Hail unto thee O Moon, O fortunate Lord, blessed, cool, moist, constant, beauteous, thou key and chief of stars, moving easily, wanderer, thou that possesseth the far reaching light, of the radiant shining, of joy, of praise and reward, thou fortunate lord, learned in religion, who deeply considereth all things, knowing, ruling subtly, who loveth music, jest and play, ruler of heralds, of messages, of the disclosing of secrets, giving, noble, mild, strong! Thou art the one whose sphere is nearest of all to us and most powerfully bring good and ill, thou art the one who makes bonds between the planets, transmitting their light and turneth to good that which favours us not; through your good will all becomes good, through your ill will all turneth to ill, thou art the first and last among all things, and to you belongeth rule and priority over all planets. Thus art thou, I ask thee, by Silijail, the angel who is set over your realm, deign to take pity on my lowly petition and prayer to you, and hearken obediently unto God and his authority, granting me what I beseech and desire of you. Behold, I invoke you by all your names: In Arabic, O Qamar, in Persian, O Mah, in Iranian, O Samail, in Roman, O Selene, in Hindi, O Soma! Hearken unto me.

AL-ISTAMATIS

This is the Book of the Seven Spirits of the Planets. Know well that each Pneuma has Seven Emanations. Six governing the Directions of Space, one governing the Orbit and Sphere of the Planet. He who knows their names may call any planetary spirit as all originate from the Spirits and their Emanations.

The Master must make his body a fit vessel for the Pneuma, by appropriate garments and rites. Know well that only by observing the correct correspondences may the rite succeed, and the Pneumas may only give you what lies within their nature. The Rites of the Pneumas are Offerings and Sacrifices, with the conjurations, all of which I shall deliver in their place. It is necessary only to make the Offering, make the Conjuration and state your desires, then consume the Offering as a Sacrament when they have used it. He who does so shall receive the Pneuma in his body and receive all he desires.

	Saturn	Jupiter	Mars	Sun	Venus	Mercury	Moon
Name	Barimas	Damahus	Dagdijus	Bandalus	Didas	Barhujas	Garnus
Height	Tus	Darmas	Hagidis	Dahimas	Gilus	Amiras	Hadis
Depth	Harus	Matis	Gidijus	Abadulas	Hilus	Hitis	Maranus
Right	Qajus	Magis	Magras	Dahifas	Damajas	Sahis	Maltas
Left	Darjus	Daris	Ardagus	Ati'afas	Ablimas	Daris	Timas
Before	Tamas	Tamis	Handagijus	Maganamus	Basalmus	Hilis	Rabis
Behind	Darus	Farus	Mahandas	Gadis	Arhus	Dahdis	Minalus
Orbit	Tahitus	Dahidas	Dahidamas	Tahimaras	Dahtaris	Mahudis	Dagajus

The Invocations

Saturn. Day of Saturn, Sun in Capricorn, Moon in Sagittarius. Place an iron footed image, dressed in green, black and red in a free field under a tree without fruit. Take a sacrificial beast, cow or calf and a chafing dish, with incense of black cats brains, wild rue, myrrh and juniper and say:

Barimas, Tus, Harus, Qajus, Gardijus, Tamus, Warijus, Tahit, Wasirah, Wamandul, come hither ye spirits, this is your offering.

Then ask what ye will.

Jupiter. Sun entering Sagittarius or Pisces, Moon in Head of Aries, day of Jupiter. In a clean, handsomely adorned sanctuary bring in offerings of moist and dry sweets (honey, butter, nuts, sugar) and rolled flat cakes of fine flour, butter, milk, sugar and saffron. Incense of musk, camphor, aloes wood, mastic (a handful).

Pile up the flat cakes in an offering bowl, layer by layer, surrounded with the sweets and place a candle over them. Place four baskets of fine bread and cold chicken and ram roast and vegetables about the bowl, with four jugs and goblets for wine, with flowers between each jug and goblet, cense the offering table (which shall be firm and placed in a corner) with Aloes wood and the Chamber with Mastic. Say seven times:

Dahamus Armas Hilis Magas Adris Tamis Farus Dahidas Afrawas Ki-Aqiras. Come together to this place, breathe the sweet perfume and the aroma of the food offering and be satisfied.

Leave the place awhile and be rested in comfort, then pass by six times asking them to come in a pleasant form and attire to attend to your desires. Then will you attain what you seek and be clothed with the pneuma of Jupiter. Then call in the disciples and consume the offering and burn the incense.

Mars. Day of Mars, Sun in Aries, Moon in Capricorn. In the open air under a fruit tree bringing a sacrifice of either a ram or a cow, with a chafing dish with Myrrh, Wild Rue and Sarcocolla, a basket of sweet-meats and pleasant foods, a jug of wine.

Say: *Dagidus, Hagidus, Gidijus, Magdas, Ardagus, Hidagidis, Mahandas, Dahidamas, this is your sacrifice, take it and do with it as you will.*

Cense the offering and slay it, remove clean and roast the liver, and spread the offering on a hide covering the table and call: *This is your sacrifice and your food offering; appear, breathe the aroma and let it suffice.* A flame-like red spirit comes to the offering, as he departs make your demands and approach the offering and consume it.

Sun. Sun in Leo, Moon in 15 ° to 19 ° of Aries on the Day of the Sun. Adorn the sanctuary, erect a golden image in the centre, lighted and polished, crowned with rubies and precious stones, clothed in red silks arrayed in rubies and gold. A row of plates of fine bread and sweets, moist and dry; wine jugs; a chafing dish of musk, camphor and amber, sprinkle the house with flowers and place a great candle before the image.

Say: *Bandalus, Dahimas, Abadulas, Dahifas, Ati-afas, Maganus, Gadis, Tahimaris.* Then state your will and consume the feast with your companions, and when you are finished and quit the temple that which you asked for will be given to thee.

Venus. Perform this with the Sun in the first degrees of Pisces, the Moon in Cancer, and on the day of Venus. Cleanse and perfume yourself. Then under a date palm or tree of Venus take a ram and slaughter knife, saying:

Didas, Gilus, Hamilus, Damaris, Timas, Samlus, Arhus, Hataris. Ask what you will, wearing the appropriate robes and only ask what is within the nature of Venus.

Mercury. Sun in Capricorn at the opening of the year, place a golden chafing dish on a gold pedestal in a solitary sanctuary. Burn Aloes wood, Myrrh, Incense, Wild Rue and Alant. Take a gold plate, bring in seven goats and slay them on a block. Say, burning incense:

Barhujas, Amiras, Hatis, Sahis, Darajas, Hatis, Dahris, Magudis; repeat for each beast, skin and lay the fat about the plate after cleansing.

Veil your face to the eyes, lay the goat hide in a vinegar pot. Present the food and bread of fine flour. Put it in baskets and say the great formula and ask what you will.

Moon. Sun entering Cancer, Moon in Aries, Day of Sun. Go out into the Sun, take a ram and slaughter knife to a fresh field with fine wood for a pyre. Take incense of Frankincense, Almond, Wild Rue, Alant, Myrrh and Aloes wood. Take food in baskets, light the great fire and be seated. It shall be beside a spring or waterfall, with a tree beside the water.

Slay the ram next to the fire, saying:

Gadnus, Hadis, Maranus, Maltas, Timas, Rabis, Minalus, Dagajus, Garnus. Burning the incense. Go to the pyre and cast incense thereon and say the invocation. Then be silent a long while before censing the offerings, take off the skin, head and hoofs, roast the flesh with the intestines and leave them with the food baskets around the tree till the morning of the day of the Moon. Then drape the tree in various bright colours and cense all, making your demands and it will be given you.

These are the invocations of the Feast Days of the Planets from the book *Al-Istamatis*, written by Aristotle for the instruction of Alexander.

Comment

In the early 16th century Pietro de Abano, supposed author of the *Heptameron*, was accused of familiarity with the *Picatrix*. The influence was not apparent to Thorndike in his classic overview of magical literature. Nevertheless, in 1978 Stephen Skinner in his introduction to the *Fourth Book* claimed the *Picatrix* heavily influenced the *Heptameron*. Another work on the Lunar Mansions, also ascribed to Abano, may be more likely to show such influence openly in its particulars. If the *Heptameron* does resemble the *Picatrix* it is conceptually, in the complex system of names used in the construction of the circle. These are readily comparable with the *Al-Istamatis* material above, and the inspiration of the *Picatrix* is not improbable. In fact, very much the same may be said and with equal justice of John Dee's *Heptarchia Mystica*, the immediate precursor, if not indeed the very root, of the much vaunted Enochian magic. The *Heptarchia Mystica* after all involves a complex series of multiple names; seven apiece attributed to each one of the seven planets. For *Al-Istamatis* delineates names attributed to positions in a sphere, while both the sevenfold schemas attributed to these magicians work with names in similar fashion.

WORKS OF THE MOON
IN THE TWELVE SIGNS

Herein I speak of the doctrine found among Kurdish and Abyssinian magicians, of the Moon dispensing the force of the planets upon the Earth. Thus it is that they use sacrifices and prayers to call upon her in the zodiacal signs, by conscious operations that they have, and which they construct around it. We have declared already what is done amongst other races, and intend to collect all examples of the Art into the Arabic tongue. As they say: when wisdom and fated-ability unite in practice they are as seeds sown in fertile ground. But Wisdom finds itself with difficulty save it be armed with a perfect understanding.

Aries

The prayer to the Moon can be performed at the Full Moon, or at the Waning, or when she is conjoined with the Sun. Drawing its power to you when she is in the Sign of the Ram you pass the night with the Moon in her passage across the sky. The place shall be a green and fertile growing place where a river or irrigation canal flows East. The sacrifice is to be a white cock, and the instrument is of bone, for iron must not touch it. Face the Moon, standing between two iron chafing dishes, causing them to flame, say:

O thou illuminating, beaming and splendrous Moon, who divides the darkness with thy exalted light, illuminating with splendid effulgence all horizons, I come to thee humbly desiring N...

Advance ten paces with one of the chafing dishes and repeat this prayer, burning four measures of storax. Draw the signs with the ash mixed with a little saffron on a leaf of the cauliflower and burning it thou shalt obtain an apparition in beautiful raiment, beaming with light. Repeat your entreaty and even thus shall it be granted thee. And this may be performed as often as thou wilt, and the signs to be drawn are these:

Taurus

The attracting of the Moon's power in Taurus. Know that the Moon has an operation in each sign, and this is what is performed when she is in the Sign of the Bull. The place, the sacrifice and the prayer are as before. The garments are of pomegranate shade and you shall have a cap upon thy head. Heat water on a fire of walnut, and with thy right hand wash thy face and underarms. Take care to keep your hat from slipping off when you wash your feet! Have with thee an untrod mat, fringed, striped with red and green, jump onto this mat, prostrate thyself and repeat these words twenty times:

Rabqar, Rabqar, Iqam, Iqam, Taqfur, Taqfur.

Stand and overpower thyself with tears of contrition. Return to the vessel and repeat thy ablutions as before. Slaughter the sacrifice and burn it with the prayer, censing all with frankincense and mastic, then a form will appear to grant thy wish. A magician who uses these arts told me of a friend who was afflicted with ill-fortune, having Saturn in his Ascendant ruling his fault. He taught him this operation so that he obtained the vision and was led to a place and bade dig it up, so that he found great treasure and transformed his poverty to wealth.

Gemini

Take yourself to a high place where the wind is restrained. The sacrifice is a hound, with incense. A brass pipe of three yards length, and a chafing dish of brass are required. Light the fire with this pipe and burn half a measure of storax, and cause he smoke to travel up thy reed to the Moon's disk. Then burn half a measure of incense and the same quantity of amber. Place yourself opposite the coal pans and with the rod draw a circle, the half width shall be the length of the rod. Take seven handfuls of wax-straw and distribute them in seven places within the circle. Divide thy offering upon them and burn them using the reed, placing thyself between them and saying:

O you illuminating Moon, whose power is powerful, whose place is exalted, whose rank is high, who governs this whole world, I ask of thee by thy spiritual power that you do N... for me!

Then you fall down and worship saying twenty times: *Hirut Hirut Garut Garut.*

Then raise your head and you will see the vision appear, ask your request and it will answer for the realisation of it.

Cancer

Perform in a high place, as a room with an altar which looks out over a great distance. Look right and left, before and behind. Have in thy hand a lark or a dove, and slay it, taking four feathers from it's right wing and likewise from the left and from the tail: cut off the quill and burn the rest (of the dove). Take those feathers and add to it two measures of coloquinth flesh and four measures of storax and tie it all in a linen cloth. Then make a picture with two measures of behen root which are mixed with the ash of the offering kneaded with aristochia water: the form of a man on a lion. Then stand before the picture censing it and saying:

O thou Moon who fulfils with light, who is great in beauty and art exalted, I raise to thee my desires, to thee I send my request aloft.

Make a cross upon the ground and place the picture in the centre, writing the name of the person whose love you seek upon it. Repeat the prayer and prostrate thyself. Raise thy head and place the image in a measure of vinegar and dissolve it, add a grain of musk, a quarter measure of amber, four of sukk and half a greater measure of lupin meal. Boil till strong and bubbling, make flat cakes of a quarter measures weight. [First measure is a dirhem, the 'greater measure' a Ritl]. Leave in the Moon's rays seven nights and then take them up, with these you may obtain all you desire if you use it as incense, to gain your desire of man or woman. The adherent of this art used it in a place full of lions, snakes and scorpions and passed by without coming to any harm.

Leo
♌

Take seven coal pans to a place without buildings and make of them a cross, with a yard between each pan. Turn towards the Moon and place between each two coal pans a goose egg marked thus... Take a thick brass nail of three spans length and hold it in your right hand, take a yellow turban and robe of yellow wool. Slaughter the white cock in the centre of the cross and divide it between the seven pans, take a drop of it's blood and sprinkle each pan and the egg. Then count two pans straight in front of you and take the egg from there and place it before yourself. Knock your nail into it censing with frankincense and yellow sandalwood saying five times: *Andab, Andab*. Then will the lord appear and you may ask of him anything concerning your desires and it will be fulfiled. Do not fear because of his appearance.

Virgo

Take thirty white starlings, slay and cook them till their feathers fall out. Salt them moderately and lift them up. This is to be done thirty days before the Moon enters Virgo [sic], and you eat one daily, fuming with a quarter measure of saffron beforehand. After each you eat not for six hours, guard yourself each day, be sure to drink wine. When all is ready wash at an eastern flowing water course, take a bottle of half a great measure of water taken when the Sun is in three degrees of Pisces and the Moon in seven degrees of Aquarius, close it with unburnt pitch. Go then and place before ye a censer with a measure [Uqija] of mastic and saffron in a wide empty place, and say:

O thou Moon, whose appearance is beautiful, whose gift is great, whose light is grand, through whose light darkness is illuminated and the soul delighted, through whose joyous light is the soul gladdened, in you rests my trust and desire of N...

Then take the bottle in your left hand and say these names 'Afut-Afut' and dig with your right hand in the earth repeating the names as you dig till you have dug a full yard deep. Then put the bottle in the hole with the mouth pointing to the south wall of the pit and you throw a handful of earth to the other and repeat the names. Then draw with a golden nail on a piece of lead the image of a beautiful person and bury it in the pit: when this is done you will obtain your desire.

Libra

Gird yourself with a belt of plaited reeds whose roots have stood in water and take yourself to an eastern flowing river with the sacrifice. The stream should flow between thee and the Moon so that you look across the water, holding in your hand a copper bow that should be made when Venus is retrograde in Taurus, and Mercury is in Aries. Five times you face the Moon, holding the bow and advancing then retreating. Then throw your bow into the river and say:

O thou magnificent, beautiful Moon, to you have I cast this here, and it is in thy power to bring my request to fulfilment and my hope to its target.

Then kindle a fire of Oleander wood and burn storax thereon. Then circle the fire, running with held breath, when you release thy breath stand and draw a line to the fire and write on it Ganiti Ganiti. Then take the earth whereon you have written, join it with the same amount of clay and knead it with still water and make from it two images, your own and that of your beloved. Your love charm works through the embracing of the images, and that immediately.

Scorpio
♏

Take yourself to a place overgrown with shrubs and also open to the water kingdom. Carve out a square figure in the earth spread out with nut leaves, quitten leaves and rushes thereon and sprinkle them with rosewater. Take seven silver censers and place them in front of you with so much fresh aloes woods, storax and incense as seems right to you. Then don a white garment devoid of any trimmings or pockets. Have two water filled clay troughs with you, with a small beaker scoop from one trough before you to one behind you, and then from that to the other. Then bring your offering, something that is under the lordship, and prostrate yourself four times, saying each time *Sarafiha-Sarafiha*. Sit down and burn more aloes, storax and incense in the coal pans and prostrate yourself four times again. Then will you see a perfect form which you will address your questions to. Then all you desire will be obtained.

Sagittarius

♐

This is of value to the magician in difficult matters, and is by union of temple and talismans for treasure seeking or sweethearts. You begin when Mercury is in 4 degrees of Cancer; take ten Ritl of brass and make thereof five snakes, distributing the work through the remaining degrees. When they are ready take yourself to a pure river, lead from it a channel, divide it into five channels and put in each a snake, each must be bored through allowing water to pass from the mouth to the tail. Be provided with five leathern bottles which you place at their mouths, and each hour take the water which has been passed through or spat out and let empty an hour on the ground. In this intermittent fashion await the time when all are full. Then take all twenty yards away from the river, place the bottles on the ground and drill each with a nail, dig a hole for the water to flow into. As the water flows out stand on and put near each bottle a serpent. Then go quickly to the river and contemplate the Moon in it. Then take the reflection of the Moon and go quickly and pour it on each bottle and each serpent. At the head of every snake place a silver coal pan burning aloes, nard and amber until all are empty. Then place the snakes in the bottles and bury them. Then stand on the place, slaughter your gift, prostrate yourself fifteen times saying each time your head rises *Harqum Harqum*. You will obtain your desires through a grand aspected image who will bear you wherever you will, east or west of the earth. I have a friend who performed this work of the sign and to them came the personage who is mindful of the talismans and knows where treasure is and can lead one to it by the hand. But the apparition told him: *Look between your feet and there you will find an iron key, and take also this elephant and go with it where you will, and where the key falls to earth there lies the treasure.* He took the elephant nearly four yards before the key fell [off the elephant?]. There he found an underground otherworldly vault. When he went therein he found it led to a huge and monstrous room in which was a chest full of gold, silver and jacinth. Of this great treasure he loaded himself with all he needed, and returned to it whenever he wanted for anything.

Capricorn
♑

Build a house for two persons with Sun in Cancer, small, not great. Each day for seven days put fresh flowers out and remove the old ones. Each day fumigate with frankincense and aloes wood. When the seven days are past go in wearing a beautiful red garment, the house should be locked so that you may be entirely withdrawn when you will. Say:

Hajawam Hajawam Balgar Balgar Naqaraw Naqaraw.

Then go outside and circle about the house seventy times. Then take within two uqija of aloes and fumigate with it in a silver chafing dish. Then go out and circle a further seventy times, then bring your gift, and on entering you shall find a spirit sitting therein and you say:

By the gleaming, beautiful and lovely Moon, be ye ready to address me now.

This you repeat three times and then it will be able to speak and you may ask what you require and carry your request. This way applies to works of love and the opportunities for it. I am told this tale by one who has used it: he sold a maid servant and soon after repented of it, and desired her with a powerful longing and passion. He tried to seize her from her master by various tricks in vain. Thereupon he used this formula of magic and thereby caused an antipathy between the girl and her master which he had aptness to use for his ends and thus she was restored unto him, with profit from the dealings. If any of these conditions are not kept, and are flouted and ignored, or if any point is omitted, or if the magician cannot keep his powers through uncleanness this will effect the light of the Moon. So that one day he sets out to call her power and will not know how, and his demands are not

due to him. Therefore did one pray everynight until a ſpirit came and
ſtopped his mouth. For forty days was he ſtruck with horror and was
mocked by all for the duration.

Aquarius
♒

The magician muſt learn that these ſtipulations concerning these
operations apply to him and muſt be met to obtain his wish or else
he works in vain, and waſtes his life in games. Many who have not
performed them correctly have received warning signs too ſtrange and
wonderful to describe at length. The simple teſt with which to guard
yourself is that only the ſtrong of soul and noble of subſtance should
venture on these works. The author of the text says: 'I have walked on
the waters of the Red Sea and this to my own amazement. On the
waters also trod a man ſtriding faſter than I. And I called this man
but received no answer from him, so I followed him by his track and
coming up to him the man asked what I wanted and I ſpoke to him
concerning the information I required and he told me what I could
not know in a hundred years and more and bade me give thanks to the
Moon. And what he told me was that he had about him something
that kept off the hands of the water from harming him. And I asked
what this might be. And he told me to scoop up a handful of water
and caſt it on my feet that it will be as a flame keeping off the water
by antipathy from my feet. And he hurried off over the water till I
almoſt loſt sight of him. Then he again appeared and said that he can
also perform this on land. I asked him of this magic and he said 'That
is one by Sargatum, the servant of the Moon when she is in the sign
of Aquarius'. And you pray to him in Aquarius and take the heads of
three ganders and cook them in old wine till they fall to pieces. Pound
them in a mortar of iron or lead, when the Moon is in Cancer, till they
form a paſte. Add a half measure (ritl), two greater measures (uqija) of
sandalwood, half a ritl of ſtyrax, quarter measure (ritl) frankincense,
and gum tragacanth. Knead the whole with the wine in which you

have cooked the heads. Make forty flatcakes and roast them in an iron roasting pan till they are dry. Then on a moonlit night take them when she is in Aquarius to a field and burn them in fifteen censers of brass and silver, and when possible of gold, one cake to each pan. Then bring your gift there. Then in the moment when the smoke ascends you shall see a form therein which comes soon and goes soon likewise. Then throw three cakes into that pan where comes the apparition saying ten times 'Hantar Asrak Hantar Asrak' then it will come to you and will communicate what is useful.

Pisces
♓

Draw out the juice of the cauliflower and take one ritl of it, and a fifth of a ritl of lettuce juice and a little juice of Aron root. Mix this and draw it out, when the Sun is in Virgo and Mercury is on a right hand course. Take care to use a marble mortar mixing four dirhem of mastic, two of amber, two of camphor, then one small measure (uqija) of Musk, and ten dirhem of sarcacolla, when you have pulverised what needs pulverising add half a ritl of the blood of a young stag who was slaughtered with a brass knife. When you have mixed it all you put it in a glass vessel, then take yourself to a place with a water fountain or a spring source and put the glass vessel by the water, take a coal pan which you have with you prepared, put it on a rock in the middle of the fountain, so that the water moistens it and kindles thereon a fire. When it is alight open the mouth of the vessel, then you put a little of the contents at once on the coal pan, and bring to him the offering there, then will the smoke bring the servant of the Moon in this zodiac sign, ask him your demands then he will fulfil your desires.

For these operations know there is a reason for every detail which they knew of old time, whose practical application is greyed with the antiquity of their origins.

Comment on the Works of the Moon

Now to ſpeak of the Times and Seasons of their [ſpirits] Appearance. The better sort of Magicians do square their times with Aſtrological hours, eſpecially of Saturn, Luna, and Venus, in the Moons increase, and the middle of the night, or twelve o'clock at noon: In which hours they do likewise compose their Garments, Caps, Candleſticks, Figures, Lamins, Pentacles, and Circles for Conjuration. As for the Times in re-ſpeɗ of their Infernal Courses, the fitteſt are when they ſpring up in the Wrath, or when they sink in the Deſpair, which is a myſtery to the learned Conjurers of Europe.

A Discourse concerning Devils and Spirits

The astrology of the *Picatrix* is often of a technical sophistication far be-yond the remit of this treatise. This can involve some very creative use of astrological rules, where what may appear to be unusual applications of astrological ideas arise. These run contrary to the general advice given, for example, by Agrippa, let alone some of the simplified concepts in current use. The Libra working above requires a copper bow made when Venus is retrograde in Taurus, with Mercury in Aries. By some lights, retrograde planets are not sought for but avoided, and Mercury has no dignity in Aries. In the next chapter, dealing with the Lunar Mansions, exception to avoidance of combust planets is found, there it is advocated as useful in *operations of the bad*. An astrological talisman in Greer and Warnock's translation of the Latin *Picatrix* involves another exception; a cursing im-age is made with the Lord of the Ascendant cadent, a weak position. The image is then buried at a crossroads while the Moon is in Via Combusta. Originally, this meant between 19 Libra and 3 Scorpio, the opposite po-sitions of the exaltations of the Sun and Moon. Later the measure was conventionalised, from 15 degrees of one sign to the same number of the other. It is said to be an unfortunate position, and such it is in many cir-cumstances, but evidently not all. The magical astrologer, like the Haitian bokor, can serve with both hands.

Venus retrograde arises on a cyclical basis, as do her stationary and direct modes. This cycle produces the transitions from Evening to Morning star and back again. As modes of the same planet there are profound implications in this cycle, which the reader may wish to explore.

In the table following, two schemas from the Papyri for relating magical workings to lunar positions are given. While different in many respects from the details of the works in the previous section, a similar method is clearly at work. It is intriguing to note that both these lists commence the lunar zodiac in Virgo, perhaps indicating a particular status for the star Spica.

Lunar Workings from the Papyri

☾	MAGICAL WORK PGM VII 284	MAGICAL WORK PGM III 275
♍	Anything may be done	Anything; bowl divination, as you wish
♎	Necromancy	Invocations, spell of release, necromancy
♏	Inflicting evil	…
♐	Invocations or incantations to the ☉ and ☾	Conduct business
♑	Recitations for any wish to best effect	Whatever is appropriate
♒	Love charms	…
♓	Works of foreknowledge	… love charm
♈	Fire divination, love charms	…
♉	Incantation of the lamp	…
♊	Spells for winning favour	Spells of binding
♋	Phylacteries	Spell of reconciliation; Air divination
♌	Rings or binding spells	…

TALISMANS & WORKS
OF THE LUNAR MANSIONS

One needs to know the constellation which is sympathetic to the talismanic rite intended. Therefore in this chapter I set forth the nature of the works performed under the lunar mansions. The maker of talismans must know the ephemeris, as also the constellations and be sure lest his works come to naught.

The Reasonable Soul is applied by Will to the World Soul and is in accord with it. By this do our works come to pass. In knowledge of the stars and planets is the beginning of that application and of the Art of Talismans. In these operations following one needs to know the position of the Moon and in which of Her Mansions She is situated; and thus it is I recount the nature of those Mansions according to the Indians, that knowing Her position, and Her potency therein you might work aright the Art of Talismans.

1 The first station of mansion is called **Al-Saratan**, of the beginning of Aries unto 12 degrees 51' 26" of Aries. In this mansion one may make journeys, it is also good for purgatives. Talismans for journeys in safety; for marriage matches and friendships when these are needed, either to make or to mend. Also to regain a runaway slave or to assist him, or to destroy associations. In operations of good take note of the evil planets and be free of them, also the combustion of the Sun. In operations of the bad, combustion may however be desirable.

2 **Al-Butan.** 12 degrees 51' 26" of Aries until 25 42' 52" of the Ram. Good for the digging of canals, fountains and the like; also to request objectives and to bury treasure or take from it. Talismans for the good of seed crops, further for the escape of slaves and the arrest of prisoners and the putting to torture.

3 *Al-Turaija* 25 42' 52" Aries unto 8 34' 18" of Taurus. Talismans for the distressed in need of liberation. Also to destroy companionship and to free or to enchain captives. Further for the success in alchemical operations, for hunting, love in marriage, injury of herds and slaves to the destruction of their lords.

4 *Al-Dabarah* 8 34 18" to 21 25' 44" of Taurus. Talismans to damage a tower or contrariwise ensure duration of buildings. Also to crops and slaves, their destruction or maintenance. Also to cause estrangement of married partners. Also for diggings, for water or treasure and buried things, it causes hostility, and to banish evil vermin, as serpents and snakes.

5 *Al-Haqa* 21 25' 44" to 4 17' 10" of Gemini. To teach and to instruct and to thrive in instruction, in religion, clerical and manual learning. To preserve travellers and enterprises. To preserve buildings and destroy company. To bring unity and harmony in marriage when the Moon and the Ascendant are in a Human Sign under good aspect. The Human Signs are the Twins, the Virgin, Libra, the Archer and the Waterbearer.

6 *Al-Han'a* 4 17' 10" to 17 18' 36" to annihilate towns and to prosecute. To chastise kings. To cover enemies with evil. To destroy crops and store of goods. Also for good relationships, good hunting, also to hinder the normal efficacy of medicine.

7 *Al-Dira* 17 18' 36" to the end of Gemini. For thriving trade, growth of crops, safety of relationships among friends. To bind vermin, as flies and such, to keep them from a place. Alchemy under this station will fail and need repeating. A talisman for demands of great men and their affection. For the flight of slaves, to gut houses and remove store of goods and possessions.

8 *Al-Natra* 0 Cancer til 12 51' 26". Talismans of love and friendship where there is none. Preserving travellers and friendships. Also to retain prisoners and cause slaves to be wicked. Further to cause the banishing of mice and bugs.

9 *Al-Tarfas* 12 51' 26" to 25 42' 52" Cancer. To destroy crops and land and travellers. To destroy companionships and damage legal proceedings.

10 *Al-Gabha* 25 42' 52" Cancer till 8 34' 18" Leo. Talismans of preserving marriage, to amaze and perplex enemies, to fetter prisoners, to procure durability of buildings and provide harmony with others for mutual profit.

11 *Al-Zubra* 8 34' 18" unto 21 28' 44" Leo. Therein one makes talismans to release prisoners and captives, to the siege of towns, for prosperity of trade, the welfare of travels, the durability of building works and of relations between companions.

12 *Al-Sarfa* 21 25' 44" Leo till 4 17' 10" Virgo. Therein one makes talismans for prosperity of crops and plants, to the destruction of the property of a people. Further talismans to destroy ships or to succeed in alchemy, to keep slaves in right condition.

13 *Al-Aiwa* 4 17' 10" to 17 8' 36" Virgo. Therein one makes talismans that trade might prosper and crops likewise. For the welfare of travellers, to bring about marriage, to free prisoners, to bring union with kings and great men.

14 *Al-Simak* 17 8' 36" till full 30 degrees Virgo. Talismans to preserve good relationships between married couples and health through medical treatment. Also talismans to damage seeds, crops and plants and the annihilation of money deposits to cause evil to happen to travellers. For the well-being of kings and luck in navigation and understanding between companions.

15 *Al-Gafr* 0 to 12 51' 26" Libra. Talismans for digging of wells and to take possession of buried treasure. To hinder travellers, to separate married couples and destroy good relationships with hostility. To expel enemies and remove them from positions as well as to destroy lodgings and houses.

16 *Al-Zabana* 12 51' 26" to 25 42' 52" Libra. Talismans to damage trade business and crops, either grown or sown. To separate friends and couples. Further if you wish to punish a woman, your wife. Talismans to cause discord amongst friends on journeys, talismans to create discord between companions and to free prisoners.

17 *Al-Ilkil* 25 42' 52" Libra to 8 34' 18" Scorpio. Talismans for well being and good condition of domestic beasts. For the siege of towns and security of buildings. Good journeys by sea. To restore friendships. Particularly good for friendship.

18 *Al-Qalb* 8 34' 18" to 21 25' 44" Scorpio. Talismans to raise the flags of conquering kings over lands of your enemies. Talismans for the solid condition of buildings. Whoever would take a wife while Mars is in this Station will leave her soon a widow, and had best avoid this Mansion. Talismans for the escaping of slaves, for prosperity of plants and secure journeys of sailors, and to the discord of companions.

19 *Al-Saula* 21 25' 44" Scorpio to 4 17' 10" Sagittarius. Talismans for sieges and the defeating of enemies and to take from them what one will. To destroy the prosperity of a people, to separate persons and create discord. Talismans for the well-being of travellers, thriving of crops, flight and escape of slaves from their masters, the sinking of ships and causing shipwrecks, discord of companions, escaping of prisoners and captives.

20 *Al-Na'aim* 4 17' 10" to 17 8' 36" Sagittarius. Talismans to tame great and difficult beasts. For the quick course and abbreviation of journeys,

to bring a person to you, for friendship. Otherwise to aggravate losses of captives and to bring good relationships of a company to ruin.

21 *Al-Balda* 17 8' 36" unto 30 degrees Sagittarius. Talismans for durability of building works, thriving of seeds, further talismans for beasts of burden and transport, as for cattle. To preserve a lords property, safe journeys, to release and keep a woman from her spouse.

22 *Sad-Al-Dabih* 0 to 12 51' 26" Capricorn. Talismans to assist the treatment of disease. Talismans to separate couples, to bring about the adultery of a married woman one desires. For the escape of slaves and their flight from the country.

23 *Sad-Bula* 12 51' 26" to 25 42' 52" Capricorn. Therein one makes Talismans for the treatment of disease, talismans for the annihilation of property, for the separation of couples and the liberation or discharge of captives.

24 *Sad-Al-Su'ud* 25 42' 52" Capricorn to 8 34' 18" Aquarius. Therein one makes talismans for the flourishing of business and the unity of married couples. Talismans for the victory of armies and troops. On the other hand for the discord of companions and the freeing of captives. Alchemical operations under this sign will fail.

25 *Sad-Al-Ahbija* 8 34' 18" to 21 25' 44" Aquarius. Talismans for the siege of towns. Talismans to the injury of enemies and victory over them, and division and hostility among them. Talismans for the consignment of messages and spies and to ensure their success. Talismans to separate married couples, destruction of plants and operations of ligature both of the genitalia and of the other members, also to bind captives (it is easy to bind captives in this station). Talismans for the foundation of building works, ensuring safety and durability.

26 *Al-Farq Al-Mugaddam* 21 25' 44" Aquarius to 4 17' 10" Pisces. Herein one makes all sorts of talismans for good purposes, and for the binding of souls in love, or whatever a traveller wishes he will obtain, talismans for successful sea journeys, for discord of companions and for binding and fettering of prisoners.

27 *Al-Farq Al-Mu'ahhr* 4 17' 10" to 17 8' 36" Pisces. Talismans ensuring the flourishing of trade and a blessed yield of crops. Quick recovery from disease, changes wealth to ruin, sows discord between couples, to prolong the captivity of prisoners and corrupt slaves.

28 *Al-Risa* 17 8' 36" to 30 Pisces. Therein one composes talismans for the flourishing of trade and growth of crops, healing diseases, that money be lost, safe journeys, reconciliation of couples, further talismans to bind captives and prevent damage to journeying ships.

Comment on Lunar Mansions

This seminal material is the source of Agrippa's Lunar Mansions and of famed astrologer William Lilly's Critical Degrees. The data on which it is based is c. 10th CE and by my reading depends in part on fixed star positions that no longer apply due to precession. As it stands the cusps also define points that remain in use, such as said Critical Degrees, and of course the Solsticial and Equinoctial points. To facilitate updated adaptation with appropriate materials, I have tabulated some current positions of principal Fixed Stars &c in relation to the Mansions as defined by Lilly's Critical Degrees and earlier convention. Rheinhold Ebertin, one of the greatest 20th century astrologers, worked with stars all over the world by relating their position to the Ecliptic regardless of distance from it (thus Polaris is associated with 27:54 Gemini). His theoretical premise, which has ancient precedent, relates stars not visible in various parts of the world to the locality. Stars outside the Northern Hemisphere – such as the Southern Cross – are just as appropriate to this schema. In effect, this provides a basis for both global and local approaches.

Mansion	Detail of Zodiac
0 Aries	Equinox 0 Aries
12 Aries	
25 Aries	
8 Taurus	
21 Taurus	Algol 26:10 Taurus
Pleiades 29 Taurus – 00 Gemini	
4 Gemini	Aldebaran 9:38 Gemini
17 Gemini	Goat Star 20:28 Gemini
0 Cancer	Solstice
12 Cancer	Greater and Lesser Dog Star 13:57 & 24:24 Cancer
25 Cancer	
8 Leo	
21 Leo	Regulus 29:41 Leo
4 Virgo	
17 Virgo	Alkaid 25:31 Virgo
0 Libra	Equinox
Gienah 10:44 Libra	
12 Libra	Spica 23:42 Libra
Arcturus 24:00	
25 Libra	
8 Scorpio	Alphecca 10:53 Scorpio
21 Scorpio	
4 Sagittarius	Antares 9 Sagittarius
17 Sagittarius	Dragons Eye 26:35 Sagittarius
0 Capricorn	Solstice
12 Capricorn	Vega 13:55 Capricorn
25 Capricorn	
8 Aquarius	
21 Aquarius	Deneb Algedi 22 Aquarius
Fomalhaut 3:52 Pisces	
4 Pisces	
17 Pisces	

ASTROLOGICAL TALISMANS

These figures are referred to particular astrological conditions, under the circumstances described herein one works for the purposes which the talismans are applicable to.

Talisman for the expulsion of mice

One draws the signs shown on a copper plate at the outgoing of the first decan of Leo. These signs are the signs of Leo. One lays the signs at a place where mice are found and they will flee the place where it is put; and this is the figure:

Talisman for the expulsion of mosquitoes

One draws the following figure on a sulphur stone at the outgoing of the second decan of Taurus. When placed where one wills no mosquito will approach that place. And this is the sign of the star, which causes the mosquitoes to vanish:

Talisman for the expulsion of flies

One paints on a tin pewter plate the following figure when Scorpio is going out, and that with its third decan. One then places this at a place and the flies will fly away from it. And this is the figure of the star which disperses the flies.

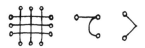

Talisman to bring a person quickly

A wonderful talisman when one wishes to bring a person one loves to one quickly. One draws the following figure on a new piece of cloth in the day and hour of Venus, when the second decan of Taurus is going out and Venus is in it. One burns the drawing in the fire and names thereby the names of the desired person. Then they will come quickly to one at the place of the operation. This figure arises when Venus has a strong signification and is in this decan. This is the figure:

Talisman for hostility

When one wants to bring separation and dissolution between two people. One draws the following figure with a black dogs tooth on a black lead plate in the day and hour of Saturn when the third decan of Capricorn is going out and Saturn is in it. Then one leaves the plate at the home of one of them or the place where they meet. Then they will be divided in all unhappy and undesirable ways. And this figure arises when Saturn has strong signification and is in this decan. And this is the figure which one must draw:

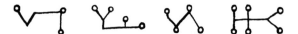

Talisman to make a place barren and to hinder cultivation

One draws the following figure with a sow's tooth on a lead plate in the day and hour of Saturn, when the second decan of Capricorn is ascending and Saturn is therein. This plate one lays at the place concerned and lets the Saturnine evil work, and it will not cultivate so long as the figure is there. And this is the drawing:

I have found no more of these talismans in the books of the masters of the art, although it is spoken of therein of the expired art of talismans. And I have found it good to continue with the use of stones and images, and the mysterious workings of the stars they belong to.

Comment

Internal evidence suggests that these symbols were not intended to be used alone; rather they were employed in addition to other symbols and images of the zodiacal zigns. Thus, for example, the *talisman to bring a person quickly* combines with an image of Venus (say with apple and comb &c.), with additions including the symbol of her planet and so forth.

CORRESPONDENCES I

The ink of Saturn is compounded of burnt wool. That of Jupiter is verdigris. That of Mars cinnabar. That of the Sun yellow sulphur. That of Venus of saffron. That of Mercury is a mixture of lacquer, sulphur and verdigris. The Moon's of white lead.

Aristotle has it in his *Book of Lamps and Banners* for the instruction of his pupil Alexander, that the images of the planets are as follows:

Saturn has the form of a black man wrapped in a green mantle, having a bald head and carrying a sickle.

Jupiter has the form of a clothed man upon a throne.

Mars has the form of a man who rides a lion and bearing a long lance.

The Sun has the form of a beardless and handsome crowned man bearing a spear. At his side is found a form with a man's head and hands, having the hands and arms raised up, his body and feet like that of a horse.

Venus has the form of a young maiden with a comb in the right hand and an apple in the other, her hair is loose.

Mercury has the form of a naked man who rides on an eagle and writes.

The Moon has the form of one riding on a hare.

Under that he writes accordingly of the precious stones and metals assigned to the planets and speaks as follows.

O Alexander, when you operate in the name of any planet, let the substances be that of the planet concerned, and likewise regarding the garments. When you undertake an operation under whatever Ascendant, proceed by wearing vestments of the corresponding nature. Those of Saturn are completely black, and when the garment is of wool it is the best. The colours of Jupiter are green, and silk is to be preferred. The colour of Mars is fire red, and when the garment is decorated with figures, or is of patterned silk, it is the best. The colours of the Sun are glistening golden yellow, and when the garment is of gold material or yellow silk, it is the best. The colours of Venus are pale rose red, and of that kind, and when the garment is of silk it is the best. The colours of Mercury are the mixed colours, and when of diverse material it is the best. The colours of the Moon are clear white, and when the garment is of linen or of pure white silk, it is the best.

And so we come to their incenses: all belonging to Saturn are evil smelling, as gum ammoniac, castoreum, asafoetida and such like. Those of Jupiter are the great harmonising incenses like ambergris and aloes. Those of Mars are called sharp incenses, such are pepper and ginger. Those of the Sun are the strong incenses like musk and ambergris. Those of Venus rose and myrtle. For Mercury mixed fumes like narcissus, myrtle and mallow. The Moon's are the cold incenses like camphor, rose and Cynomorium coccineum.

The inks of the operations of the decans, for use with the images:

The first sign is Aries, and the first decan is fox-red formed of a part of green gall-apple powdered fine, gum Arabic and vitriol, the latter two in equal parts, bound with egg white and made into pills. Keep in a vessel until needed and then dissolve it. The second decan of Aries has ink of gold yellow, its recipe is as follows: magnesia and copper vitriol in equal parts, pulverised and mixed with an equal quantity of club honey mixed and made into pills. When desired take pestle and mortar, reduce to powder and dissolve in gum Arabic. The third decan of Aries is of white made of magnesia and white lead.

Next is Taurus and its first decan is of dust grey smoke colour, for which one collects lamp black mixed with fish glue and gum Arabic lightened with white lead. The second decan: gold yellow made of gall apple broken in pieces, extract the liquid from its black interior, mix with gum Arabic. The third decan is gold, made as above described.

The decans of Gemini: first decan, gold as above; second decan, red, distillation of vitriol and cinnabar mixed with a little gum Arabic. Third decan yellow as above described.

Cancer: first decan white as above; second decan gold-yellow as described above; third decan black made similarly to the first decan of Aries only the vitriol and gall apple are in equal parts.

Leo: the first decan is dust grey tar colour. The second decan gold yellow. The colour of the third decan is pomegranate red formed of cinnabar, sulphur mixed with water of gall apple, left to dry, with a little gum Arabic and lacquer added when one would write.

Virgo: the first decan is red formed with bruised saffron mixed with green gall apple water, left to stand and diluted with a little gum Arabic when one would use it. The second decan is smoke grey tar. The third reddish yellow made of sulphur, saffron water and gum Arabic.

Libra: first smoke grey; second black; third white.

Scorpio: first black; second yellow, third smoke grey.

Sagittarius: first red, second yellow of sulphur set over a fire over night then mixed with white lead and gum Arabic to write. The third decan is smoke grey.

Capricorn's first decan: green of verdigris and gum Arabic; the second decan is red of cinnabar, gum Arabic and glue. The third is black.

Aquarius: first decan musk red of dragons blood and gum Arabic; the second is black, for every part of good Persian ink add gum Arabic, gall apple and a half part of sieved burnt paper. Thicken with egg white breaded into pastilles until one needs it when it can be dissolved for use. The third decan is green formed of the gall of a wild beast mixed with a little gum Arabic when one writes.

Pisces: the first decan's ink is blonde, formed of red lead and lead white, with a little gum Arabic. The second decan is dust grey, of tamarisk, burnt thorns and gum Arabic. The third decan is red.

These inks are used in rites and upon talismans. And just as we have said regarding planets and their influence, even as Utarid [Hermes]the Wise has written that the nature of a planet is drawn down when its nature is emulated by the operator: in food, drink, incense, times, rites, inks, invocations, sacrifices, amulets, stones and jewels in the form of talismans. Thus the spirits of the planets appropriate to the force required in one's undertaking are united with one's efforts and one proceeds with success.

Comment on Correspondences I

This chapter accords perfectly with the concept of Sympathia fundamental to Greek astrological cosmology. Many of the correspondences involve familiar ideas despite some variation. Black for Saturn, red for Mars, yellow or gold for the Sun and mixed colours for Mercury is common enough in the grimoires; using a mixture of ingredients for Mercury's ink alone is a nice touch. Naturally, the author of this material was not Aristotle, but the appeal to Greek authorities is sincere enough.

That the symbol of Saturn should bear a sickle is natural, while an enthroned Jupiter is equally expected. These are pictures of the classical gods. Mars' lion is not typically Greek, though the association of the beast to Nergal is certainly appropriate.

While there are examples that are more classical elsewhere in the *Picatrix*, the solar image is intriguing. The heroic spearman and the centaur suggest Achilles and Chiron, or indeed the initiation of any such hero. In the image of Venus holding an apple we have an allusion to the triumph of Aphrodite in the Judgement of Paris, an icon older than the Homeric occurrence of it. This is a classic talisman, and Catherine de Medici possessed one with this image its principal motif, surrounded with additional magical characters.

Grimoire aficionados will note the resemblance of these images to the planetary talismans found in *Le Petit Albert*. Another resemblance is important to take away from this study into modern practice. This is the resemblance of such images of the gods to some species of clay or cast metal votives once obtained for offering at pagan temples. Once this is noted, it becomes very apparent that talismans and such votives have a substantial amount in common. While modern occultists generally think of talismans as occult jewellery, or as items carried on the person, the *Picatrix* contains many formulae that broaden this view. Talismans are equally a part of image magic and general spell work. It is perfectly appropriate to add the votive function to talismans when operating within a pagan framework or indeed simply a more 'spirit friendly' ritual context.

The votive is generally understood as involving positive favours, but this too is but part of their range. A very common spell type in the ancient world, with many archaeological examples from Alexandria through Rome to the English city of Bath and beyond, is the defixione. This is essentially a negative votive, frequently inscribed on lead. The choice of this material involves many considerations, besides the association with malefic planets (the *Picatrix* ascribes lead to Mars; the usual ascription is to Saturn). It was readily obtained, stolen from piping for example, and could be easily written on. Rolling up for placing in a crack in a wall or tomb was a typical means of deposit, and lead sheet favours this practice.

A drawn image of a god or daimon as well as a written spell underlines the connection with votives, as does the depositing of the defixione at a temple, or in a grave or even a bathhouse. These did not ask for positive favours, but for retribution, or defeat or other misfortune to befall a victim. The targets ranged from thieves to opponents in politics, to rival teams at the chariot races. Some locations were so favoured for depositing these that excavation occasionally locates dozens at a single place. Incidentally one reason lead may have been associated with Mars is the astrological rule of elemental water by this planet.

The colours listed in this section are similar to those of the grimoires, with a couple of exceptions, green for Jupiter and pale rose red for Venus, the latter suggesting the not infrequently found pink, as in candles for love magic in Hoodoo.

The thinking behind the incenses is evidently the source of similar ideas in western grimoires, and we may be certain which end of the spice trade they originate. The use of such ingredients to manufacture inks is hopefully sufficiently interesting to justify the inclusion of the remainder of this excerpt. The closing passage gives a clear description of Sympathia active in astrological magic, attributed to Utarid the Wise, which is to say Hermetic sources. The use of these substances also resembles the basis of statue animation, concepts present equally in Hermeticism and Theurgy in the Hellenistic era.

CORRESPONDENCES II

To Saturn is assigned the following stones: iron, diamond, lead lustre [antimony], onyx, the pure black jet, the turquoise, lodestone and magnesium. It has also a share of gold, ruby, coins of gold and haematite.

To Jupiter is assigned the tin-pewter, white and yellow jacinth, and it has a share of cornelian, gold, chrysolith, crystal and every brilliant white colour stone.

To Mars is assigned brass, catstone [?], sulphur with its occult ways, and it has a share of coins, bloodstone, lodestone, glass, cornelian and onyx. It is also assigned all red, dark coloured stones.

To the Sun is assigned gold, sulphur, garnet, diamond, pharoah's glass, the red mussel shell, and all brilliant stones, and has its share of bloodstone, sapphire, and ruby.

To Venus is assigned the lapis lazuli, the pearl, the mussel shell, malachite and coral, and it has a share in silver, pearl, crystal and the magnet.

To Mercury is assigned quicksilver, sapphire, emerald, has its share of chrysolith, tin-pewter, glass and marble.

To the Moon is assigned silver and silver coins and seed pearls, it has a share in crystal, lapis lazuli, onyx and pearl.

The planetary talismans make use of the signs following, which are the symbols of the planets and lead to victory in their workings:

| Saturn | Jupiter | Mars | Sun | Venus | Mercury | Moon |

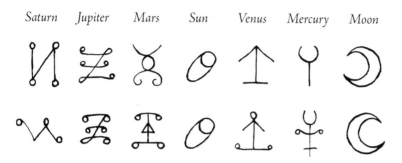

Now we continue with the images of the planets, and with what we have taken from *The Book of the Uses of Stones* and the *Book of the Talismans of the Spirits*.

Sun

The Book of the Wise Apollonius describes the image of a woman in a carriage drawn by horses. In her right hand she has a mirror and in her left she holds a whiplash to her breast. She has a brightness about her head. *The Book of the Uses of Stones* describes a man standing as if saluting someone opposite him, in his left hand he holds a shield and under his foot the image of a dragon. *The Book of the Talismans of the Spirits* describes the image of a king who sits upon a throne, with a crown upon his head, before him the image of a raven and under his feet a dragon.

Elsewhere I have found that the great luminary has the form of a crowned man who stands in a chariot, pulled by four horses. In his right hand is a mirror, in his left a shield, and his form is entirely yellow. Each of these images has influence and workings in the talismans of this book.

Venus

Apollonius the Wise said that it has the form of a standing woman with an apple in her right hand. *The Book of the Talismans of the Spirits* has it that the image is a standing woman bearing an apple in the right hand and in the left a comb, and there are signs on the tablet. Utarid's [Hermes'] *The Book of the Uses of Stones* describes a man having the face of a bird and the feet of an eagle. It asserts also that it has the form of a naked woman, behind her stands a child, while Mars stands before her, and at his neck is a chain. Another form is of a woman with loosened hair who rides upon a stag; she holds an apple in her right hand and flourishes herbs in her left. Her dress is a skein of white.

Mercury, the Scribe

Apollonius says that his image has the form of a bearded young man, with a staff in his right hand, and on the inner side is a cat. *The Book of the Talismans of the Spirits* describes a man with a rooster on his head, sitting on a stool, his feet are those of an eagle; on his left hand sits a falcon and under his feet are the figures of Mercury. Utarid's *Book of the Uses of Stones* describes the form of a standing man, with two spread wings; on his left side is a small rooster, in his right he holds a staff and in his left a round clay vessel. On his head is a comb like that of a rooster, and also on each foot. Elsewhere I found the image of Mercury described as a crowned man riding upon a horse, with a staff [stylus?] in the right hand and a sheet of paper in his left. The colouration of this image is dappled.

Moon

Utarid's *Book of the Uses of Stones* says that the image of the Moon is like the form of a woman with a beautiful face, girdled with a dragon, on her head are two serpents, she is horned, she wears as bracelets two snakes, at each wrist a snake, under and over her head are two seven-headed dragons. The wise Apollonius says that the Moon has the form of a woman, who is upon two bulls or a seven-headed snake as before. *The Book of the Talismans of the Spirits* says the lesser luminary has the form of a man on whose head is a bird. He walks leaning upon a staff and before him is a tree. Another source gives to the Moon in her sphere the form of a crowned youth, standing upon a chariot drawn by four bulls. In his right hand he has an ox goad and in the left a mirror. His form is white and green.

Saturn

In *The Book of the Talismans of the Spirits* he has the form of a man with the face of a raven and the feet of a camel. He sits upon a stool, bearing a stick in his right hand and dice in his left. In the book of the philosopher Apollonius he has the form of a man who stands before a lecture desk. Utarid has it that his form is that of a standing man, his hands over his head and the image of a lizard under his feet. Elsewhere I found that Saturn in his sphere has the form of a man standing upon a snake, he has a sickle in his right hand and a stick in his left. His image is dust coloured and black.

Jupiter

Apollonius the Wise says that he has the form of a man wearing vestments in which he wraps himself, he sits on an eagle with his feet on its shoulders, and has the furled end of his vestment in his right hand. In *The Book of the Talismans of the Spirits* he has the form of a man with the face of a lion and the feet of a bird, under his feet is a many headed dragon, and he bears a lance in his right hand with which he stings the head of the dragon. In the *Book of the Uses of Stones* he wears a cloak and rides a vulture, he bears either a lance or a staff. Elsewhere I found that Jupiter in his sphere has the form of a man with a roll in his right hand [holding his vestment as in the image given by Apollonius, or a scroll?] and a nut in the left. His garment is yellow and green.

Mars

Apollonius says of it that it has the form of a man with a helmet, with armour of the lower legs and upon his arms. He is girt with a sword. *The Book of the Talismans of the Spirits* says that he has the form of a crowned man bearing a sword, upon which are signs. *The Book of the Uses of Stones* of Utarid says that he has the form of a naked man, standing, and to his right is Venus who strokes her hair back. Mars has his right hand behind her neck and his left to her breast and looks at her. This he asserts has many workings which he quotes in his book. By another I found that Mars in his sphere has the form of a man, who rides upon a lion, he bears a sword in his right hand and a man's head in the left. He is dressed in iron and silk.

These are the images of the planets after the teachings of the Masters. And these forms are for the special and specific workings which they are appropriate to.

Comment on Correspondences II

The correspondence of planets to metals and minerals is problematic, in terms both of accuracy of translation and of the attribution. There are differences from those given in the Latin and Spanish editions, which conform more closely to Western usage and have likely been adapted to do so. This note of caution aside, the principle is well illustrated and the inclusion of the material sufficiently justified. The second row of planetary symbols is from elsewhere in the text.

The planetary order employed here is very curious, it adjusts the Chaldean order not to place Sun and Moon in most prominent position, but Sun and Venus. A female figure for the Sun is not surprising, being apparently natural to some Sabean sects. In any case, Hecate, Medea and Circe are all relatives of Helios, and alternative male figures quickly follow. A crowned and throned figure suggests a solar Baal rather than the Jovian. The resemblance of the figure to Helios is striking, it possesses all the attributes of his classical image. Although the mirror may be the remains of a whip, its use in Mystery rituals is significant. Retaining the whip we have a perfect Helios, and the image also adapts to an Abraxas by adding a rooster's head and snaky legs.

The Venus image includes two typical images of a woman bearing an apple, with variations. More complex images with a child probably representing Eros, and Mars mentioned by name, obviously draw on classical imagery. So too the woman with apple reflects Aphrodite's triumph at the Judgement of Paris, the ancient precursor of all these survives in the biblical Eve. The supposedly solar lion in the martial image reminds us that Mars was the later attribute of previously solar Nergal. One must also be careful in examining older syncretism. Symbols are not necessarily exclusive; the martial lion can also equally represent Jupiter or the Sun as kingly figures. However, they are not all inclusive either. Not all synonyms of related figures are mutual; martial Nergal was also the Sun, but Apollo, while frequently associated with solar Helios and lunar Mēn, never became Mars. This is a timely reminder of the relations and distinctions between gods and celestial bodies.

Such images of star-daimons as that of Jupiter: a man with the face of a lion and the feet of a bird, are plainly the inspiration for similar descriptions of demons in texts such as the *Goetia*. Similar images were attributed to the decans, which were completely personified in ancient magic, frequently as demons. If such spirits are infernal, the term obviously does not apply in the assumed subterranean sense.

THE FIGURES OF THE STONES

Regarding engravings for seal rings of the seven planets:

Engravings of the Sun

1 Concerning the engravings appropriate to the Sun: when one draws talismans under the greater Luminary on a ringstone of ruby of a pure red colour the picture of a king, who sits on a throne, with a crown on his head and the image of a raven before him and this figure under his feet, one conquers all kings. So it is written in the *Book of Explaining of Spirit Talismans*. Therein it is asserted that the Sun must be in his exaltation when one works.

2 Among the Solar signs is that given by Aristotle in instruction to Alexander, writing: who draws on a jacinth the picture of a lion with this sign thereon, with Leo ascendant and the Sun therein, with the unfortunate planets afar off, such a one is unconquerable and likewise whatsoever they undertake they will readily press on therein. Also they will be free of affliction of any frightening dreams.

△

3 Also under this star one draws on a diamond the picture of a woman, who sits on a carriage, which four horses pull, with a mirror in the right and a whip in the left hand, and seven candles on her head, with a 'pond' on the innerside of the ringstone [a hollow or a sign?]. This also is done in the exaltation. Having procured such an engraving, all the one who bears it meets with or opposes shall do him reverence.

4 Also to his engravings belongs the figure on a haematite in the first decan of Leo, which protects from the lunar diseases [epilepsy and lunacy &c.], and this is the figure:

5 Also to his engravings belongs that which Hermes mentions in his book *Al-Haditus*, saying: take a stone named the samalinun that is a yellow stone with black dots and green eyes, it is light and of brilliant colour; in the hour of the Sun, and under his ascendant, engrave the figure of a fly; fire does not hurt him who bears it through the flames. He asserts that this stone is to be found in Persia.

6 And to the engravings of the Sun also belongs a figure to expel snakes, engraved on a ringstone the image of a serpent, in the hour of the Sun when he is in the seventh degree of Aquarius, Saturn in the seventh degree of Aries, the Moon in the seventh degree of Scorpio, Jupiter in the second degree of Sagittarius and the Tail in ten degrees thereof. On the back of the serpent are drawn these signs:

and around it these signs:

and one sets this stone in a seal ring of gold and thus can remain with it in any place free from reptiles and serpents.

7 And to his engravings also, one for the expulsion of woodlice; drawn on a ringstone of carnelian is the image of a woodlouse, in the hour of the Sun in his exaltation, Saturn in seventeen degrees Aquarius, Mercury in 20 degrees Gemini, Moon in 2 degrees Cancer and Mars in the last degree of Libra. Draw thereon these signs and put it in a gold seal ring, then no woodlice appear at the place where one is, and its wearer shall see none.

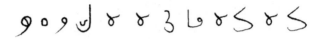

Engravings of Venus

1 One engraves for Venus on a ringstone of ruby the image of a woman with an apple in her right and a comb in the left hand. One draws this on the comb. The image has a human body with a bird's face and eagle feet. This image gains the love of all persons and is done in the day and exaltation of Venus.

2 Also to her belongs that on a ringstone of white jacinth, of a woman with an apple in her right hand and a comb in her left. Make it in the first decan of Libra. He who wears this ringstone is ever glad and laughing so long as he wears it.

3 Under her workings belongs the engraving in her hour on a lapis lazuli the image of a naked young woman; next to her is a man with a chain about his neck, behind her a little boy who carries a sword. Whoso wears this will subject women and they will never decline him.

4 Further belongs to her: one engraves likewise on a lapis lazuli the image of a standing woman with an apple in the right hand and on the inner side of the stone a mother sheep. Who wears this ring, by his hand sheep will thrive when he attends them. This is to be done in her exaltation and hour.

5 From the book of Kriton *About the Talismans*: one engraves on a pearl the image of a snake and under it a scorpion, on the morning of Monday in her hour and exaltation, who wears this will suffer no

snake bites, and if he would cure them he places the ring in liquid and uses it as medicine.

6 Further belongs to her: one engraves the following signs, on a pearl. Do this in her hour and whoso wears this stone shall enjoy the company of boys, coming near their hearts, and they know not of their keeping away when they are in the company of the wearer.

$$\Lambda\ o\ |\ o\ \Lambda\ o$$

7 One engraves on a pearl the picture of a sitting woman with two pigtails behind, with two winged boys in her bosom, in her hour and exaltation. For the wearer of this stone journeys will be made light, and near and far no accident shall befall them.

8 Further belongs to her: one engraves on a ringstone of crystal in her hour three joined forms. The bearer will have blessing and luck in transactions, as much as he wishes.

9 Further belongs to her: one engraves on a coral the image of two cats and a mouse between them, in her hour and her ascendant when she is in it. Then it serves for the expulsion of mice from that place, and one knows they do not exist therein.

10 Further belongs to her [for the expulsion of leeches]: one engraves on a malachite stone, on the obverse the image of a leech and on the reverse two leeches, of which one has its head in the direction of the tail of the other; take this stone to the place where leeches are. One seals with it in her hour and her ascendant, and likewise is the use of the other engravings of the stones that you know of.

11 Further under her rule: one engraves on a pearl the image of a standing fat-bodied woman. This serves for love and is well known.

12 Likewise under her rule: one engraves on a cornelian stone the image of a woman with a coiled cloth in one hand, and scaly skin, and a thing like an apple in her other hand. Therein one seals in wax for children's illnesses, and all that you will. This too is to be done in her hour and her ascendant.

13 Further belongs to her: one engraves on a cornelian stone the image of a wild asses head with a fly's head upon it as a 'small addition'. This is done in her hour and her ascendant. With this stone one seals in wax against colic. This is proven and the Egyptian temples made use of it.

Engravings of Mercury

1 In the *Book of the Explaining of the Spirit Talismans* translated by Bugratis [Hippocrates] I found: one engraves on a ringstone of green topaz the picture of a man with a rooster on his head, he is seated on a chair, his feet are the feet of an eagle, on his left hand sits a falcon, and under his feet are these signs, and this is done in his hour and exaltation. This talisman brings about the liberation of captives and the like.

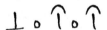

2 Further under Mercury: one engraves on a ring stone of emerald in his hour and his ascendant the following signs, he who wears this will be the writer, calculator and manager among subjects.

3 Further belongs to him: one engraves on a stone, which is the renowned manatas stone, the image of a man who sits on a canopied chair, with a quill in the right hand and a scroll, on which he writes, in the other. This is done in his hour and exaltation. When one who is expert in writing arts wishes to work for the sultan he wears this ring stone and is employed in his service and made confidante in his affairs and beloved by him in all matters.

4 And in Kriton's *Book of Talismans*: one engraves on an emerald the picture of a frog, in his hour and his ascendant. Whoso wears this ringstone, no-one does damage to, and no-on gossips about him. He is as worthy men and prospers in all his works.

5 And from the same book one engraves on a ringstone of emerald the picture of a lion and a lion head and writes under it Alif [ا] and over that a Dal [د] in his hour and his ascendant. He who puts on this ringstone is beloved and respected by all people in his cause and secure before the pursuits of kings.

6 And from another book further belongs to him: one engraves on a ringstone of green chrysolite the picture of a scorpion in his hour and his ascendant. When this ringstone is put on his child remains preserved from all ill chance.

7 And further belongs to him: one engraves on glass in his hour and his ascendant a man's hand holding a balance. And with this ringstone one seals against all kinds of fevers and heals them. It is proven, and all find it effective.

Engravings of the Moon

1 When one engraves on a bezoar stone the picture of a scorpion, when the Moon is in Scorpio and the hour is hers and Scorpio is in one of the anguli of the ascendant, it must be fixed in a gold seal ring and sealed with consecrating incense. When the Moon is in Scorpio and one censes the scorpion bite and gives to drink of water which the

ring has touched so will it heal at once, and that is proven, and we have explained it before in this chapter.

2 Further belongs to her: when one engraves on a ringstone of lasur these signs in her hour and ascendant and dips this ringstone in a drink and give it to three or more persons, unity arises between them where before was enmity.

$$ 2 \circ \curlyvee \curlyvee 4 \ominus | \ominus $$

3 Further belongs to her, from *The Book of Explaining the Spirit Talismans* of Bugratis, when one engraves on a ringstone of pearl the figure of a man with a bird's head, he has a cut staff, and before it is something like the image of a camomile, and be sure that it is done in her hour and ascendant and her exaltation. Then the wanderer will not tire so long as he bears it on a long journey from home.

4 And from another book: when one engraves on a crystal the image of a woman with a forelock standing with two bulls under her, each of them has its feet on the head of the other. And on the inner side of the stone is the image of a standing woman with a type of crown on her head and a whip in her right hand, and one engraves thereon these signs, so one must seal with this stone in wax and leave it at a place at which live doves, then will they become innumerable in their increase. And it must be engraved in her hour and ascendant as before said.

$$ \llcorner I \ominus \downarrow $$

5 And further belongs to her: One engraves on a ringstone of cornelian the picture of a fly in her hour, when she is in two degrees Libra, Jupiter two degrees Sagittarius, Saturn one degree Capricorn. On the body of the fly one writes these signs, and on the stone these others, and fasten it in her hour and ascendant in a seal ring, even as with the engraving, and place under the ringstone a snakeskin, then no flies come in the house or at the place where this ring is found, in no manner whatever.

Figures of the fly:

Figures of the stone:

6 And further belongs to her: When one engraves on a lasur-stone the picture of a lion with a man's face with a Moon on his back. In her hour and her ascendant, so is the working of this ringstone which protects children from any attack they might befall.

7 And further belongs to her: one engraves on a bezoar stone in her hour, in the first decan of Cancer, this figure. So it helps especially the banishing of scorpions.

8 And further belongs the stone which has the colour of the Anbars, which many call the Anbari. It has extreme antipathy for bugs. When one engraves on it in her hour and her ascendant the picture of a bug and on it this sign. Thus no bugs appear at the place where it is found, and as few where its seal is made in wax in the same hour and ascendant.

9 And further belongs to her: one engraves on a bezoar stone or a green malachite stone the image of a serpent with this on its head, and in her hour and ascendant. This stone has special powers to banish vipers and snakes, and the image and the astrological alignments strengthen it.

10 Further belongs to her: one engraves this on an emerald and seals it with consecratory incense and swallows up the smoke as medicine. It greatly strengthens memory and intellect. And this in its hour and ascendant.

Engravings of Saturn

1 When one engraves on a bezoar stone in the hour of Saturn, when he is ascending in twenty-one degrees of Libra, the picture of a man with broad brow and long face, with wrinkled eyebrows, driving a plough with two oxen before it. He has a collar at his neck at which his head and that of a fox are found. So has this image power to preserve fields and cattle, seeds and plants, and the sustenance thereof by springs and waterfalls, stability of the building, and to tread upon open hostility and banish secret hate. It chases away troubles and preserves its wearer from all fear of men.

2 Further under his rule: one engraves on a diamond, the stone of stones, in the hour of Saturn, and his is the ascendant, these signs, and seals with it in wax for hostility and aversion between people, friends and lovers. This seal of division is left at whatsoever place one would work it. The maker of it should avoid its contact besides when it is with him.

3 Further belongs to him: in his hour and his ascendant one engraves on a turquoise the image of a man sitting on a chair at a lecture desk. He wears on his head something like a coiled turban and bears a sickle. The object of this working is longevity and safety for the wearer.

4 Further belongs to him: one engraves a ringstone of yellow amber with the image of a wolf, in his hour, when Capricorn ascends and Saturn is in twenty-three degrees of Leo, Mercury in two degrees of Virgo and Mars in nineteen of Libra. About it one engraves the following characters, and fasten it in a sealring of silver. When put on the wolf flees from the place where on is, no will any wolf be found there or wherever the wearer goes.

5 Further, for protection from locusts, one engraves on a sabarg stone (jet) the image of a locust in the hour of Saturn when he is ascending in two degrees Aries, Mars in five of Cancer and Moon in three degrees Capricorn. Through these degrees it gains its power. One engraves about it these signs. In a cavity beneath the stone, place a piece of the hide of a hare. Then will no locusts come where it is.

6 Further under Saturn, engrave on any appropriate stone the picture of a hare with Libra ascendant, Saturn in thirteen degrees of Gemini, and the Sun five degrees of Cancer and engrave about it these signs; then one fastens it to a seal ring and fixes it. Then will the woman who the wearer has not leave him so long as he keeps it on him.

Engravings of Jupiter

1 One engraves for him on a ringstone of white korund (jacinth) the image of a man crowned and enthroned on a four legged throne, each leg is upon the neck of an upright man. The men have wings, and he prays with lifted arms. This is done in his hour and exaltation. The working of it is for the esteem and prosperity of the wearer; to put him in a good position, with children in great numbers; his affairs will be well settled and his works accomplished. It protects against enemies and destroys their efforts. He is successful and safe from assassination.

2 Further belongs to him: engrave on green korund the image of a man having a lion's face and birds feet, under his feet is a dragon. He has a lance in his right hand thrust in the head of the dragon. It is done in his hour in the first decan of his exaltation. This working confers the vanishing of foes and fear, and instils great fear in the enemies of him who wears it.

3 Further belongs to him: engrave on a crystal the picture of a beautiful man with a round cap, who rides on an eagle. And his working is to gain power in the religious sphere. And it is done in his hour and exaltation.

4 Further: one engraves a vulture on the stone known as midwife. This is done in the hour of Jupiter when the first decan of Sagittarius is ascending. By this, the wearer can cause birds to gather and attend him. In addition, health and well being are assured, and love of the people. And this stone is that with reddish strokes within it. It moves itself when rubbed; white water comes forth from it. Its quality is to give pregnancy when a woman bears it. And Hermes says that the stone is blessed among stones. He says that the image of a fox drawn thereon in Jupiter's hour with the Moon aspected to Jupiter in Pisces causes men to fear the bearer. Further, one engraves on it a nightingale in his hour and exaltation. The liquid immersing it gives visions of the spirits, and one may command them. Hermes also taught this with many references and suggestions.

Engravings of Mars

1 On a lodestone, the image of a man riding a lion, bearing a naked sword in his right and a man's head in his left hand. This both in the hour of Mars and the second decan of Aries. Its working is both evil and good, but it is greater in evil.

2 Further belongs to him: when one engraves on the stone of Mars the image of a man standing in armour, girt with two swords and one drawn in his right and a man's head in his left hand. In his hour with Mars in his sign. This confers respect and majesty, all who see the bearer or have dealings with him are respectful. I have seen these images upon a ringstone of carnelian amongst magicians.

3 Further belongs to him: when one engraves in an onyx the image of a lion with these signs before it. Do this in his hour and with his sign ascendant. When this stone is applied to the blood coming from a member the blood goes back and its course is blocked. But you must know whereof I speak!

Other Planetary Talismans

One can make other talismans for the planets besides, with wonderful workings through appointed astrological alignments. I quote:

☉

For the Sun, in his hour when he is in the first decan of Leo: to cause attacks on the soul to cease; to relieve pains in the stomach and other illnesses and towards the bringing of peace.

☽

For the Moon, in her hour, when she is in the first decan of cancer: a talisman for the thriving of seeds and trees of all kinds.

♄

For Saturn, in his hour, when in the third decan of Aquarius: a talisman which heals dysentery and curbs the menses of a woman.

♃

For him, in his hour, when he is in the second decan of Sagittarius and when the Sun is applying to him: a talisman to stop rain when flooding is feared.

♂

For Mars; his hour; when in the first decan of Scorpio: a talisman to make cowards brave, to break the sultan's fury, to ward off damage by robbers, lions, wolves and every cause of destruction.

♀

For Venus; her hour, when she is in the first decan of Pisces, a talisman to cure the ills of women, pain of the abdomen, afflictions of the soul in melancholia, to make cheerful the heart and increase fertility. And when she is in the first decan of Taurus a talisman for stout and exalted workings to come to pass.

☿

For him, in his hour, when he is in the first decan of Gemini; a talisman to sharpen the reason and to promote the meditative faculties, to facilitate knowledge and investigation. Also for esteem among men &c.

Comment on Figures of the Stones

It remains now only to comment on *Figures of the Stones*, which encapsulates my whole purpose in writing *Geosophia*. Take the astrological images and the instructions for their manufacture; the images are evidently related on occasion to the gods of the Classical world and ancient near East. The engraving on a hæmatite in the first decan of Leo suggests talismans known from the Papyri and in archaeology. Let us multiply the significant exemplars: an archaic image of Venus from this source was used on the talisman of Catherine de Medici; one of the most educated women of the Renaissance. Clearly, as with many images of the *Picatrix* subsequently retained in Agrippa and elsewhere, this was derived from ancient pagan iconography. Other images, of male and female figures, bound and threatened with swords, are also clearly described centuries earlier in the Magical Papyri. Indeed, the whole field of aggressive love magic in the grimoires and elsewhere has clear classical roots. Some of the roots of *Picatrix* material far exceed even such a vintage; note particularly the *standing fat-bodied woman* which *serves for love and is well known*. This is enough to place the section, and the *Picatrix* itself, as firmly in the context of ancient magic as of Renaissance astrology. It is worth noting too that the curious prescriptions for astrological degrees in this section bear no obvious relation to conventional astrology. What they are – Babylonian omens or degree gods of Egypt or Petra – awaits further elucidation. Nevertheless, while a good deal remains to be explored in this important volume, it clearly connects two eras of Western magic; the periods of the Papyri and the grimoires are a continuum. Understanding the *Picatrix* solely as an Ur book for Renaissance Christian magic addresses only half of this equation. This indeed is the heart of the paradox of my own book. Magical traditions emergent from Africa and the New World are fully integrated in their own way with Christianity. Yet, while Western magic was christianised in the medieval and Renaissance period, in order for modern Western magic to properly interconnect with the African and New World systems, a re-examination of our pagan past is both necessary and unavoidable. The necessity of such a re-examination is not solely based on the potential for such an alignment, but to raise our revival to a living tradition.

APPENDIX:
ASTROLOGICAL NOTES

A STROLOGICAL MAGIC is largely pursued by ultra-traditionalists who work entirely by Renaissance rules, omitting the trans-Saturnine planets and other innovations. There are more experimental and forward looking schools, particularly those espousing the English Qaballistic approach. Despite its centrality to the inherited traditions of magic, many modern occultists neglect the art, and not always through lack of interest. Often they are aware of its place, and desirous of applying it, but encounter various impediments. There is for example a lack of widespread contemporary linkage to magical practice in modern astrology textbooks. Perhaps a still greater obstacle to good intentions is the complex manner many of these same manuals adopt regarding drawing a map of the heavens. A very brief and straightforward summary of practical technique in the works of Aleister Crowley could obviate this difficulty if better known. The following is slightly abbreviated but gives all relevant information:

It is a very easy matter to set up a figure of the heavens suitable for astrological judgement... the first thing to be done is to provide yourself with an Ephemeris... the present generation of astrologers employ that issued by 'Raphael' and we shall suppose the student to possess it. At the left hand of the left hand page will be found the date and the day of the week. Pick out the day which you require... In the next column is given the Sidereal Time. We need not here enter into what that means. We merely give the rule. If the hour and minute for which you set up the figure is for afternoon, add that hour and minute to the Sidereal Time for the day. If it be before noon, find out how much before noon, by subtracting the hour and minutes from twelve hours (thus eight o'clock in the morning is four hours before noon) and subtract the result from the Sidereal Time. If, in the first case, the time obtained is more than twenty four hours, subtract twenty four hours from it. In the second case, if the time before noon is greater than the sidereal time, add 24 hours to the Sidereal Time. You then turn to the end of the book and look at the Tables of Houses for the place you wish to set up the figure. Now, take the blank form with which you have provided yourself, a circle divided into 12 parts. At the top of the Tables of Houses you will see the Sidereal Time marked on the left-hand side. Run your eye down the column until you find the nearest approximation to the new Sidereal Time which you have made by adding or subtracting the hours as stated above. Now, against the house in your blank figure which is marked ten, put the sign and degree which is given in the column next to the Sidereal Time in the Table of Houses, and fill in the others as far as the third house accordingly. From the 4th house to the 9th no figures are given, and it is not necessary that they should be give, for the 4th house is equal and opposite to the tenth, the fifth to the eleventh and so on. Thus if 16 Cancer be on the cusp of the 10th, 16 Capricorn will be on the cusp of the 4th... You then proceed to insert in this figure [the chart] the planets in their proper places. For example, suppose 24 Virgo is on the cusp of the 11th house, and you find the Sun marked as 22 Virgo, you put him slightly in front of the cusp; if in 26 Virgo slightly behind it. The daily motion of the Sun is always within about 3 minutes of a degree and it therefore quite unnecessary to make any calculations depending on the hour of the horoscope... We then consider the position of the Moon; the Moon's daily motion is very large; it is sometimes as much as 15 degrees or even a little more. It is sometimes as much as 12 degrees or even a little less, but this works out approximately as a degree every two hours. In the Ephemeris, the [lunar] positions for both noon and midnight are given. You should take noon or midnight according to whether the hour of the horoscope is nearer the one or the other. By allowing half a degree an hour you will get the Moon's position [approximately and close enough to] correct... Thus suppose the time you want is 9 o'clock PM and the Moon at midnight is 8 degrees 37 minutes of Taurus... subtract a degree and a half = 7 degrees Taurus. You then go to the right hand page of the Ephemeris, which will give you the positions of the other planets.

I have here docked his remarks on the Moon's Nodes and on the relative motions of the planets; it is only necessary to take a little care with Venus and Mercury – who though fast are appreciably slower than the Moon – and then only if super accuracy is required, which it rarely is. These instructions are not much abbreviated here, and compared to many manuals are extraordinarily concise and permit the beginning student to set up a chart with minimal confusion. This is particularly true for locations covered by the short Table of Houses in back of *Raphael's Ephemeris*; a larger book of Tables is also available from Raphael's which greatly extends the range. It should be noted that the format of *Raphael's Ephemeris* has slightly changed since Crowley wrote. For most purposes, including rite timing, when it comes to plotting aspects the 'Ptolemaic' ones are almost all that is really needed: conjunct, opposition, sextile, square, and trine. The only exception being inconjunct or quincunx (the name differs depending which side of the Atlantic the astrological manual consulted was written) which does seem more important than other minor aspects not occurring in Ptolemy's writings. Following these instructions you can set up a chart, which is usually the biggest obstacle to beginning the study of astrology.

One problem with the practice of astrological magic in modern times is the uncritical use of Renaissance techniques. The avoidance of modern elements is understandable within limits, but the neglect of Hellenistic astrology demonstrates the narrowness of such partiality. An historical analysis shows that certain elements of the Renaissance method were heavily influenced by Arab innovations which were not necessarily improvements on their Greek sources. The Arabic Parts are a major case in point, being an elaboration upon the Lots employed in the Hellenistic method. These so proliferated among the ivory castle mathematicians of

Baghdad as to become both absurd and a major obstacle to appreciation of the original schema. An important writer among modern astrological traditionalists is Robert Zoller, whose research deserves major credit. On the other hand however his *Lost Key to Prediction* exemplifies these trends, dealing as it does with the Arabic parts in astrology. Important translations of Guido Bonatti and other sources form a key part of the text. Bonatti incidentally was a very important practitioner of astrological magic; he was also a thoroughly irascible personality as deserving of a movie biography as Aleister Crowley, if not more so!

Returning to Zoller's text however, therein we find the use of these so called Arabic parts in commodities speculation; involving formulae for plotting the future value of various crops. For example, in the case of lentils: subtract the degree of Mars from that of Saturn, add the result to the degree of the Ascendant, project the result from the Ascendant to find the position of the Part of Lentils; and form your judgement therefrom. After two dozen such examples there follows thirty-seven other Arabic parts, following Al-Biruni, for employment in judging horary figures. The enormous proliferation of these abstract calculations in the Arab period is adequately demonstrated by these examples. The precedent in Hellenistic astrology has been elaborated to the point where the original idea is completely swamped.

The Greek formulæ were elegant and focussed; they were also much less numerous, and deserve attention from modern astrologers and magicians applying astrological methods. They involve important elements of the philosophical and theoretical basis of Hellenistic magic, which the majority of Arabic parts clearly do not. Seven of these formulæ are pre-eminent: two of them represent the Sun and Moon, the others the five planets of traditional astrology. The most important of these is that nowadays known as the Part of Fortune; the Hellenistic astrologers referred to this as the Kleros Tyches or Lot of Tyche (Fortuna in Latin) which is lunar in nature. Next in status, though less well known to the average reader is the Part of Spirit or Kleros Daimonos, which is of solar nature. Two methods of working out the positions of each of these were known to the ancients, depending whether the time of the chart was day or night. Thus, according to this doctrine, by day the position of the Part of Fortune is discovered by the formula Ascendant + Moon − Sun, while by night the formula is Ascendant + Sun − Moon. Similar formulæ are used to discover the position of the Lots of the other planets.

	Titles	Diurnal Formulæ	Nocturnal Formulæ
☽	Kleros Tyche Pars Fortuna	Asc. + ☽ − ☉	Asc. + ☉ − ☽
☉	Kleros Daimon Pars Spirit	Asc. + ☉ − ☽	Asc. + ☽ − ☉
♄		Asc. + Fortuna − ♄	Asc. + ♄ − Fortuna
♃		Asc. + ♃ − Daimon	Asc. + Daimon − Planet
♂		Asc. + Fortuna − ♂	Asc. + ♂ − Fortuna
⚥O		Asc. + ⚥O − Daimon	Asc. + Daimon − Planet
☿		Asc. + Fortuna − ☿	Asc. + ☿ − Fortuna

However the earliest known Hellenistic horoscope in which the Lot of Fortune is used employs the so called day formula for a night chart, and comments that the reverse formula is the usage of 'ignorant people.' At least then modern differences in practice – in which distinguishing night or day in the calculation is followed by some and by others ignored – both follow ancient precedents.

Certainly there is considerable precedent for the day/night formulae. The Latin astrologer Vettius Valens gives 50 cases where the rule applies; later authors of the period add a further 13. However, the Loeb Classics edition of Ptolemy's *Tetrabiblos* notes his supposed preference for different night and day formulae as later interpolations; in some texts they are attributed to Ptolemy, but they originate in scholiasts confused with the original text by later copyists. His original material clearly states the formula to be the same by day and by night (*Tetrabiblos* III.10 & IV. 2). Here

I follow the first mentioned chart and Ptolemy, which is to say those precedents in which the formula is consistent regardless of the hour. Following the undifferentiated formulæ for Fortuna and Daimon, the formulæ add the degree occupied by the planet in question to the Ascendant in every case, as follows:

Fortuna = Ascendant ° + Lunar ° − Solar °
Daimon = Ascendant ° + Solar ° − Lunar °
Saturn = Ascendant ° + Saturn ° − Fortuna °
Jupiter = Ascendant ° + Jupiter ° − Daimon °
Mars = Ascendant ° + Mars ° − Fortuna °
Venus = Ascendant ° + Venus ° − Daimon °
Mercury = Ascendant ° + Mercury ° − Fortuna °

The calculation is made easier by combining the 30 degree divisions of the signs into 360 degrees of celestial longitude as follows:

Aries	0–29
Taurus	30–59
Gemini	60–89
Cancer	90–119
Leo	120–149
Virgo	150–179
Libra	180–209
Scorpio	210–239
Sagittarius	240–269
Capricorn	270–299
Aquarius	300–329
Pisces	330–359

Next determine the celestial longitude of the Ascendant (and other elements of the equation in question), thus if the Ascendant is at 21 Taurus the value is 51. If the total exceeds 360 degrees deduct 360 from it. The final result in each case is projected forwards from the Ascendant.

While reprising some aspects of Hellenistic astrology it is as well to demonstrate their utility through more direct means than the consideration of these abstract formulæ. The following table shows the house meanings of Greek horoscopes, which as will readily be seen have more connection with spiritual experience and with magic than the more conventional meanings in modern use. House titles are in bold type.

I **Life**, *also body, spirit or breath.*

VII **Marriage**, *Relationships with others connected to the question.*

II *Livelihood, property; Partnership, business. Also* **Gate of Hades** *through relation with the* VIII.

VIII **Death**; *trial, penalty, loss, weakness. But also sex and magic. Profit from inheritance through relation with* II.

III **Brothers**; *also* **Goddess** (*Moon*); *living abroad, prominent persons, wealth, friends, relatives.*

IX **Travel**; *also* **God** (*Sun*). *Friendship, travel, benefit from prominent persons, revelations, manifestations of gods, soothsaying. The state of mind of the inquirer.*

IV **Home**, *Parents; spirits, spiritual life in relation to others, repute, children, etc.*

X **Career and Honours**; *accomplishment, reputation, But also status as concerns children and marriage partner through relation with* IV.

V **Children**; *also* **Good Fortune**. *Friendship, matters in question. Venus.*

XI **Good Daimon**. *Friends, hopes, gifts, children, freed persons; accomplishments.*

VI **Bad Fortune**. *Illness, enmity, infirmity. Service. Mars.*

XII **Bad Daimon**. *Enmity, foreign country, loss of freedom, illness, dangers, court trials, infirmity, death.*

APPENDIX II
TYPHONIAN STAR-LORE

THE ANCIENT CULT OF URSA MAJOR finds its reflection in many cultures, as does the motif of the World Centre – represented by the Pole Star. A fair amount of astronomical knowledge is required to follow the course of the lore of the stars. To enable the student to overcome this obstacle to some extent we write this chapter. Ursa Major and several other non-zodiacal stars and constellations will appear in the course of this section and I shall endeavour to amplify any obscure points as they occur.

That Ursa Major is associated with the World centre is not surprising, as the Northern Height would represent such an association to any race dwelling in high places in Northern latitudes. The World Centre was not always identified with Polaris, although some forms of the motif strongly suggest a connection with the theme from early times. Ursa Major and the World Centre motif in mythology predate Ursa Minor's arrival at the Pole position by many thousands of years. Polaris, the Pole Star, of the constellation Ursa Minor is a comparative newcomer to the Northern Height. 3000 years BCE when Sumerian and Egyptian cultures were already both established the Pole Star was Thuban, the brightest star in the constellation Draco, the celestial dragon that winds sinuously around both of the stellar Bears, Major and Minor.

Astronomers call the phenomenon of changing Pole Stars the precession of the equinoxes. The same phenomena causes the zodiacal signs attending the equinoxes to change every 2000 years. This is the explanation of the cycle of astrological ages, such as the Age of Pisces and the future Age of Aquarius. Aries is traditionally the sign of the Spring equinox, but in fact precession caused Pisces to usurp this position hundreds of years ago. About a third of the constellation Pisces has to move over the Vernal equinox point before the much-vaunted Age of Aquarius comes to pass.

The legend of the dragon-slayer refers to the change from Thuban to Polaris. Many dragon slayers are in fact named bear, as Beowulf = Beewolf = Bear, and Arthur = Ursa = Bear. Interestingly, Arthur's surname was Pendragon meaning Dragons Head. Other dragon slayers are identified with the constellation Orion, occasionally said to stand on the Dragons Head, although the constellation Hercules more usually receives this dubious honour. Hercules and Orion are major figures in stellar lore, identified with the consorts and co-regents of the Goddess.

Orion in Egypt is seen as Osiris, and the constellation Lepus, below him, as his funerary boat. Draco in this case would be Apep. The original dragon slayer was the Sumerian deity Marduk, later to become Adad and Melqart and so on. This slaying in fact asserts the dignity of the deity, no longer content to be a doomed and dying god. He becomes the undying co-regent or even supreme God.

A more important form of the boat of the Underworld is the constellation Argo that in conjunction with Sirius, Orion and Canis Major and Minor has attracted attention from various authors. But Ursa Major and Minor and their key role in stellar myth cycles have been curiously overlooked. Ursa Major's role in the dark cults of antiquity may be exemplified in the 'witches' widdershins dance. This does not seem to be explained by a conscious reversal of the direction of the Sun. It is more likely a continuation of the earlier practice emulating the anticlockwise direction of Ursa Major. It is this constellation that marked out the cross-quarter days of the witches' year – thus indicating the position of the four major Sabbats. The holy place of the witches and their antecedents was the northern quarter, the place of the circumpolar constellations Draco and Ursa Major.

The Yezidis have their holy place in the North, practice widdershins circumambulations and so on. The origins of such rites can only come from a culture practicing some form of astronomy. The Sabeans derived their knowledge from Chaldean – that is to say, late Babylonian sources, which in turn stemmed from Sumeria. The Yezidis as a people (as opposed to a sect for the name indicates race as well as religion) claim descent from the Assyrians, another nation which obtained much of its culture and beliefs from Sumeria.

The position of the Sabbats in the calender is curious. In old style astrology the constellations equivalent to their dates are a most remarkable group. Every occultist worth their salt knows that the four directions have symbolic creatures associated with them. These are of course the Bull, the Lion the Eagle or Snake and the Man. These in turn represent the constellations Taurus, Leo, Scorpio and Aquarius. Scorpio has three symbols: the Eagle, the Snake and the Scorpion hence the complication of the third symbol. These archetypal symbols date from the time when Taurus was the sign presiding at the Spring equinox. The Lion thus represented the Summer solstice, Scorpio the Autumn equinox and the Water Bearer the Winter solstice. However the precession of the equinoxes changed all that and these signs were displaced. Due to this they came to occupy the points in the solar year that the Sabbats now occur in. This can only represent a stellar survival within a later calender.

Sabbat	Hebrew Month	Zodiac Sign
Halloween	Bul	♏
Candlemass	Shebat	♒
Walpurgis	Iyar or Zif	♉
Lammas	Ab	♌

Shebat is from Shabatu the old Babylonian month of Aquarius.

In the Northern Hemisphere various curiously apt astronomical phenomena attend the dates of the Sabbats. At Walpurgisnacht Draco is at its highest point in the course of its cycle.

Position of Bears and Dragon at Walpurgisnacht

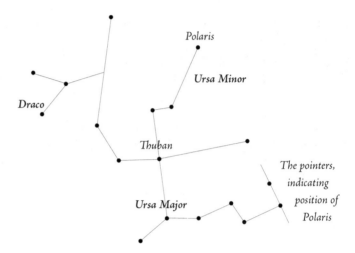

At Lammas Capricorn reaches its height, while Halloween sees Orion at his highest point. At the Winter solstice Sirius reaches its greatest Southern declination and is for a short time visible to observers in our latitudes.

As we have stated above Ursa Major has a connection with distinctly sinister, that is left-handed, deities. As the Foreleg this constellation was early identified with the Egyptian Deity Set, whose worship was ancient before the Second Empire. At one time Set was a popular deity and had no evil connotations, being the god presiding over the Upper Kingdom as Horus represented the Lower. The Typhonian Animal, the totem of Set was probably associated with this constellation rather than a bear. The long tail of this beast lends itself to this interpretation at very least for artistic purposes.

Typhonian Animal overlaid on Ursa Major

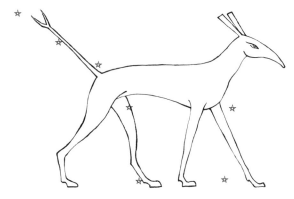

In the Solomonic black book known as *The Testament of Solomon* the Persian counterpart of Set – Aeshma-Dæva, known in demonology as Asmodai or Asmodeus – is also identified with Ursa Major. Deep in antiquity the seven demons of Sumeria (and later Babylonia and Assyria) were identifed with this constellation. Idpa (*Fever*), Namtar (*Magician of the Underworld*), Utuk (*Spirit*), Alal (*Destroyer*), Gigim (*Spirit*), Relal (*Wicked Demon/Warrior*) and lastly Uruku (*Larvæ*). These were the great demons of the Middle East at that time.

These demons were associated with the archetypal seven heads of the Dragon, Ursa Major being conceived as part of the constellation Draco. Apep, the seven-headed dragon of Egypt has been identified with Tiamat, the great dragon of Sumeria, slain by Marduk. This primordial goddess is the prototype of the biblical monster Leviathan. It is little known that in the *Book of Revelation* this same dragon makes an anonymous guest appearance. Nowhere in biblical literature, apart from *Revelations* where the Dragon is not named, is Leviathan described as seven-headed. But in Ugaritic tablets this identification is plainly made. Much of the later Biblical literature finds its prototype in Ugarit and is considerably amplified by the Ugaritic texts. Tiamat or Leviathan was an early biblical image for 'the wicked city' so it is apt that the Whore of Babylon should ride a seven-headed dragon in the *Book of Revelation*.

The zodiac contains the best known constellations, although few could recognise them today almost everyone knows their names. Many can even list them in order, but few can recognise the constellations. They are extremely ancient, Babylon gave them most of their present definitions, but obtained their knowledge of them from the pre-Polaris astronomy of the Sumerians. Amongst the oldest constellations are Cancer and Capricorn, curiously enough, for they are very vague and unspectacular constellations even through a telescope. These anciently represented the Summer and Winter Solstices. In Chaldean (ie. Babylonian) astronomical lore Cancer was called the Gate of Men, the entrance point for souls seeking incarnation in human bodies. Capricorn was called the Gate of the Gods by which souls passed into Heaven.

The myth cycle of the constellations in this part of the sky is briefly as follows, drawing on Greek and Egyptian symbology although predating them both. The Underworld river is typified by the Milky Way, its celestial counterpart, intersected at two points namely Cancer and Capricorn in the band of the Ecliptic, called the zodiac. The boat of the Underworld, that of Ra in Egypt, Charon in Greece, is the stellar ship Argo-Navis, whose fifty oars represent the cycle of Sirius' companion Sirius B (*and* also the Great Year of Antiquity likewise measured in double periods, thus one hundred years, but based on Lunar time). These oars also indicate the Judges of Sumeria, the Anunnaki. The god of the Underworld is the constellation Orion in his boat, the constellation Lepus. The guardian of the Gate of the Underworld is the Greek Cerberus, the Egyptian Anubis, represented by Canis Major and its principal star Sirius the Dog Star. The Underworld, or Zodiac, has twelve divisions, and escape is only possible through the Gate of Men or the Gate of the Gods. These lead from one river (the Zodiac) to another (the Milky Way). The two rivers are reminiscent of crossing rivers in Greek and Semitic legend. They also suggest the White and Blue Nile of Egypt. Originally they were associated with Sumeria's Tigris and Euphrates. The goddess Tiamat, the celestial dragon, has been identified with the Milky Way by some students. But the Underworld Dragon was always the Zodiac itself, through whose body the traveller made their way. On the other hand, Tiamat has been identified with the cloak of mist over the rivers of Sumeria, spread out on the plain like an immense serpent. It is more likely however, that Tiamat had a physical as well as a celestial counterpart.

Position of Sirius at Winter Solstice

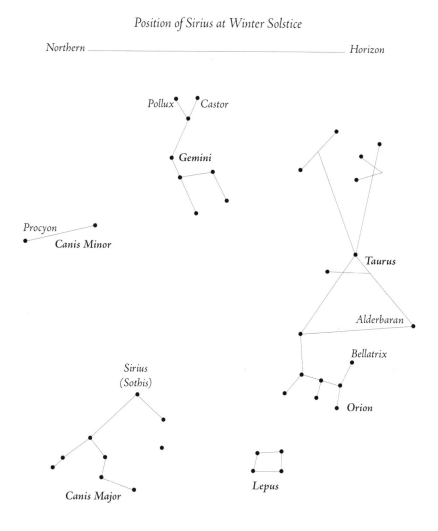

The dragon of the zodiac is necessarily circular, the serpent with its tail in its mouth in fact. Not only is the serpent said to encircle the world in this form, but to coil about World Mountains and Trees. In Greek and Semitic mythology it guards the forbidden fruit at what is recognisably an archetypal World Centre. Draco has been identified with all these mythological dragon guardians. We should also note that the Sumerio-Babylonian stellar lore recognised two kinds of celestial spirit. The first kind are the children of Anu, the infernal judges, the Anunnaki – identified with the oarsmen of Argo Navis. These are the spirits of stars below the horizon, in the Underworld. The other kind, the Igigi are spirits of the stars above the horizon, and were also associated with Anu, the Sumerian Sky and Heaven god. In Mesopotamia (and points north) Draco, Ursa Major and the circumpolar stars are Igigi, they never set. Canis Major, Argo Navis and Orion are invisible much of the time in northern latitudes and are thus Anunnaki. Tiamat fulfills both roles, as celestial dragon she is Igigi, as Underworld river Anunnaki.

Ursa Major is always Igigi, the seven heads of the Dragon and the seven gods of the world centre or high place, the holy place of the stellar cults: the Northern Height. The sinister role of the seven spirits is late, post Polaris in fact. They were originally the seven sages and teachers (as the seven spirits of Mount Meru, the Indian world centre, situated *in the north*). Elsewhere, particularly in the shamanic lore of Siberia and Mongolia they retain that status.

SELECT BIBLIOGRAPHY

AGRIPPA, CORNELIUS: *The Three Books of Occult Philosophy.*

AGRIPPA, CORNELIUS (attrib): *The Fourth Book of Occult Philosophy.*

BARB, A.A: *Three Elusive Amulets.* Journal of the Warburg and Courtauld Institutes, vol. 27, 1964.

BARRACLOUGH, G. & PARKER, G: *The Times Atlas of World History,* fourth edition. BCA, 1994.

BETZ, HANS DIETER (editor): *The Greek Magical Papyri in Translation.* University of Chicago Press, 1986, 1992.

BETZ, HANS DIETER: *Fragments from a Catabasis Ritual in a Greek Magical Papyrus.* History of Religions, vol. 19, no. 4 (p. 287–295), May 1980.

BLACKWOOD, R; CROSSET, J; LONG, H: *The Socratic Oath "By the Dog".* Classical Journal no. 57, (p. 318–9), 1962.

BLOOMFIELD, MAURICE: *Cerberus, Dog of Hades; the History of an Idea.* Kegan Paul, Trench, Trubner & Co. London, 1905.

BURKERT, WALTER: *Greek Religion.* Basil Blackwell ltd. & Harvard University Press. Oxford, 1985 (first English translation).

BURKERT, WALTER: *Goes – Zum griechischen 'Schamanismus'.* Rheinisches Museum für Philologie (Frankfurt a. M.), n.s. 105: 35–55, 1962.

BURKERT, WALTER: *Weisheit und Wissenschaft. Studien zu Pythagoras, Philolaus und Platon.* Nuremberg, 1962.

CLARK, RAYMOND J: *Trophonios: The Manner of His Revelation.* Transactions of the American Philological Association, vol. 99 (1968), pp. 63–75.

COLLINS, DEREK: *Magic in the Ancient Greek World*. Blackwell Publishing Ltd, 2008.

COOK, ARTHUR BERNARD: *Zeus: A Study in Ancient Religion*. Cambridge University Press, 1914.

COPENHAVER, BRIAN P: *Hermetica: the Greek Corpus Hermeticum and the Latin Asclepius in a new English translation, with notes and introduction*. Cambridge University Press, 1992.

CULIANU, IOAN PETRU: *Psychanodia – A Survey of the Evidence Concerning the Ascension of the Soul and its Relevance*. E. J. Brill, Leiden, 1983.

CUMONT, FRANZ: *Oriental Religions in Roman Paganism*. NY, 1956.

D'ESTE, SORITA AND RANKINE, DAVID: *Hekate – Liminal Rites*. Avalonia Books, 2009.

DODDS, E. R: *The Greeks and the Irrational*. University of California Press, 1951.

DORESSE, JEAN: *The Secret Books of the Egyptian Gnostics*. Inner Traditions International, 1986.

ELIADE, MIRCEA: *Shamanism: Archaic Techniques of Ecstasy*. Princeton University Press, 1964.

ELIADE, MIRCEA: *Zalmoxis: the Vanishing God*. University of Chicago Press, 1972.

FAIRBANKS, ARTHUR: *The First Philosophers of Greece*. Kegan Paul, Trench and Trubner, London, 1898.

FLINT, VALERIE: *The Rise of Magic in Early Medieval Europe*. Oxford University Press, 1991.

FLOWERS, STEPHEN EDRED: *Hermetic Magic – The Postmodern Magical Papyrus of Abaris*. Weiser, 1995.

FOL, ALEXANDER & MARAZOV, IVAN: *Thrace and the Thracians*. Cassell and Co. Ltd, 1977.

FOSSUM, JARL & GLAZER, BRIAN: *Seth in the Magical Texts*. Zeitschrift für Papyrologie und Epigraphik 100, p. 86–92, 1994.

FRAZER, J.G: *The Golden Bough – A Study in Magic and Religion*. The Macmillan Press Ltd, London, 1922.

GRAF, FRITZ: *Magic in the Ancient World*. Harvard University Press, 1997.

GREER, JOHN MICHAEL & WARNOCK, CHRISTOPHER: *The Latin Picatrix Books I & II*. Renaissance Astrology, 2008.

GREY, PETER & DIMECH, ALKISTIS (editors): *Diabolical*. Scarlet Imprint, 2009.

HYDE CLARKE: *On the Proto-Ethnic Condition of Asia Minor, the Khalubes (Chalybes), Idaei Dactyli, &c, and their Relations with the Mythology of Ionia*. The Journal of the Ethnological Society of London (1869–1870), vol. I, no. I. (1869), pp. 39–50.

JOHNSTON, SARAH ILES: *Restless Dead – Encounters between the Living and the Dead in Ancient Greece*. University of California Press, 1999.

KAHN, CHARLES H: *Religion and Natural Philosophy in Empedocles' Doctrine of the Soul*. Archiv fur Geschichte der Philosophie (Berlin), XLII (1960), pp. 3–35.

KIESEL, WILLIAM: *Picatrix – The Goal of the Wise, Volume I*. Ouroboros Press, Seattle, WA, 2002.

KIESEL, WILLIAM: *Picatrix – The Goal of the Wise, Volume II*. Ouroboros Press, Seattle, WA, 2008.

LEITCH, AARON: *Secrets of the Magical Grimoires*. Llewellyn Publications, 2005.

Liddell and Scott's Greek-English Lexicon. Oxford University Press.

LUCK, GEORG: *Arcana Mundi: Magic and the Occult in the Greek and Roman Worlds; A Collection of Ancient Texts*. The John Hopkins University Press, second edition, 2006.

MCDONALD, WILLIAM A: *Progress into the Past: The rediscovery of Mycenaean Civilisation*. 1967. (English edition: *The Discovery of Homeric Greece*. Elek Books Limited, 1968).

MEAD, G.R.S: *Thrice-Greatest Hermes: Studies in Hellenistic Philosophy and Gnosis*. 1906. (Watkins edition, 1964).

MELLERSH, H.E.L: *Chronology of the Ancient World – 10,000 BC to 799 AD*. Barrie & Jenkins Ltd, 1976; also BCA 1976.

MILIS, LUDO J.R. (editor): *The Pagan Middle Ages*. The Boydell Press, 1998.

NEUGEBAUER, O. & VAN HŒSEN, H.B: *Greek Horoscopes*. The American Philosophical Society, 1959.

OGDEN, DANIEL: *Greek and Roman Necromancy*. Princeton University Press, 2001.

OGDEN, DANIEL: *Magic, Witchcraft and Ghosts in the Greek and Roman Worlds*. Oxford University Press, 2009.

OVID: *Metamorphoses*. Penguin Classics, 1955.

PETERSON, JOSEPH: *Twilit Grotto*: CD & online archive: http://www.esotericarchives.com

PINCH, GERALDINE: *Magic in Ancient Egypt*. British Museum Press, 1994.

PRICE, SIMON & KEARNS, EMILY: *The Oxford Dictionary of Classical Myth & Religion*. Oxford University Press.,Oxford and New York, 2003.

RICKARD. T. A: *The Primitive Smelting of Iron.* American Journal of Archaeology, vol. 43, no. 1. Jan–Mar, 1939, pp. 85–101.

RIEU, E.V. (translator): HOMER: *The Iliad.* Penguin Classics, revised edition 2003.

RIEU, E.V. (translator): HOMER: *The Odyssey.* Penguin Classics, revised edition 2003.

RIEU, E.V. (translator): APOLLONIUS OF RHODES: *The Voyage of the Argo.* Penguin Classics, 1959.

ROLLER, LYNN E: *In Search of God the Mother.* University of California Press, 1999.

SMITH, MORTON: *Jesus the Magician.* Harper San Francisco, 1978.

STRATTON-KENT, JAKE: *The True Grimoire.* Scarlet Imprint, 2009.

STOYANOV, YURI: *The Hidden Tradition in Europe – The secret history of medieval Christian heresy.* Penguin Arkana, 1994.

TAKÁCS, SAROLTA A: *Politics and Religion in the Bacchanalian Affair of 186 BCE.* Harvard Studies in Classical Philology, vol. 100 (2000), pp. 301–310. Department of the Classics, Harvard University.

THOMAS TAYLOR (trans): IAMBLICHUS: *On the Mysteries of the Egyptians, Chaldeans, and Assyrians.* Wizards Bookshelf, San Diego, 1984.

TEMKIN, OWSEI: *The Greeks and the Irrational by E. R. Dodds* (review). Isis, vol. 43, no. 4. (Dec. 1952), pp. 375–377.

THEODOSSIEV, NIKOLA: *The Thracian Ithyphallic Altar from Polianthos and the Sacred Marriage of the Gods.* Oxford Journal of Archeology 13 (3), pp. 313–323, 1994.

TESTER, JIM: *A History of Western Astrology.* The Boydell Press. Boydell & Brewer Ltd, 1987.

WAITES, MARGARET C: *The Deities of the Sacred Axe.* American Journal of Archaeology, vol. 27, no. 1. (Jan-Mar, 1923), pp. 25–56.

WEINSTOCK, S: *Lunar Mansions and Early Calendars.* Journal of Hellenistic Studies LXIX (1949): 48ff.

WENDER, DOROTHEA (trans): *Hesiod and Theognis.* Penguin Classics, 1973.

WENZEL, MARIAN: *The Dioscuri in the Balkans.* Slavic Review, vol. 26, no. 3. (Sep. 1967), pp. 363–381.
YATES, FRANCES: *Giordano Bruno and the Hermetic Tradition.* Routledge and Kegan Paul, University of Chicago Press, 1964.

YONGE, C.D (trans): *Diogenes Laertius' Life of Empedocles, from 'Lives of the Philosophers'.* Henry G. Bohn, London, 1853.

INDEX

A

Abano, Pietro de 249

Abaris 7, 14, 182, 194, 195, 314

Abramelin 62, 182

Abraxas 58, 62, 148, 159, 160, 162, 163,
    164, 177, 182, 184, 282

Acheron 48, 131

A Discourse of the Nature of Spirits 68

Aeacus 87, 114

Aeschylus 104, 176

    Prometheus Bound 104

    Seven Against Thebes 176

*A form of conjuring Luridan the Familiar,
    otherwise called Belelah* 69

African Traditional Religions 129, 215,
    219

Agrippa, Cornelius 14, 16, 19, 27, 37, 40,
    131, 144, 159, 168, 183, 186, 187,
    195, 228, 230, 231, 260, 267, 297

    Three Books of Occult Philosophy 16, 27,
        40, 144, 228, 313

        De incertitude et vanitate scientiarum
        187

        Scale of the Number Ten 183

Albertus Magnus 56, 222, 231

    Speculum Astronomiae 231

Al-Istamatis 8, 244, 248, 249

Al-Tabari 233

amber 86, 87, 89, 91, 247, 252, 253,
    256, 259, 293

animal sacrifice 26, 46, 47, 53, 73, 80, 81,
    82, 86, 87, 98, 100, 101, 102, 110,
    116, 117, 123, 173, 186, 198, 199,
    203, 217, 230, 234, 241, 253, 259,
    275, 295

Anubis 132, 133, 134, 135, 137, 138, 139, 140,
    141, 142, 143, 144, 145, 146, 152,
    154, 184, 310

    Anuberos 132, 152

Aphrodite 21, 22, 59, 90, 128, 129, 161,
    166, 172, 184, 240, 242, 276, 283

    Judgement of Paris 22, 276, 283

Apollo 5, 8, 14, 17, 20, 29, 30, 34, 42, 44,
    51, 91, 112, 117, 121, 124, 127, 129,
    130, 160, 167, 169, 171, 172, 194,
    195, 212, 232, 283

    Baal 162, 167, 168, 184, 232, 239, 282

    Nergal 160, 232, 283

    Reshef 160, 162

Apollodorus 105, 172

Apollonius of Rhodes 20, 21, 23, 28, 49,
    53, 68, 86, 87, 88, 89, 91, 92, 99,
    101, 102, 103, 104, 105, 106, 109,
    110, 113, 114, 116, 118, 123, 125, 126,
    130, 159, 171, 188, 189, 199, 279,
    280, 281

Apollonius of Tyana 188, 189

    Nuctemeron 188, 189

Apsyrtus 20, 24, 86, 87, 88, 89, 98, 103

Ares 1, 5, 9, 24, 25, 30, 31, 33, 59, 129, 161,
    166, 167, 176, 184, 240, 241

    Mars 10, 11, 25, 59, 106, 129, 162, 167,
    176, 223, 230, 232, 234, 237, 241,
    245, 247, 265, 272, 273, 275, 276,
    277, 278, 279, 280, 281, 282, 283,
    285, 293, 295, 296, 301, 303, 304

Argonautica 7, 20, 21, 24, 26, 28, 31, 86,
    89, 90, 92, 130, 135, 175

Ariadne 115, 116

Arimazpi 17, 18, 19

Aristæus 50, 102, 118, 121, 174

Aristeas 7, 17, 19, 194

Artemis 1, 5, 7, 8, 28, 47, 86, 110, 119, 120, 121, 129, 172

Asclepius 34, 314

Asia Minor 2, 6, 8, 10, 13, 29, 47, 135, 167, 170, 178, 197, 198, 209, 227, 231, 315

Astaroth 61, 95, 97, 101, 107, 138, 140, 143, 146, 158

Astarte 95, 138, 142, 184, 242

Atargatis 95, 107

  Dercetis, Derceto 95. See also Astarte, Dirce

Athena 8, 21, 22, 30, 88, 113, 114, 172, 205

Athens 8, 111, 113

B

Baalbek 162

Baalit 184, 232, 239

Babalon 51

Bacchus 3, 83, 131. See also Dionysus

Barrett, Francis 168

Bendis 7, 8

Betz, Hans Dieter 56, 57, 157, 160, 226

  The Greek Magical Papyri in Translation 156, 226

Black Pullet, The Cabala of 19, 53, 54, 55

Book of the Talismans of the Spirits, The 279, 280, 281

Book of the Uses of Stones, The 279, 280, 281, 282

Book of the Wise Apollonius, The 279

Boreas 173

Brimo 26, 27, 32, 57

Brotherhood of the Green Wolf 152

Brujeria 220

Bruno, Giordano 40, 195, 196, 318

Burkert, Walter 92, 115, 210

Byzantium 80, 88, 135, 156, 166, 168, 184, 227, 228

C

Caca 211, 212

Cacus 211, 212, 213, 214

  Cæculus 213, 214

Cadmus 30, 31, 88, 172

Calypso 88, 98

Carpathian Mountains 19

Cassandra 118

Cassiopeia 175

Castor and Pollux 68, 97. See also Dioscuri

Cellini, Benevenuto 69

cemeteries 221

Cerberus 27, 57, 102, 117, 130, 131, 132, 133, 134, 135, 136, 137, 138, 140, 141, 142, 143, 144, 145, 148, 154, 165, 174, 189, 310, 313

Çabala 132

Chaldea 191, 197, 227

Chaldean Oracles 180, 181, 188

Chalybes 21, 88, 110, 167, 173, 315

Chango 97, 127, 128

Charon 89, 131, 134, 310

Chiron 104, 130, 276

Cilicia 172, 173, 174, 175

Circe 20, 52, 89, 93, 98, 99, 100, 101, 102, 103, 109, 213, 282

Claunech 141, 146

Clymene 89, 90

Colchis 9, 20, 21, 27, 29, 86, 88, 93, 103, 130

Cook, Arthur Bernard 166, 167

Corinth 8, 48, 49, 50, 93

Coronzon 77, 79, 80, 82

Corybantes 48, 68, 117

Corycian cave 171, 172

Cotys 8

Crete 2, 5, 9, 47, 122, 123, 193, 197, 202

Crossroads 221

Crowley, Aleister 65, 66, 298, 300, 301

Book of the Law 51
Liber Pyramidos 63
Liber Resh vel Helios 62
Liber Samekh 62, 65
Cumæ 22
Cumont, Franz 161, 163
   Oriental Religions in Roman Paganism 161
Curetes 48, 94, 207. *See also* Corybantes, Dactyls
Cybele 1, 3, 6, 7, 9, 25, 47, 94, 97, 110, 120, 130, 209
Cyzicus 17

D

Dactyls 21, 48, 56, 57, 58, 83, 193, 194
Dante 133
   Inferno 133
Dee, John 79, 80, 195, 249
   Heptarchia Mystica 249
   Hieroglyphic Monad 195
defixiones 156, 177, 216, 276
Delphi 2, 29, 47, 50, 51, 89, 90, 100, 118, 119, 171, 175, 192
Demeter 5, 6, 7, 8, 24, 43, 50, 97, 106, 107, 109, 110, 124, 125, 143, 172, 174, 191, 194, 199, 203, 209, 215
   Hymn to Demeter 109
Deucalion 29, 31
Dionysus 1, 2, 3, 5, 6, 7, 9, 11, 15, 30, 31, 34, 50, 59, 83, 88, 90, 94, 102, 108, 109, 110, 111, 112, 113, 115, 118, 120, 121, 125, 129, 131, 160, 163, 167, 168, 172, 173, 174, 176, 177, 199
Dioscuri 68, 93, 94, 95, 96, 97, 98, 130, 318
Dirce 50, 93, 94, 95, 97, 107
Dodona 88, 93
Draco 305, 306, 307, 309, 312
Dragon Rouge, Le 155

E

Echidna 134, 174
Eleusian Mysteries 2, 107, 109, 136
Eleusis 6, 13, 107, 124
Eliade, Mircea 13, 15
Ellegua head 216
Elysian Fields 11, 31, 104
Empedocles 7, 35, 37, 38, 39, 41, 42, 43, 44, 63, 92, 159, 193, 195, 200, 315, 318
   Purifications 41
Enoch 64, 184, 229
Ephesian letters 57
Ereshkigal 56
Erinyes 26, 106
   Furies 145
eschatology 133, 223
Etna, Mount 33, 43, 74, 173, 174
Euripides 34, 111
   Bacchæ 30, 31, 34, 111
Eurypylus 117, 118, 119, 120, 121

F

Ficino, Marsilio 186, 228
Fourth Book of Occult Philosophy 68, 70, 77, 228, 249, 313
Frazer, James George 149, 152, 230
   Golden Bough 149, 230
frenzy 114, 123
Frimost 27, 61, 131, 146

G

Gaia 5, 9, 172
Glycon 34
Goetia of Solomon 79, 107, 131, 141, 215, 283
Golden Dawn 82
Golden Fleece 23, 24, 30, 32, 58, 86, 113

Gorgias 37, 39, 144

Grand Grimoire 10, 65, 83, 127, 141, 155

Graves, Robert 130

Greek Magical Papyri 8, 27, 31, 32, 53, 56,
58, 60, 61, 63, 67, 132, 137, 138, 139,
143, 144, 145, 154, 156, 163, 164,
165, 168, 170, 175, 180, 181, 182,
184, 224, 226, 227, 261, 313

Greek shamans 15, 42, 196

griffins 17, 18

Grimorium Verum 12, 54, 61, 62, 83, 146,
155, 165, 207, 219, 220, 224, 225.
See also True Grimoire, The

H

Hades 5, 7, 9, 22, 23, 38, 40, 43, 44, 45,
50, 57, 96, 101, 104, 107, 108, 116,
122, 123, 124, 131, 133, 134, 135, 140,
142, 143, 147, 148, 154, 160, 161,
174, 192, 193, 203, 215, 304, 313

Dis Pater 133, 147, 148, 203

Hael 153, 154

Hecate 7, 20, 24, 25, 26, 27, 28, 31, 32, 43,
56, 57, 58, 94, 102, 107, 112, 128,
129, 137, 138, 139, 140, 142, 143,
170, 184, 209, 282

Helios 20, 22, 23, 50, 52, 58, 59, 62, 87,
89, 90, 91, 92, 93, 103, 122, 123,
128, 135, 136, 157, 159, 160, 161, 162,
163, 164, 165, 166, 168, 184, 240,
242, 282, 283

Hephæstus 9, 21, 22, 23, 24, 25, 68, 74,
83, 90, 92, 99, 104, 109, 118, 128,
129, 135, 136, 168, 171, 173, 174, 205

Heptameron 77, 80, 81, 230, 249

Hera 5, 13, 21, 22, 23, 24, 38, 45, 48, 49,
88, 103, 104, 105, 109, 129, 171, 172

Hercules 130, 136, 211, 212, 214, 306

Hermanubis 133, 142

Hermes 7, 5, 23, 25, 30, 59, 93, 125, 129,
131, 136, 138, 139, 140, 141, 142,
143, 154, 159, 161, 166, 172, 184,
192, 209, 240, 243, 275, 280, 285,
294, 295, 316

Hermes Chthonios 131, 140, 141, 142,
143

Hymn to Hermes Chthonios 140

Herodotus 15, 17, 48, 49, 192, 195, 197

Hero 7, 4, 5, 7, 64, 200

Hesiod 5, 6, 10, 20, 41, 92, 107, 133, 172,
173, 318

Hesperides 33, 105, 130

Hestia 5, 100, 103, 209, 210

Hittites 2, 168, 175

Holy Guardian Angel 62, 182, 200, 219

Homer 2, 3, 5, 20, 22, 41, 43, 92, 98, 99,
102, 103, 107, 108, 121, 133, 167, 173,
174, 175, 176

Iliad 22, 176, 317

Odyssey 20, 41, 43, 88, 99, 102, 109, 317

Homeric Hymns 92, 115

Hoodoo 63, 142, 220, 226, 277

Horace 207

Epode 207

*How to conjure the Spirit Balkin the
Master of Luridan* 77

Huictigaras 141, 146, 153, 154

hydromancy 143, 195

Hygromanteia 156

Hyperborea 14

I

Iamblichus 35, 41, 158, 179, 180, 181, 182,
183, 185, 186, 187, 195

Mysteries, The 182, 183

Theurgy 158

Idæan cave 22

Idaean Dactyls 56, 193. *See also* Dactyls

India 5, 8, 39, 59, 115, 132, 198, 199, 228,
240, 312

Invisibility 154
Isis 46, 135, 136, 138, 139, 140, 317
Isle of Amber 87, 88
Isles of the Blessed 108
Italy 1, 4, 17, 22, 87, 107, 139, 174, 192, 201,
    202, 205, 209, 211, 212, 227

J

Jason 7, 9, 20, 21, 22, 23, 24, 25, 26, 28, 29,
    30, 31, 32, 33, 34, 50, 52, 58, 86, 87,
    98, 99, 100, 103, 104, 110, 111, 113,
    114, 116, 122, 124, 125, 126
Johnston, Sarah Iles 46
    Restless Dead 46, 315
Jupiter Dolichenus 167, 168
Jupiter Heliopolitanus 162, 165, 168

K

Kabbalah 3, 163, 222
Kabirs 38
Key of Solomon 79, 156, 168, 216, 217,
    220, 230
Kosingas 13
Kronos 5, 9, 10, 11, 12, 33, 59, 80, 110, 123,
    128, 136, 139, 161, 166, 167, 172,
    184, 240, 241

L

Laërtius, Diogenes 37, 43, 192
    Life of Empedocles 43, 318
Lamiae 75
Lares 75, 94, 206, 207, 208, 209, 213
Larvæ, Lemures 204, 309
Lemegeton 187
Lévi, Eliphas 131, 133
    Mysteries of the Qabalah 131
    Transcendental Magic 133
Liber Troisième 224, 225

Libya 86, 91, 112, 113, 116, 117, 118, 121, 122,
    125, 130, 169
Life of Apollonius of Tyana 68
ligature spells 145
Lilly, William 267
Linear B 111
Lucifer 141, 146, 147
Lucifuge Rofocale 65
Luck, Georg 58
    Arcana Mundi 58
Lunar Mansions 8, 58, 59, 146, 249, 260,
    262, 267, 318
Lunar Workings from the Papyri 261

M

Mænads 34
Magi 16, 191, 197, 198
main de gloire 142, 154
Manes, Dii Manes 147, 167, 202, 203,
    204, 206, 207, 208
Manetho 135, 136
Marsyas 93, 212
Medea 7, 9, 11, 20, 22, 24, 25, 26, 27, 28,
    29, 31, 47, 50, 51, 52, 86, 87, 98, 99,
    100, 101, 102, 103, 104, 110, 111, 112,
    113, 116, 123, 124, 125, 130, 282
    Scarlet Woman 7, 51, 52
Medusa 101, 117, 129, 211
Melissa 7, 46, 47, 48, 49, 50, 103, 104
Mercury 59, 106, 133, 162, 208, 209, 231,
    234, 235, 237, 238, 242, 245, 248,
    255, 256, 259, 260, 272, 273, 275,
    278, 279, 280, 285, 288, 293, 300,
    303
mia labores 215, 220, 221
Milton, John 18, 147
    In Quintum Novembris 147
    Paradise Lost 18
Mirandola, Pico della 37, 40, 186, 187,
    195

Mithras 56, 172
Mopsus 28, 116, 121
Morail 146, 153, 154
Moses 44, 64, 65, 66, 157
Mount Casius, Kasion 175
Mount Hecla 68, 70, 74, 75, 77
Mount Nysa 172, 173
mugwort 151
Mycenæ 201

N

Nabateans 227, 238
Naiades 101, 102
Naxos 115
Nebiros 7, 61, 131, 132, 138, 140, 141, 142,
    143, 144, 145, 146, 147, 148, 152,
    153, 154, 155, 158
Neoplatonism 37, 163, 180, 188
    Ammonius Saccas 180
    Porphyry 180, 183, 193
Nepthys 53, 55, 134, 138, 139

O

Ode to the Sun 169
Ogden, Daniel 49
    Greek and Roman Necromancy 49, 316
Olaus Magnus 70, 75, 84
Olympus 3, 21, 96, 124, 172
Orpheus 2, 14, 15, 58, 94, 117, 118, 136,
    140, 156, 160, 192, 197, 198
    Hymns of Orpheus 140
Orphism 1, 46, 47, 108, 160, 191, 199
Osiris 11, 134, 135, 136, 137, 138, 143, 145,
    169, 176, 224, 306
Ovid 107, 147, 167, 173, 174, 203, 204, 207
    Fasti 204, 207
    Metamorphoses 107, 173, 316

P

Pæeon 116
    paeoniae herbæ 116
Palladium 14, 182
Pan 94, 172
Papyrus of Unas 144
Parmenides 35
Pausanias 42, 43, 118, 120
Pelasgian 1, 25
Peleus 87, 104, 105, 114
Penates 75, 205, 206, 207, 210, 213
Penates, Dii Penates 75, 205, 206, 207,
    210, 213
Pentheus 30, 31, 115
Periander 48, 49, 50
Persephone 6, 7, 8, 14, 27, 38, 43, 49, 50,
    59, 94, 101, 104, 106, 107, 108, 115,
    129, 133, 135, 136, 143, 160, 161,
    174, 194, 203, 209, 215
Petit Albert, Le 276
Phæthon 87, 89, 90, 91, 92, 101
pharmakos 27, 52, 98
Pherecydes 191, 193
Phoenicia 30
Phrygia 2, 3, 17, 194, 197
Picatrix 8, 80, 158, 159, 162, 188, 196, 216,
    217, 227, 228, 229, 230, 231, 239,
    240, 249, 260, 276, 297, 315
Pindar 118, 122, 125
Plato 7, 14, 15, 105, 108, 144, 160, 185,
    191, 195
    Gorgias 144
    Laws 160
Pleiades 22, 118, 268
Plotinus 35, 37, 180
Plutarch 49, 134, 136, 139, 145
Pluto 89, 134, 135, 142, 144, 147
Polaris 267, 305, 306, 310, 312
Pomba Gira 147
Poseidon 5, 9, 44, 51, 114, 117, 118, 122

Potnia Theron 7, 121, 143

Priapus 210

Proclus 180, 185

Prometheus 21, 26, 29, 90, 99, 104, 174

Ptolemy 134, 135, 195, 228, 300, 302, 303
  Almagest 228
  Tetrabiblos 302, 303

Pythagoras 8, 14, 15, 17, 39, 41, 42, 63, 185,
    191, 192, 193, 194, 195, 196, 197,
    198, 199, 200, 313

Python 89, 90, 145, 171

Q

Quimbanda 60, 61, 127, 129, 147

R

reincarnation 198, 199

Reuchlin, Johann 40, 196
  De Arte Cabalistica 40, 196

Revelations 51, 309

Rhea 5, 6, 7, 9, 47, 130, 209

Rhodes 50, 90, 92, 93, 123, 166, 171, 174

Rig Veda 93, 132

S

Sabaoth 163, 164

Sabazius 15, 34, 163

Sabbats 307

Sabeans 8, 229, 230, 233, 236, 239, 240,
    282, 306

Sabians 227

Samothrace 2, 14, 56, 205

Santeria 97, 127, 129, 217, 222, 223

Satanachia 141, 146

Saturn 10, 11, 12, 59, 106, 162, 188, 223,
    233, 236, 240, 241, 245, 246, 251,
    260, 270, 272, 273, 275, 276, 278,
    279, 281, 285, 290, 292, 293, 296,

301, 303

Scirlin 61, 219

Scot, Reginald 40, 69, 71, 79, 80, 141
  Discoverie of Witchcraft 69, 71, 79, 80

Scylla 109

Scythians 18, 192

Segal 146, 147

Sergulath 153, 154

serpent 7, 24, 30, 31, 32, 33, 34, 57, 105,
    116, 133, 134, 160, 164, 172, 206,
    256, 285, 292, 311, 312

Set 8, 11, 134, 136, 139, 145, 162, 170, 171,
    175, 176, 177, 178, 224, 308, 309

sexual mysticism 8

shamans 14, 15, 16, 19, 39, 42, 47, 57, 71,
    139, 142, 194, 196, 327

Sibyl 101, 113, 118

Sicily 8, 37, 41, 43, 44, 49, 107, 148, 173,
    175

Sirens 105, 106, 109, 195
  La Sirène 106

snakes 31, 33, 34, 67, 94, 96, 97, 101, 133,
    163, 164, 176, 189, 201, 202, 207,
    211, 253, 256, 263, 280, 281, 285,
    286, 287, 292

Solstice 142, 143, 146, 147, 148
  St. John's Eve 142, 148, 149, 152

Spartans 96

Spell for All Occasions or Consecration of
    all Purposes 164, 165, 166
  The Orison of the Instrument 165

Strabo 167, 174

Styx 91, 134

Sumeria 306, 309, 310, 311

Summanus 147, 148

Sympathia 7, 35, 36, 37, 151, 159, 182, 183,
    186, 187, 275, 277

Syria 90, 161, 162, 172, 174, 175, 227

T

Tartarus 9, 167, 172, 173
Telauges 39, 43
Telchines 90, 110, 172, 174
Testament of Solomon 156, 309
Thebes 30, 31, 50, 66, 93, 94, 95, 176
Thesprotia 49
Thetis 104, 105, 114, 128, 129
Theurgy 35, 158, 179, 180, 181, 182, 183,
    185, 186, 187, 188, 277
  Julianos the Theurgist 180, 182
    Chaldean Oracles of Zoroaster 180
Thrace 2, 4, 14, 15, 34, 86, 88, 173, 197,
    200, 315
Thracians 1, 2, 3, 4, 5, 6, 7, 8, 13, 14, 15, 16,
    17, 18, 31, 33, 34, 44, 63, 64, 88, 92,
    104, 111, 131, 199, 315, 317
Tiamat 174, 309, 310, 311, 312
Titans 9, 108, 110, 160, 174
Tree of Life 146
Trithemius 40, 196
  De Septum Secundeis 196
  Steganographia 196
Trophonios 44, 56, 94, 148, 313
True Grimoire, The 27, 31, 35, 61, 62, 87,
    107, 131, 138, 140, 141, 143, 145,
    146, 151, 152, 154, 155, 158, 163,
    207, 224, 231, 317
Turkey 3, 173, 175
Typhon 8, 33, 53, 62, 89, 109, 134, 136,
    139, 160, 167, 169, 170, 171, 172,
    173, 174, 175, 176, 177, 178, 184
Typhon-Set 8, 170, 171, 177, 178

U

Undines 45, 102. *See also* Naiades
Ursa Major 305, 306, 308, 309, 312
Utarid 243, 275, 277, 280, 281, 282

V

vegetarianism 187, 198, 199
Vepar 107
Veritable Key of Solomon 156
Vesta 103, 205, 209, 210, 211, 214
  Hestia 5, 100, 103, 209, 210
Vesuvius 22
violets 167, 203
Virgil 121, 133, 174, 203, 205, 211, 214
  Aeneid 49, 121, 133
Vision of Er 105, 195
Voodoo 106, 107, 127, 148
votives 216, 276, 277
Vulcan 25, 74, 129, 211, 213, 214

W

witchcraft 20, 149, 151, 220
Sabbath 131, 133

Y

Yezidis 306

Z

Zalmoxis 7, 14, 15, 16, 314
Zeus 5, 6, 7, 9, 11, 12, 22, 33, 38, 45, 47, 48,
    59, 88, 90, 91, 93, 94, 97, 100, 101,
    102, 103, 104, 107, 108, 112, 118,
    120, 123, 126, 128, 129, 134, 140,
    148, 161, 162, 163, 165, 166, 168,
    172, 173, 174, 175, 184, 193, 194,
    240, 241, 314
  Zeus Kasios 175
Zoller, Robert 301
  Lost Key to Prediction 301
Zoroaster 16, 180, 197, 198